CHASING SUCCESS
AND CONFRONTING
FAILURE
IN AMERICAN
PUBLIC SCHOOLS

LARRY CUBAN

CHASING SUCCESS AND CONFRONTING FAILURE IN AMERICAN PUBLIC SCHOOLS

HARVARD EDUCATION PRESS
Cambridge, Massachusetts

Paperback ISBN 978-1-68253-454-0
Library Edition ISBN 978-1-68253-455-7

Library of Congress Cataloging-in-Publication Data

Names: Cuban, Larry, author.
Title: Chasing success and confronting failure in American public schools / Larry Cuban.
Description: Cambridge, Massachusetts : Harvard Education Press, [2020] | Includes index. | Summary: "The history of American education is rife with calls for school reform and efforts to turn so-called "failing" schools into "successful" ones. Cuban argues that, in the history of American education, standards of success and failure-as well as the reform efforts issuing from them-have been neither stable nor consistent"— Provided by publisher.
Identifiers: LCCN 2019052575 | ISBN 9781682534540 (paperback) | ISBN 9781682534557 (library binding)
Subjects: LCSH: Educational change—United States. | School management and organization—United States. | Educational accountability—United States. | Education and state—United States. | Academic achievement—United States. | Teaching—United States.
Classification: LCC LB2806.22 .C83 2020 | DDC 371.010973—dc23
LC record available at https://lccn.loc.gov/2019052575

Published by Harvard Education Press,
an imprint of the Harvard Education Publishing Group

Harvard Education Press
8 Story Street
Cambridge, MA 02138

Cover Design: Ciano Design

The typefaces used in this book are ITC Legacy Serif and Solano Gothic

In Blessed Memory of

Norton Cuban
(1926–2018)

CONTENTS

Introduction 1

CHAPTER 1 How Have "Success" and "Failure" Been Defined
and Applied to Schools Past and Present?................... 11

CHAPTER 2 From Where Do These Ideas of "Success" and
"Failure" Come? 41

CHAPTER 3 How Were These Ideas and Values Transmitted
to Americans Then and Now?............................ 61

CHAPTER 4 Who Decides (and How) Whether Schools
"Succeed" and "Fail"? 81

CHAPTER 5 What Does Institutional and Individual "Success"
and "Failure" Look Like in Two Contemporary Schools?.... 109

CHAPTER 6 MetWest High School in Oakland, California.............. 145

CHAPTER 7 So What?.. 185

Notes 215

Acknowledgments... 245

About the Author 249

Index 251

INTRODUCTION

Here is why I have become hooked on determining what "success" and "failure" mean in American public schools.

In the mid-1960s, I taught in and later directed a federally funded teacher-training program located in several Washington, DC, public schools.[1]

The Cardozo Project in Urban Teaching (CPUT), as it was then called, prepared in one year returned Peace Corps volunteers to teach in urban elementary and secondary schools. The "interns" taught for half-days under the supervision of master teachers in elementary school grades and English, science, math, and history in junior and senior high schools. They took on-site university-sponsored seminars after school, and in evenings developed curriculum materials for their lessons and worked in the community. At the end of the year the CPUT "interns" were certified to teach in the District of Columbia and were on the way to earning a master's degree in their field through local universities.[2]

An independent evaluation confirmed that sixty-one interns had completed training between 1963 and 1967. Of the fifty-six who had finished (two had died and three left the program for various reasons), forty-two (or 75 percent) were teaching in urban schools, other federally funded programs, or overseas—one goal of the program. The on-site training, the supervision by DC master teachers, and after-school seminars involving both interns and regular faculty from the participating schools were put into practice and seemed to be a fruitful mix for channeling rookie teachers into the system. The evaluation and praise for the program led the DC school board to fund and rechristen the program as the Urban Teacher Corps in 1967. Getting a school board to use its limited monies to continue a federally funded pilot program meant that school officials saw its worth in attracting a different pool of teaching candidates.[3]

Consider further that the CPUT model of recruiting and training new teachers became the poster-child for funding a federal initiative to prepare teachers nationally for high-poverty urban and rural schools. The National Teacher Corps legislation (1966) adopted the model used by CPUT for training teachers on-site, but rather than fund districts, federal officials funneled monies to universities that took responsibility for the training program and awarding degrees.[4]

Surely, the pilot program had achieved its goals: three of four interns became full-time teachers after completing the program. And the program was adopted by an urban district using locally budgeted funds. Accomplishing both goals suggests program effectiveness, a sign of clear success. That the pilot program became the model for a National Teacher Corps further cements the sweet smell of success.

As a twenty-nine-year-old teacher/director of the project, I did inhale that sweetness. After leaving the project to return to teaching high school history, I believed I had been part of a "successful" reform. And I felt good about my part in the innovation.

There is a "however" to this seeming "success" story that needs to be noted. After the Urban Teacher Corps became part of the DC schools, the board of education fired its superintendent and in 1970 appointed Hugh Scott as its first black superintendent. During Scott's brief administration (he resigned in 1973), he dismantled the Urban Teacher Corps. Together the federally funded pilot program and locally funded UTC existed for just under a decade.

Similarly, with the election of Ronald Reagan in 1980, the National Teacher Corps disappeared as federal monies for education went to the states in block grants rather than to specific programs. The NTC had lasted just over a decade.

The disappearance of both teacher-training programs within ten years suggests "failure" even though they could be fairly characterized as "successes" in achieving their primary goals.

Program "success" or "failure"? If it is a binary either/or conclusion, then determining whether CPUT should go down in the books as a "successful" reform in a district recruiting and training new teachers and then have it disappear raises questions about how one defines program "success"—Being adopted? Fully implemented? Achieving goals? Longevity? Or are there gray areas in defining "success" that seldom get attention?

I want to add two pieces to finish the story.

First, an assumption (not an explicit goal) was that the pilot project with ten returned Peace Corps volunteers, seven of whom were white and three were African American, would somehow influence staffing Cardozo Project schools whose faculties were then 80–90 percent black. That is, a majority white teacher-training project would produce, over time, an integrated faculty at each of the schools.

Changes in faculty demographics did occur in subsequent decades but can hardly be attributed to CPUT or the subsequent Urban Teacher Corps. In 2008, for example, Cardozo High School was closed for persistently poor academic performance. It reopened with different teachers hired to replace existing ones. As a result, percentages of white teachers increased to over one-third in 2009. While in 2017 the district has 32 percent white administrators and teachers, the original schools in CPUT continue to have predominantly black staffs.[5]

Second, before leaving the Cardozo Project in Urban Teaching in 1967, I asked a professor at the University of Maryland to find out if the students in classes of elementary and secondary school interns achieved less, about the same, or more than students who had nonintern teachers. While raising student achievement was not an explicit goal for the Cardozo Project in Urban Teaching or the Urban Teacher Corps, there was a staff assumption (which I shared) that well-trained teachers creating engaging lessons and working in the community would eventually lead to better teaching and better teaching would lead to higher student achievement.

The professor designed a study where students in classes taught by interns were matched with students taught by regular DC teachers. With no districtwide standardized test available then, the professor used the Iowa Test of Basic Skills as the outcome measure of teaching in reading, math, and other skills. About a year later, the professor called me up—I was then teaching history at a DC high school—and said he had the results. We met for coffee and he showed me what he had found.[6]

In both elementary and secondary classrooms of interns and regular teachers, students in *regular* classrooms did marginally better than those in "intern" classrooms. While the percentile scores in both sets of classes were fairly low compared to the national average, I was still shocked. I had believed that the teacher-training program I had taught in and eventually directed was so strong that even in one year with "interns," DC students would do better academically than in nonintern classrooms. I was wrong.

Although standardized testing was becoming common—the year is 1968—as a consequence of the Coleman Report (1966) and the federal Elementary and Secondary Education Act (1965) that required outcome measures to hold districts accountable for the federal dollars they received, I knew little then about the design and methodology the professor had used to evaluate student achievement.

Of course, now I realize that there were flaws in the evaluation design—it was not a random sample of students or interns; the test questions covered content and skills that students had not yet been taught in the DC curriculum; only one year was covered—still I was shaken by the results.

So I come to the end of my story and the puzzle of defining program "success," one that a half-century later still bothers me. Here is an example of a pilot that initially appeared as a "success" in achieving its primary goals. The Cardozo Project in Urban Teaching baptized later by the DC Board of Education as the Urban Teacher Corps serving the entire district had the fragrance of success. Adding to the scent was the founding of the National Teacher Corps. Yet within a decade both teacher-training programs had disappeared.

And as an afterthought, in examining the underlying assumption that a majority white teacher-training project might have effects on prevailing faculty demographics, I found that African American teachers with a gradual smattering of Hispanics in the early 2000s continued to dominate the racial profile of faculties in these schools and across the district. Faculty demographics had changed minimally over time.

Finally, I discovered that students achieved less well in classes taught by interns than did students in regular classrooms. Even though raising student achievement was not one of the program's goals, the results turned my assumptions inside out. Reform outcomes, I discovered, are seldom tidy.

Why this story? Puzzling then as it was to me, I still have not figured out a satisfying answer to the direct question of whether the Cardozo Project (and its progeny—the Urban Teacher Corps and the National Teacher Corps) was a "success." Surely, it was not a "failure." What lies between "success" and "failure" in a reform or when applied to a particular school or program?

Any answer to the question has to deal with what the concepts mean when applied to reform, organizations or individuals, who decides what they mean, the criteria used in making judgments, and whether these concepts have shifted in their meanings over time. Although determining "success" and "failure" remains puzzling to me, I have discovered that policy makers, administrators, practitioners, and political leaders also stumble over judging a particular innovation, program, school, classroom teacher, and individual students. And unraveling this enduring puzzle is one to which this book is devoted.[7]

LOOKING BACKWARD AT DETERMINING "SUCCESS" AND "FAILURE" IN SCHOOLING

My experience in one reform-driven project does not mean that there have not been clear "successes" in improving schools. I describe briefly one educational institution that has weathered decades of political conflict and demonstrates resilience in its durability even today. I use the criteria of institutionalization of a reform and its longevity as measures of "success." Political action, that is, gathering support from teachers, parents, voters, and taxpayers to adopt and sustain an organization is essential in determining "success" and "failure." If a structure, program, or school process began as an innovation, was fully implemented, and then incorporated into the organization long enough to become taken for granted as is a drain in the kitchen sink or a sofa in the living room, the reform has been a "success." Where these notions of "success" come from I take up in chapter 2.

Consider the mid-nineteenth century age-graded school imported from Prussia as an innovative reform to the then-dominant public school organization: the one-room schoolhouse. Horace Mann, Henry Barnard, and others were evangelists for age-graded Common Schools in New England and elsewhere. These reformers built political coalitions in various states that persuaded legislatures and town officials to fund these Common Schools. They succeeded in establishing such age-graded schools across New England, the mid-Atlantic states, and the Midwest prior to the Civil War.[8]

Since the late nineteenth century, the age-graded school (e.g., K–5, K–8, 6–8, 9–12) has become the mainstay of school organization in the twenty-first century. Today, most taxpayers, voters, and readers of this book have gone to kindergarten at age five, studied Egyptian mummies in the sixth grade, taken algebra in the eighth or ninth grade, and then left twelfth grade with a diploma.

If any school reform—in the sense of making fundamental changes in organization, curriculum, and instruction—can be considered an institutional "success," it is the age-graded elementary and secondary school. In providing access to all children and youth, longevity as a reform, and global pervasiveness, the age-graded school is stellar.

But there is far more to the age-graded school. Its structures and rules such as a teacher for each classroom, daily schedules, homework, tests, report cards, and annual promotion are intrinsic to the organization. Students move sequentially through the school curriculum each month. If they pass tests and make "normal" progress, they advance to the next grade or can move from algebra to geometry. The age-graded school defines what is "normal" academic progress and behavior. These structures become what others and I call the "grammar of schooling."

These structures and rules also instruct those in the organization about what adults and children are to do and how to behave inside classrooms, hallways, lunchrooms, and auditorium assemblies. In short, the "grammar of schooling" is the genetic code of the age-graded school.[9]

The age-graded school and its "grammar of schooling," then, have been a robust "success." Think about its longevity—the first age-graded structure of eight classrooms appeared in the Quincy Grammar School in Boston, Massachusetts, in 1848. Within a half-century, it had begun to replace one-room schoolhouses in urban and rural schools.[10]

Or consider access. Between 1850 and 1913, over thirty million Europeans crossed the Atlantic and settled in the United States. The age-graded school has enrolled millions of students over the past century and a half, assimilated immigrants into Americans, sorting out achievers from nonachievers, and now graduates over 80 percent of those entering high school.[11]

Or ubiquity. The age-graded school exists in Europe, Asia, Africa, Latin America, and North America covering rural, urban, and suburban districts. What other school reform has been this "successful"?[12]

Habit and tradition play a part in the longevity of the age-graded school. The lack of recognizable alternatives that have been around sufficiently long to compete with the prevailing model is another. Sure, occasional reformers created nongraded schools and similar singletons, but they were outliers that disappeared after a few years.[13]

What is too often ignored in explaining the durability of the age-graded organization, however, are the widely shared social beliefs among parents and educators about what a "real" school is. After all, nearly all US adults—save for the tiny number who are home schooled—have attended both public and private age-graded schools. Addition, subtraction, and multiplication are taught in primary grades; the nation's history is taught in the fifth, eighth, and eleventh grades. This is what a school is and does. American as apple pie and the Thanksgiving holiday.

For example, when charter school applicants propose a brand-new innovative school, the chances of receiving official approval and parental acceptance increase if it is a familiar age-graded one, not one where most teachers team teach and groups of multi-age children learn together.[14]

External pressures also constrict reformers' maneuverability in trying other organizational forms. State-mandated grade-by-grade curriculum standards—college entrance requirements calling for which academic subjects have to be taken and passed are located in the ninth to twelfth grades, and the federal Every Student Succeeds Act determining what grades elementary and secondary school will be tested—are all married to this taken-for-granted institution.

The unintended (and ironic) consequence of frequent and earnest calls for radical change in instruction through nontraditional teachers and administrators, charter schools, nifty reading and math programs, digital devices for kindergartners, and other reforms assumes that such innovations will occur within the traditional school organization, thus inadvertently preserving the age-graded school and freezing classroom patterns that so many reformers and entrepreneurs want to alter.

Beyond the age-graded school, there have been other fundamental and incremental changes that have, intentionally or not, sustained the structure and culture of this organization. The striking emergence of the junior high school and then the comprehensive high school in the 1920s, offering students an array of academic and vocational courses leading to graduation, remains a mainstay in US secondary schools in 2020. These new age-graded organizations appealed to families wanting their sons and daughters to have a high school diploma, at that time a prized piece of parchment.

Cementing that high school structure in grades nine through twelve has been the Carnegie unit—student contact of 120 hours in a class over a school year of at least twenty-four weeks—installed as another innovation in the early twentieth century. It has been used as a basis for students graduating high school and continues into the twenty-first century.[15]

These triumphs of reform came about because every policy aimed at solving a district or school problem contains three essential elements that demand attention prior to making judgments about overall "success" and "failure": the *process* of adopting a policy, the *programs* that enact the policy, and the *politics* necessary to put the policy into practice. Thus, there can be a lasting institutional "success" in all three realms— see above examples—but more often than not, there are temporary and partial "successes" leading to mixed judgments; for example, the policy was a "success" in getting adopted but "failed" in securing sufficient political support from teachers for classroom implementation (e.g., school vouchers, open space schools). Noting these three strands of organizational policy recognizes that "success" and "failure" are not binary judgments. There may be early victories and later defeats in one realm and not another. Puzzling contradictions and ambiguities that accompany so many judgments about policies as "winners" or "losers" become clearer and richer in acknowledging these political dimensions of reform-driven policies.

Recognizing these often-overlooked facets of policy helped me make sense of my experiences in a federally funded program to train teachers on school sites a half-century ago. Such analyses of policy also help unravel ambiguities and contradictions in assessing "success" and "failure" in noneducational domains such as starting and sustaining business and providing health care.

This brings me to the questions that drive this study of organizational "success" and "failure" in school reform and judging the quality of public schools in the nation.

1. How have "success" and "failure" been defined and applied to schools past and present?
2. From where do these ideas of "success" and "failure" come?
3. How were these ideas transmitted to Americans then and now?
4. Who decides (and how) whether schools "succeed" and "fail"?
5. What does institutional "success" and "failure" look like in two contemporary schools?
6. So what?

My journey from the Cardozo Project in Urban Teaching in the mid-1960s to now has been both meandering and long. Whether that project, one that led to a career as an administrator and then professor, was a "success" or "failure" is a question that has dogged me for over a half-century. As a teacher and superintendent, I thought I knew the answer, but as a researcher looking back to what I did and what I have learned from investigating reforms and similar projects, I now understand how notions of "success" and "failure" I took for granted, I had never questioned. Reflecting on my experiences and research over decades, I remain uncertain and ambivalent about these common terms to describe schools and life itself. Thus, this book.

The following chapters answer the above questions. The answers I constructed give me a hand-hold—but not a full grip—on figuring out what these common terms mean in judging school reform, applying them to school innovations, programs, individual teachers, and students. And, I have discovered that reconsidering key events in my life has brought me full circle to where I began in Washington, DC, where I became hooked on determining what "success" and "failure" mean in American public schools.

HOW HAVE "SUCCESS" AND "FAILURE" BEEN DEFINED AND APPLIED TO SCHOOLS PAST AND PRESENT?

In the four decades between when I started teaching English at T. C. [Williams High School in Alexandria, Virginia] in 1970 and my retirement this year [2013], I saw countless reforms come and go; some even returned years later disguised in new education lingo. Some that were touted as "best practices" couldn't work, given Alexandria's demographics. Others were nothing but common-sense bromides hyped as revolutionary epiphanies. All of them failed to do what I believe to be key to teaching: to make students care about what they're studying and understand how it's relevant to their lives.

—PATRICK WELSH[1]

Success For All, a comprehensive schoolwide reform program, primarily for high-poverty elementary schools, emphasizes early detection and prevention of reading problems before they become serious. . . . We know it works because a study that randomly assigned 41 schools across 11 states to an experimental or control group found improved reading skills, including comprehension, in students in the experimental group. Most of the students were black or Hispanic, and from low-income families. Success For All was awarded $50 million to more than double its network of schools over five years, to train teachers and to improve effectiveness in new sites.

—RON HASKINS[2]

The two views above express different definitions of institutional "success" and "failure." Welsh says that reform after reform in the Alexandria public schools over forty years failed "to make students care about what they're studying and understand how it's relevant to their lives." No mention of state test scores. What was of crucial importance to this high school English teacher were students' passion for learning and seeing connections to their lives outside of school. Hardly quantifiable. That was this teacher's view of "success." Many teachers, principals, superintendents, school board members, and parents would nod in agreement.

However, the program Success For All "succeeded" because it supposedly raised test scores in reading skills as proved by an experimental/control group study. Two different criteria for "success" and "failure."[3]

Differences in defining "success" and "failure" are not new. They have existed for as long as there have been tax-supported public schools. While few distinguished between institutional and individual "success," over time certain organizational definitions became dominant among educators, parents, and voters while competing views remained on the fringes. Today, test scores, the percentage of students graduating high school, and the number of graduates who attend college are signs of district and school institutional "success" and "failure." Yet even with the constant drumbeat of test scores, other voices echoing an earlier generation of reformers call for tallying individual student outcomes (e.g., independent decision-making, problem solving, caring for others, collaboration, and humaneness) that cannot easily be translated into numbers. These institutional and individual differences in viewing "success" and "failure," then, have a history.[4]

PAST VIEW OF "SUCCEEDING" AND "FAILING" SCHOOLS (1890s–1970s)

In the late nineteenth century, a generation of reformers—called "Progressives"—rolled up their sleeves—most were men—and worked hard to change America and its schools. And they did.

Facing decades of political corruption at all levels of government, and wave after wave of immigrants settling into urban slums enduring crime and health problems, a new generation of reformers vowed to create a better America cleansed of slums, corrupt political practices, and retrograde schooling.[5]

Filled with admiration for what business leaders had done in industrializing the economy and for what scientists had achieved in the late nineteenth and early twentieth centuries, these determined Progressive reformers, using the latest corporate and scientific practices, identified national and local problems that had to be solved.

Intense criticism of "traditional" schooling out of step with the growing industrial economy led business-oriented reformers—historians labeled them "administrative Progressives"—to call for many changes in public schools. Or as the *Saturday Evening Post* magazine put it in 1912: "Our Medieval High Schools—Shall We Educate Children for the Twelfth or Twentieth Century?"[6]

They saw the sad state of public schools at the beginning of the twentieth century as a ripe candidate for modernizing education in order to assimilate millions of immigrants and fit them to a swiftly changing economy and society. They wanted to make schools "efficient" in being aligned to the workplace and larger economy while ending wasteful practices in classrooms and schools.

Joseph Rice, a pediatrician-turned-school reformer, visited public schools across the country in 1892. In one of Boston's celebrated grammar schools, he observed "three lessons in geography so perfectly mechanical [intended as a criticism] that they were altogether out of harmony with the reputation of the school."[7]

In one of the lessons, the teacher began with a question:

With how many senses do we study geography? "With three senses: sight, hearing, and touch," answered the pupils.

The children were now told to turn to the map of North America in their geographies, and to begin with the capes on the eastern coast. When the map had been found each pupil placed his forefinger upon "Cape Farewell," and when the teacher said, "Start," the pupils said in concert, "Cape Farewell," and then ran their fingers down the map, calling out the name of each cape as it was touched. . . . After the pupils had named all of the capes on the eastern coast of North America, beginning at the north and ending at the south, they were told to close their books. . . .

"How many senses are you using now?" the teacher asked.

"Two senses—touch and hearing," answered the children.

Rice concluded: "The lesson throughout consisted of nothing beyond thus studying in concert a number of cut-and-dried facts; it could hardly have been more mechanical."[8]

In the last decade of the nineteenth century, "traditional" teachers routinely used rote recitations anchored in a prescribed curriculum for students who sat at bolted-down desks and obeyed teachers. Children dropped out of school in droves.[9]

Moreover, urban politicians pressured school boards and superintendents to hire teachers they recommended and, God forbid, they should ever fire one endorsed by a local boss. Principals were unaware of how much money they spent buying books, providing inkwells and paper for students, and heating schools. Policy makers, administrators, and practitioners made decisions based on personal opinions, crude guesses, and occasional comparisons with neighboring schools and districts.

The *Ladies' Home Journal*, a popular magazine of the day, quoted James Russell, Dean of New York City's Teachers College, about the nation's schools in 1912:

> We desiccate, sterilize, petrify, and embalm our youth. Our children learn by rote and are guided by routine. The present school system squanders the resources of the country and wastes the energy and the lives of our children. The school system should be abolished. Our educators are narrow-minded pedants, occupied with the dry bones of textbooks and the sawdust of pedagogics, who are ignorant of the real, vital problems of human interest.

He concluded his rant with: "Our educational system is wasteful and inefficient."[10]

These doyens of reform saw wasted effort and money everywhere in existing schools. They wanted competent governance, efficient school operations, and trained professionals doing their job.

They sought elected school boards where civic-minded citizens make decisions for the public good rather than appointed political hacks seeking dollars to line their pockets; they wanted schoolhouses that would be well lit and amply heated at the least cost; they sought knowledgeable teachers who could teach math, reading, composition, handwriting, and spelling using every single minute profitably; they wanted more than a one-size-fits-all academic curriculum since they knew that most students would enter the workplace. A "successful" teacher, principal, or district superintendent was one that met prescribed standards set by "efficiency experts" who sniffed out wasted time and pursued productivity in every classroom, school, and district nook and cranny. And students had to be efficient. Enter tests.

Urban students began taking standardized achievement tests after World War I. These "efficiency experts" saw results on these tests as an indicator of student efficiency. A later generation would call these "administrative Progressives," technocratic reformers.[11]

These "administrative Progressives," the education experts of the day, imbued with the ideas of "scientific management" then sweeping corporate America, installed the latest business innovations to make classrooms, schools, and districts efficient. Enter cadres of "educational engineers." Enter time-and-motion studies with outsiders holding stopwatches to measure educator actions. Exit nepotism and political payoffs to mayors and party bosses. Exit personal opinions, guesses, and anecdotal comparisons in making decisions. Prizing data-driven standards and careful accounting of dollars to achieve efficiency became the Holy Grail of the New Education.[12]

Between the early 1900s and the late 1960s, then, a "successful" school that employed the latest scientific evidence and business practices to reduce waste while providing with its limited resources an array of curriculum services to students was labeled "efficient."

Keep in mind that this generation of reformers assumed that efficient schools and districts were also effective in doing what they were supposed to do, that is, make children—now taking the innovative standardized achievement tests—into literate adults who would contribute to their communities and be prepared to enter the workplace. Using established standards of efficiency, they believed, would naturally lead to effectiveness. As Superintendent Frank Spaulding, from Newton, Massachusetts, said at the 1913 annual meeting of the nation's superintendents, there are three essentials of scientifically applied efficiency to schools that had to be put into practice:

1. The measurement and comparison of comparable results.
2. The analysis and comparison of the conditions under which given results are secured—especially of the means and time employed in securing given results.
3. The consistent adoption and use of those means that justify themselves most fully by their results, abandoning those that fail so to justify themselves.

Later in the same speech, Spaulding made clear that these essentials would lead to conclusions about "the quality of the education that the school affords."

Efficiency and effectiveness were as one in the minds of these twentieth-century reformers.[13]

Challenges to this dominant view of an engineered, efficient school being an effective one arose from another wing of school reformers—historians called them "pedagogical Progressives"—who sought the same goals as "administrative Progressives"—literate and engaged citizens prepared for the workplace—but mainly through new curriculum and instruction that emphasized individual children and youth "learning by doing," intellectual inquiry across the curriculum rather than in separate subjects, and developing the "whole child." Another challenge came from educational conservatives of the day whose views of what schools should do countered both wings of educational Progressives.

Pedagogical Progressives

Reformers of this stripe, echoing a historically humanistic approach to schooling, sought to create classrooms and schools that gave individual students more choices, positioned teachers as guides rather than drill sergeants, created curricula that crossed disciplinary boundaries, and integrated family, community, and the larger world into classroom experiences. To these reformers, "success" and "failure" went far beyond adhering to "efficient" classroom and school standards measured by "educational engineers." The definition of "successful" schooling that they constructed sought different social ends rooted in individual student well-being and agency and intellectual, social, emotional, and physical growth in becoming literate, engaged, and employable citizens.[14]

John Dewey's words rang in their ears:

> What avail is it to win prescribed amounts of information about geography and history, to win ability to read and write, if in the process the individual loses his own soul, loses his appreciation of things worth while, of the values to which these things are relative; if he loses desire to apply what he has learned and, above all, loses the ability to extract meaning from his future experiences as they occur?[15]

To these reformers, schools had to be both institutionally and individually "successful." They had humanistic goals embedded in a wide-ranging curriculum encompassing academic disciplines and life outside of the school. The daily schedule of activities, how individual students were grouped, and personalized teaching practices that accounted for student differences in how much and how fast they learned characterized such schools.

Consider two brief examples. Superintendent Carleton Washburne (1919–1943) developed the Winnetka Plan that included ways for individual children to master "Common Essentials," work on projects that connected to life inside and outside the school, and make choices. In Washburne's words: "The individualized learning system allows each student to do each grade's work at his or her own natural rate of progress, unhurried by those who are quicker and unhampered by those who are slower."[16]

Similarly, Helen Parkhurst's Dalton Plan in the early twentieth century individualized elementary school work through a signed contract between teacher and student. Students worked at their own pace and finished what they could when they could, made choices in organizing their time, and stayed with the same teacher for more than one year. These examples of pedagogical Progressives turned upside down the traditional elementary school of the day. What determined "success" was achieving these humanistic goals for each student.[17]

But these challengers, while earnest and vocal in articulating a different version of schooling children and youth (as well as a competing definition of "success"), were a scattered minority. They seldom were part of the reigning policy elites and, most important, lacked political muscle among administrators and teachers. Their efforts to overcome the dominant view and the structures of the age-graded school crumpled although their humanistic definitions of a "successful" school have persisted in a sprinkling of schools until the present day.

Educational Conservatives of the 1930s

Another small group of academics and allies, wanting the same long-term goals as the administrative and pedagogical Progressives—literate and engaged citizens prepared for the workplace—challenged mainstream school-based Progressivism's dominant efficiency beliefs and practices—by questioning reformer's basic assumptions.

Diane Ravitch, in *Left Back: A Century of Failed School Reform*, resurrects critics William Bagley and Isaac Kandel who—from the same pulpit that Teachers College, Columbia Progressives Edward Thorndike, William Kirkpatrick, and Harold Rugg preached—wanted a common academic curriculum for all children and youth, not a differentiated one allowing the young to choose among varied courses of study. They wanted children and youth, in Bagley's words, to acquire knowledge and skills in "industry, accuracy, carefulness, steadfastness, patriotism, culture, cleanliness, truth, self-sacrifice, social service, and personal honor." They wanted teachers to inculcate in students self-discipline, character, and patriotism. They respected the traditional ways teachers taught. They called for some changes but not to either the scale or substance that both kinds of administrative and pedagogical Progressives wanted. They, like their contemporaries, wanted "successful" schools, but their version of institutional "success" differed from those of the two strands of Progressivism.[18]

Historian of education, Adam Laats, in *The Other School Reformers*, points to what conservatives of the day argued in the Tennessee Scopes Trial in the mid-1920s over the teaching of evolution in schools and the struggle over Progressive social studies textbooks in the late 1930s. Each episode, Laats asserts, reveals the strong countervailing effort by conservatives to slow down the steamroller of Progressive curricular and instructional reform.[19]

The back-and-forth between the two wings of Progressives and conservative critics revealed starkly a contradiction that tax-supported public schools have faced since their founding in the mid-nineteenth century. Public schools are both conserving institutions and agents of reform. These competing responsibilities (and visions of "success" and "failure") appeared time and again.

The first responsibility of tax-supported public schools is to imbue and prepare children and youth with knowledge, skills, and values that they would use to become politically engaged citizens who participate in a democracy, can find jobs in a competitive market-based workplace, and gain, again through competition, personal "success."

Also at this moment of change, Progressives added a responsibility in wanting schools to make America a better place to live in. The duty of public schools was to be an agent of societal reform. This idea took off in the early twentieth century and has been in the educational bloodstream ever since.[20]

So here is a national institution that has had from its very earliest years conflicting goals—reform and conserve. Even though there were splits among Progressives during their heyday of reform (1890–1940)— efficiency-minded and pedagogical wings—they sought and achieved, in spite of educational criticism from scattered conservatives, major changes in what many reformers then and now sneeringly called "traditional schools." These contradictory obligations of reforming schools, while conserving traditional knowledge and classroom practices, have been in the genetic code of tax-supported public education for well over a century.

Times change, however. So do purposes shift for tax-supported public schools. The Great Depression of the 1930s and World War II became the crucible in which the United States moved from economic scarcity and high unemployment to becoming a world power and a beacon for democracy afflicted with domestic problems of race and inequality, but nonetheless, a commanding, prosperous nation opposed to the Soviet expansionism that historians called the Cold War. In these decades, civic and business leaders turned to public schools for solutions to these national problems.[21]

In these years, the prevailing progressive consensus over attaining efficient schools and what constituted institutional "success" and "failure" eroded as conservative attacks gained adherents. By the mid-1960s, a later generation of school reformers had risen to challenge what had become the orthodoxy of a "one best system" of "efficient" schooling. Progressive ideas and practices still persisted, and conservatives even embraced some of the changes that the previous generation of reformers had enacted in curriculum and instruction, but different contexts created different reform agendas.[22]

CONTEMPORARY VIEWS OF "SUCCEEDING" AND "FAILING" APPLIED TO SCHOOLS (1970s–PRESENT)

For over a half-century, then, efficiency-driven Progressive policy makers, academics, and practitioners had concentrated on establishing rational standards for what goes into schooling, such as per-pupil expenditure; hiring of college-trained, knowledgeable teachers; and improved school facilities. Professional educators, using efficiency measures to cut perceived waste while increasing teacher and student productivity, determined organizational "success" and "failure."

But rising criticism of the dominant Progressive curriculum and "efficient" teaching practices in the 1950s grew into a tsunami of censure aimed at "failing" and mediocre US schools in the wake of an emerging Civil Rights movement and following the Soviet Union's launch of Sputnik into space (1957). Growing disapproval of American schools from both liberals and conservatives cracked the ideological cocoon of Progressive educators' dominance in state and district rhetoric and policies that they had enjoyed for a half-century.[23]

Disparaging schools as "failing" the nation after the *Brown* decision (1954) and the unfolding of the Civil Rights movement as it spilled over from protests against segregated buses and disenfranchised black voters onto low performing poverty-wracked urban and rural schools across the country made the 1960s a tumultuous decade.

The assassination of President John F. Kennedy elevated Vice President Lyndon Johnson to the highest office, giving him the chance to enact his vision of a "Great Society," one rooted in the federal government working to end poverty and improving the lives of the poor and disenfranchised. Through the Civil Rights Act, Voting Rights Act, and the Elementary and Secondary Education Act (ESEA), the "Great Society" unfolded but eventually collapsed as it became harnessed to the tragic Vietnam War.[24]

During these years, federal and state policy makers—as well as corporate leaders and donors—became committed to decision-making based on quantitative data (e.g., body counts in Vietnam, zero-based budgeting in government). The technocratic approach to schooling revealed in the "scientific management" of an earlier generation got updated with new technologies, data gathering, and decisions anchored in data.

These reform-minded policy elites had little patience with traditional educators using older, obsolete ways of managing data and making decisions, particularly because these educators were insulated from the hurly-burly of political negotiations which was becoming a staple of the new technocrats. Innovative ways of calculating effectiveness in terms of outcomes rather than inputs and the inevitable trade-offs that occur in running large corporate and government organizations were seemingly beyond the ken of the current generation of educators.[25]

Groupthink among educators that "good" schools were efficient and met research-based standards of earlier decades left advocates of the Great Society rolling their eyes. As data increasingly revealed that poor and minority children and youth were failing to read, understand math, and write coherently, federal policy makers leapfrogged the political educational establishment and the insularity those educators had prized to impose politically a different definition for "successful" schools. By 1970, student outcomes and quantifiable results to establish both efficiency and effectiveness had seeped into reformers' vocabulary and thinking about school improvement.

This generation of civic, business, and philanthropic leaders supported federal legislation that distributed for the first time large sums of money to districts to better educate poor students and, they hoped, move their families into the middle class. With the flow of money went federal regulations on how that money should be spent to avoid waste—efficiency criteria to determine institutional "success" re-emerged.

Legislators, also aware of new ways to analyze systems and manage organizations through quantitative reports of results, for the first time paid more attention to school-by-school test scores and student outcomes such as graduation and dropout rates and college admissions.

This shift from "efficient" schools using resources wisely to "effective" schools determined by student outcomes traces the path that definitions of organizational "success" and "failure" took in schools and districts over the past half-century. Both efficiency and effectiveness, however, remained important within schooling, but the center of gravity had clearly shifted to a primary focus on overall student results and holding districts and schools responsible for those outcomes.

HOW THE CHANGE IN DEFINITIONS OCCURRED

This seismic shift in institutional definitions of "success" and "failure" began in ESEA hearings held in 1965 when dueling views of whether distribution of funds to states should be evaluated for students' effects or simply efficiency, that is, what districts did with the money. Some legislators expressed open distrust of educators' judgment when it came to children of the poor. Disagreements boiled over as to who should do the evaluations—educators or independent evaluators. Most important, however, to Senator Robert Kennedy (D-NY) was that federal funds not be wasted. He asked repeatedly, "I wonder if we couldn't have some kind of system of reporting either through some testing system that would be established which the people at the local community would know periodically as to what progress has been made under this program."[26]

Kennedy's questions and views about importance of results and accountability for outcomes prevailed—tests would be given and results would be made public; expert evaluators, not educators, would do the assessment work. Within a few years, educators and informed community activists, prodded by federal grants, accelerated the move toward testing students (and publishing those results) to determine whether the federal dollars made a difference in their academic performance.

No longer was the adjective "efficient" dominant in describing a "good" school; now the pervasive adjective was "effective" when student academic outcomes improved seemingly as a result of new funding, tougher curriculum standards, better teaching, and other factors. Thus, the center of gravity shifted from inputs to outputs.

Effectiveness as Criterion for Determining "Success" in Schools Since ESEA

Since the late 1970s, "successful" schools have been called "effective," "high performing," "good," "excellent," and similar phrases. Institutional measures of success for these "effective schools" were scores on state standardized tests, dropout rate, numbers of students graduating high school, and proportion of graduates attending college. These numbers counted.

In these years, a civic and corporate-led political movement grew to tie the national economy, buffeted by foreign competition and sagging productivity, to improve schools. The resurrection of schools seeking "social efficiency," that is, linking education to a stronger economy, echoed an earlier generation of "educational engineers."

Employers worried about having sufficient high school graduates who could easily move into a workforce shifting from industrial and manufacturing jobs to ones rooted in information and service-based occupations. They and civic leaders saw public schools as the vehicle to do just that. Probably the shortest national report on education, the thirty-six-page *A Nation at Risk* captured both the fears and hopes of corporate and civic elites, including donors, as it laid out a raft of recommendations aimed at marrying education to a strong economy:

> *We report to the American people that while we can take justifiable pride in what our schools and colleges have historically accomplished and contributed to the United States and the well-being of its people, the educational foundations of our society are presently being eroded by a rising tide of mediocrity that threatens our very future as a Nation and a people.*

And that "rising tide of mediocrity" was apparent to the Commission in how US students compared with other nations' students on international tests:

> *If an unfriendly foreign power had attempted to impose on America the mediocre educational performance that exists today, we might well have viewed it as an act of war. As it stands, we have allowed this to happen to ourselves. We have even squandered the gains in student achievement made in the wake of the Sputnik challenge.*[27]

Within the next three decades, national goals, rigorous curriculum, ample use of standardized test scores, and accountability regulations had spread across the United States. So had the concept of "mediocrity" as a tainted word in policy elites' vocabulary that was (and is) perilously close to damnable "failure."[28]

None of this should surprise readers knowledgeable about the early decades of the twentieth century. Then "scientific management" and public schools mimicking corporate practices to become "efficient" infused reformers who saw Great Britain and Germany as economic competitors for global markets.[29]

Also partnerships between government leaders and the business community have existed since the founding of the nation—recall the National Banks of the late eighteenth and early nineteenth century, the federal patent system, financiers lending the government money, and joint efforts to build public roads and improve education.[30]

The intersection between public education and business, civic, and donor leaders has had another twist over the decades. These leaders turned to public schools time and again to solve national problems. Since tax-supported schools were founded in the early nineteenth century, they have been a profoundly political institution that elite leaders had established to serve larger purposes in the nation (e.g., produce patriotic, literate citizens with solid character prepared for the workplace). US public schools are (and have been) state and locally controlled and financed political institutions vulnerable to popular movements and consequential events coursing through the nation such as Civil Rights protests, economic depressions, and wars. "The nation has a cold and schools sneeze" may be a cliché, but it is accurate at its core simply because public schools are dependent upon taxpayers and voters for political and financial support.

Close relations between corporate America and public schools throughout the 1980s and 1990s showed up in top federal officials' and business leaders' embrace of national goals, tougher curriculum standards, standardized testing, and ways of holding students, teachers, schools, and districts accountable for outcomes. So reforms aimed at restructuring schools to make them "effective" by using new technologies and repeated calls for schools to innovate were common in these years. The "effective schools" movement that emerged in these years fit the times.[31]

Spread of "Effective" Schools

Anchored in the features of schools located in low-income neighborhoods that defied predictions of mediocre performance by scoring high on standardized tests, "effective schools" surged across the nation's urban districts in the mid-1980s and extended through the 1990s. So-called effectiveness features (e.g., strong principal, focus on academics, frequent assessment, close work with community) extracted from studies of high performing schools in poor neighborhoods became converted into formulas for "success." Remember, however, that these effective schools were outliers. Most schools enrolling largely poor and minority children and youth scored low on state tests and were viewed as mediocre or failing.[32]

In 1998, President Bill Clinton signed the Comprehensive School Reform Act, which converted concepts of the Effective Schools movement into law. Federal officials identified seventeen models of whole school reform backed by research evidence such as Success For All, Direct Instruction, and New American Schools, a joint venture between selected corporations and educational policy makers. Districts awarded grants could put into practice one or more of these models. Improved test scores were again the primary measure of "success" in putting these whole-school reform models into practice.[33]

With the bipartisan passage of No Child Left Behind in 2002—the Comprehensive School Reform Program was folded into NCLB—test results continued as triggers for federal and state actions. Business leaders cheered NCLB and its desired results that fit corporate America's balance sheet. Steel-reinforced curriculum standards, more tests, and accountability mechanisms that penalized low performance would produce high school graduates prepared to enter college and the workplace.[34]

Minority access to better schools would reduce inequalities rife in American society, reformers believed. Disadvantaged children would have a shot at climbing the social ladder of financial success. The return of "social efficiency" promoted by earlier generations of reformers heralded another generation imbued with technocratic values, beliefs in both excellence and equity and making schools "good."

Schools that met NCLB's "Adequate Yearly Progress" on standardized tests of reading and math—proxies for college and job preparation—were designated as "successful" while those that did not were labeled "failing." A national report card of "success" and "failure" appeared in districts receiving federal funds. By 2011, however, nearly half of the nation's schools were judged to be "failing" by NCLB criteria. Subsequent reauthorization of ESEA now called Every Student Succeeds Act (2015) loosened federal control of accountability, returning much authority for determining "successes" and "failures" to state officials. Much of the previous law, however, remained in its replacement.[35]

Yet by 2019, no recipe for creating and sustaining schools identified as "effective"" had emerged. In the 1980s and 1990s, researchers Ron Edmonds and later Anthony Bryk had identified common structures and practices found in effective schools, but sustaining those easily measured outcomes and less quantifiable humanistic features over time, that is, trust and respect for students, teachers, and community, was unrelentingly steady work that often eroded as falling student test scores, decreasing graduation rates, and lower admissions to college occurred, forcing districts to replace principals and staffs or close schools. For poor and minority students, inequalities in academic achievement and access to "good" schools persisted.[36]

In the twenty-first century, effectiveness, as measured by test scores and other quantitative markers, remains among reformers on the political left and right the primary criterion to determine institutional "success." Since the early 1990s, the policy strategy of expanding parental choice through public charter schools, a political goal of contemporary (mostly politically conservative) school reformers, had already enrolled over 6 percent of all public school children and youth. Just as in regular public schools, academic "success" and "failure" among charter schools also hinge upon test scores, college admissions, and entering the workforce. Yet that coalition of liberal and conservative reformers focused on measurable student outcomes had begun to fray and split.[37]

If effectiveness is now in the foreground from both wings of the current generation of school reformers as the primary organizational criterion of "success" or "failure," efficiency—the cutting of waste in time and money while increasing student and teacher productivity (as measured by test scores)—continues quietly in the background as a powerful force when leaders make policy decisions. After all, local and state voters determine what monies to allocate to schools, and those funds are often below what educators seek. Hence, figuring out to the dollar what instruction, curriculum, and facilities cost and continually reducing waste in spending money remain ever-present concerns. The technocratic tradition harking back to "administrative Progressives" is alive and well in 2019.

Traditional reliance on both effectiveness and efficiency over the past half-century got a booster shot when school reformers latched onto new technologies. With the rapid expansion of computers in schools since the 1980s—the business sector was far ahead of education in automating work and increasing productivity of workers—and recent advances in analyzing large data sets and using artificial intelligence, policy makers have increasingly relied upon data-driven algorithms to make district, school, and classroom decisions that seemingly increase both effectiveness and efficiency.[38]

NEW TECHNOLOGIES ENTER SCHOOLS AGAIN TO INCREASE BOTH EFFICIENCY AND EFFECTIVENESS

The current crusade among reformers for data-driven decision-making and evangelizing for new technologies in schools and classrooms resurrects Frederick Winslow Taylor's application of scientific methods on how workers did their jobs a century ago.

In the decade before World War I and through the 1930s, Taylor's acolytes with ever-present stopwatches in their hands reigned. Institutions as varied as agriculture, medical practice, municipal government, criminal justice, and schools adopted Taylor's techniques of time-and-motion studies to increase employee efficiency and find the "one best way" of doing work well at the least cost. Experts, then, assumed that an efficient operation was an effective one. Educators grasped "scientific management" eagerly and employed it religiously in these years.[39]

Here is Newton, Massachusetts, superintendent Frank Spaulding telling fellow superintendents at the annual conference of the National Education Association in 1913 how he "scientifically managed" his district. The crucial task, Spaulding told his peers, was for district officials to measure school "products or results" and thereby compare "the efficiency of schools in these respects." What did he mean by products?

> *I refer to such results as the percentage of children of each year of age [enrolled] in school; the average number of days attendance secured annually from each child; the average length of time required for each child to do a given definite unit of work.*[40]

Spaulding and other superintendents inspired by measurement gurus of the day such as Teachers College psychologist Edward Thorndike measured in dollars and cents whether the teaching of Latin was more efficient than the teaching of English, algebra, or history. These "administrative Progressives" recorded how much it cost to teach vocational subjects versus academic subjects.[41]

What Spaulding described in Newton as increased efficiency (and the assumption that it led to effectiveness) spread swiftly among school boards, superintendents, and administrators. In the 1920s and 1930s, districts hired academic experts such as Stanford University's Ellwood Cubberley and University of Chicago's Charles Judd to gather data. Using high-tech devices and methods then present in the early twentieth century such as stopwatches to count minutes and hours to complete tasks, teams recorded results meticulously. They described and analyzed inside and outside buildings, how much time principals spent with students and parents, and what teachers did in daily lessons.[42]

Between the 1920s and 1950s, technological devices called "teaching machines" appeared. They were touted to teach individual students more content and skills faster and better at less cost than teacher-led whole-group lessons. Influenced by the work of psychologist Edward Thorndike, Ohio State University professor Sidney Pressey patented a teaching machine using a typewriter that displayed a question followed by multiple-choice answers. He sought to help the teacher by incorporating drill-and-practice exercises for students to do alone. In Pressey's words: "Lift from her [the teacher's] shoulders as much as possible of this burden and make her free for those inspirational and thought-stimulating activities which are, presumably, the real function of the teacher."[43]

Pressey's teaching machine flopped. Few superintendents bought the devices. Not until the 1950s did a similar invention by Harvard University's B. F. Skinner make a larger splash than the earlier Pressey device. As Skinner put it:

> The greatest single source of inefficiency in American education is our practice of moving a whole group of students at the same rate. That's bad for the fast student who has to be held up. He gets bored. But it's particularly bad for the slow student. The slow student falls behind in the present system and then he goes even slower. Finally, he gives up and you lose him. The whole point of individually programmed or prescribed instruction is to move the student along as rapidly as he can or as slowly as he needs.[44]

Skinner's critique of the age-graded school fell on deaf ears. While Skinner's teaching machines were manufactured and sold in the 1950s and 1960s to K–12 schools, universities, and corporate trainers, they seldom took hold in classrooms beyond pilot programs and occasional experiments. Not until the early 2000s with the spread of computing devices at all levels of K–12 schooling did the press for increased productivity and efficiency bring updated versions of Sidney Pressey's and B. F. Skinner's ideas to policy makers, practitioners, and donors.

Altogether, then, the efficiency-driven progressive crusade for meaningful data to inform policy decisions about classroom, school, and district effectiveness that began in the first half of the twentieth century continued in subsequent decades and took on renewed vigor with the ubiquity of devices and software in the early decades of the twenty-first century.

CONTEMPORARY ENTHUSIASM FOR TECHNOLOGY-DRIVEN EFFECTIVENESS AND EFFICIENCY IN SCHOOLS

The current donor and business-led resurgence of a "modern cult of efficiency," or the application of technocratic approaches, can be seen in many companies and US schools.[45]

Consider Amazon, a company that earned little revenue in its early years yet in 2018 was valued at over $700 billion. Using technology including robots to track inventories, customers' preferences, and rapid delivery is part of its "phenomenal success." Amazon's quest for efficiency in swiftly delivering purchases to customers' doors would put a smile on Frederick Winslow Taylor's face.[46]

One observer, for example, reported in 2015 on the newly opened one-million-square-feet Amazon warehouse in Robbinsville, New Jersey, where orders are "fulfilled":

> Upon arrival, each new product is identified using a computer vision system that catalogues it rapidly, feeding its weight and dimensions into a central tracking system. At the heart of the building, items stored on tall, square shelves are kept stocked by humans working with a team of 2,000 squat orange robots. The robots zip around the storage area, picking up shelves and either arranging them in neat rows for storage or bringing them over to the human workers, who stack or pick from them. Further along the fulfillment line, workers charged with packing up orders for shipping are automatically given the optimal size of shipping box and even the correct amount of packing tape. Before those boxes are sent to trucks, a system weighs them to make sure the correct products are inside.[47]

Amazon has updated century-old Taylorism practices to produce "standardization, . . . the setting of precisely defined tasks, the emphasis on efficiency, and productivity to the exclusion of all else."[48]

Turn now to schooling. The current incarnation of "Taylorism" can be seen in the standards, testing, and accountability movement launched over three decades ago in the wake of the report *A Nation at Risk*. The application of business practices and lingo under the umbrella of scientifically acquired evidence reappeared anew albeit with different labels. Increasing the effectiveness and efficiency of public schools would increase "human capital" and stimulate worker productivity, thereby strengthening the national economy.[49]

With the increased power of computers to gather and analyze data, new techniques appeared to prod schools to teach more, better, and faster. The frequent gathering and parsing of student-by-student, school-by-school, district-by-district, state-by-state, and national test data became a major enterprise. The lure of increased productivity and efficiency through evidence-based decision-making in light of huge data sets and faster computers has led to increasing use of software algorithms to grade performance of individual schools, evaluating individual performance of teachers, and customizing online lessons for individual students.

Many states and districts now evaluate the performance of schools based on test scores, growth in achievement, graduation rates, and other measures and then assign rankings by issuing a report card grade to each school ranging from an A to an F, awarding one to five stars, or similar rating systems. Such report cards signal parents which schools are high performing and attractive to enroll their children and which schools are to be avoided—an efficient way for parents sorting through options since parental choice in public schools has expanded.[50]

Determining which teachers are productive, that is, "effective," using students' test scores has occurred in many states and big city districts. Fueled by extensive donor grants, such outcome measures should not shock anyone familiar with the spreading influence of the business model and its vocabulary into schooling (e.g., calling superintendents CEOs and parents "customers," seeking a larger "market share" for charter schools, tying employee evaluations to student test scores, and stressing "return on investment").[51]

And do not forget students. Within classrooms, both effectiveness and efficiency have come to the fore in customizing lessons for individual children and youth. Earlier efforts to introduce "teaching machines" in the 1920s and later in the 1950s testify to the history of educators seeking ways to tailor teaching and learning to fit individual students and overcome common practices of whole-group teaching in the age-graded school.[52]

The spread of faster and cheaper technologies since the 1990s, harnessed to the growth of large data sets on student performance in math, reading, and other school subjects used to meet state accountability requirements, has led to a Niagara of academic software spilling over schools in the past two decades. The rationale for extensive buying and distributing of new devices and software has been to make teaching and learning faster, better, individualized, and, yes, cheaper. Former US Secretary of Education Arne Duncan made this point in 2010:

> Technology can play a huge role in increasing educational productivity, but not just as an add-on or for a high-tech reproduction of current practice. Again, we need to change the underlying processes to leverage the capabilities of technology. The military calls it a force multiplier. Better use of online learning, virtual schools, and other smart uses of technology is not so much about replacing educational roles as it is about giving each person the tools they need to be more successful—reducing wasted time, energy, and money.[53]

An administrative Progressive, circa 1910, could not have said it better.

Those sentiments continue to reign supreme among contemporary policy elites when it comes to schooling. Efficiency, productivity, and effectiveness, a holy trinity to earlier generations of educators, remain sacred to current federal officials and philanthropic leaders, a moment that Frederick Winslow Taylor would have thoroughly relished.[54]

The recent surge of technology-enhanced schooling called "personalized learning" merges the polestars of school reform since the 1890s. First, there is a renewed stress on effectiveness and efficiency as seen in the "effective schools" movement of the 1980s, and second, the century-old two wings of the Progressive movement—"administrative" and "pedagogical" reformers—have re-emerged under different aliases. Both mergers have become evident in 2019 as a renewed "cult of efficiency." The language, images, and practices that promoters use to characterize "personalized learning" have re-established these historic twin goals for US schooling.

PERSONALIZED LEARNING

Today's reformers promoting "personalized learning" seek what their much older cousins among Progressive educators sought a century ago. Then, reformers, albeit split between two wings of the movement, wanted public schools to turn children and youth into thoughtful, civically engaged, whole adults. Both pedagogical and efficiency-minded Progressives used John Dewey's words to justify their positions.

But philosopher Dewey was not easy to parse. While many academics and practitioners cited Dewey's writings and reduced his ideas to aphorisms "learning by doing" and "start where the child is," other academics such as behaviorist John Watson, who had studied with Dewey, said: "I never knew what [Dewey] was talking about and, unfortunately, I still don't." Psychologist Edward Thorndike, a colleague of Dewey's at Teachers College, stated outright: "I just cannot understand Dewey."[55]

Nonetheless, doyens of efficiency Ellwood Cubberley and Edward Thorndike using Deweyan ideas to overhaul inefficient traditional schools triumphed over those pedagogical Progressives who called for teaching the "whole child." Although Dewey's notion of growing a full human being through active problem solving and inquiry has persisted, effectiveness and efficiency-minded reformers prevailed in early twentieth century schools. This institutional definition of "success" drowned out the rival definition of the well-being of a growing individual child promoted by pedagogical Progressives.

In 2019, however, both behaviorists and believers in the "whole child" wear the same clothes and mouth the same phrases of school reformers and educational entrepreneurs seeking "personalized learning." They tout scientific studies showing that lessons tailored for individual students produce higher test scores than before, or that project-based learning or social-emotional skills create independent, creative, and smart students who go on to lucrative careers and help their communities.[56]

What exists now is a re-emergence of the efficiency-minded "administrative Progressives" from a century ago who now, as entrepreneurial reformers, want public schools to be more business-like where supply and demand reign, and more realistic in preparing the "whole child" for a competitive workplace. These champions of "personalized learning" fall into three categories.

Visualize a spectrum that at one end are entrepreneurs and technology advocates including practitioners who want individual students to master the content and skills found in state curriculum standards in less time than teachers typically use in lessons while spending fewer dollars to achieve that mastery—as measured by required state tests. Aware of the bind they find themselves in wanting to meet state and district accountability requirements for improved test scores while "personalizing" learning to meet each student's strengths and limitations, these advocates embrace a menu of different programs that carry labels such as "competency-based education," "mastery learning," and "proficiency-based learning."[57]

Examples would be current versions of competency-based learning aligned to, say, Common Core standards or programs such as Teach To One that follow prescribed skills to be learned in, say, math. Consider David A. Boody Intermediate School in Brooklyn, New York:

> Teach to One: Math . . . combines small group lessons, one-on-one learning with a teacher, learning directly from software, and online tutoring. . . .
>
> One key feature of the program is apparent even before instruction begins. The entrance to the math class at David A. Boody looks a bit like a scene at an airport terminal. Three giant screens display daily schedule updates for all students and teachers. The area is huge, yawning across a wide-open space created by demolishing the walls between classrooms.
>
> "There is a great deal of transparency here," said Cathy Hayes, the school's math director, explaining the idea behind the enormous classroom [that holds 150 sixth graders]. "Children and teachers can see each other, and that transparency works to share great work. This isn't a room where you can shut the door and contain what you are doing."
>
> The open design is meant to encourage collaboration; teachers can learn from each other by working in close proximity. Shelves, desks, and whiteboards divide the large room to create nooks for small-group instruction. Each area has a name, such as Brooklyn Bridge or Manhattan

Bridge, which helps [the 150] students know where they are supposed to go. Sometimes students are instructed by teachers; other times they work in sections monitored by teaching assistants. Some stations use pencil-on-paper worksheets with prompts to help guide students through group projects; stations in another part of the classroom are for independent computer-guided lessons and tutoring. . . .

All this activity in the large, high-ceilinged room creates a constant buzz, which seemed to distract some students. Teachers had to remind them not to peer around the big room. Students seated in the back appeared to have trouble hearing the teacher.

Math class spans two 35-minute sessions, with students and teachers rotating to new stations after the first session. The school has about 300 students in the math program. Half of them report to class at one time.

The program's computer system coordinates where everyone will go based on how the children perform on a daily test at the end of class. The next day's schedule is delivered electronically. Teachers, students, and parents can log on to a website to see it. . . .

The software used by the Teach To One system pulls lessons from a database created and curated by the program's academic team. When Teach To One staffers discover a lesson that fits their program, they negotiate with the publisher to buy the lesson à la carte—sort of like buying one song from iTunes instead of buying the entire album. Staffers say they examined about 80,000 lessons to create a library of 12,000 from 20 vendors. A room in the office of the nonprofit is filled with stacks of math textbooks. . . .

Supporters say the program gives every student a custom-designed math class, allowing students to get different lessons, and move faster or slower than peers in the same class.[58]

At the opposite end of this "personalized learning" spectrum are practitioners and entrepreneurs who see schools as places to create whole, knowledgeable human beings capable of entering and succeeding in a world far different than their parents faced. To these technology-friendly reformers (e.g., private AltSchool, Khan Lab Schools, and public Summit School charters), student interests and passions are integrated efficiently into daily activities in which they, with the help of teachers, make decisions about projects they will work on and how long it takes to demonstrate mastery while meeting curriculum standards and posting high scores on state tests.[59]

For example, the principal of a Wisconsin school described a "typical day" of "personalized learning" for Cal, a real middle-school student, at the Waukesha STEM Academy.

... Starting the Day

Cal's learning begins at home as he prepares for his school day. He checks his Google Calendar schedule while eating breakfast, and he texts the members of his Future City team to plan where to meet later in the morning to work on their design project. Upon entering school, he approaches one of the badging stations at the front door and scans his ID, which tells the school office he's safely at school. The attendance process that used to require the first 10 minutes of each class is now done within seconds. ...

... Advisory Time

Cal's school day begins as students move to advisory time. Today's advisory activity is updating the students' learner continuums. Cal already did this a few days ago, when he revised his learner profile to reflect current proficiency levels in his classes and projects. Still, while reflecting on his learner profile and continuums during advisory, Cal realizes he has acquired a few more skills and demonstrated mastery across more content areas on his learner continuum than he had identified earlier. Although the system is not grade-bound, Cal is still able to confirm that he's on track to be fully prepared for high school. ...

... [Project] Time

This school doesn't have bells or four-minute transition times between classes, but Cal knows when it's time to head to [find] . . . his Future City team in the space where they had decided to meet when they texted earlier in the morning. Two teammates walk up with an assortment of building supplies that they've brought in to continue building portions of their project, which centers around "public spaces that encourage interaction and interconnectedness throughout the community."

Each member of the group plays a specific role to complete the overall project. At the meeting today, the students review due dates and begin to plan the next stages of their project. With the incorporation of actual models into the main project, the team is now ready to begin composing their narrative description of their ideas and key concepts. One of the project facilitators, a math teacher, asks the team, "Are you going to be ready for the check-in on Friday? Are you feeling good about the timeline you created? What successes and challenges are you going to share with the other groups?" Cal and his teammates discuss their progress and work to get ready for the Friday check-in. . . .

. . . Self-Paced Mathematics

Cal moves on . . . to work on mathematics in an open commons area. He opens his Google Classroom app to look over his current tasks and review progress on his learning goals in a document titled "Math Learner Continuum." Cal is working on the standard "understanding and applying operations with fractions to add, subtract, multiply, and divide rational numbers." He notices that he has not yet shown proficiency on all parts of this standard and decides that he needs additional coaching. So he opens a series of videos and online tutorials, as well as tutorials prepared by his teacher. He takes notes, rewinds to review a few components, and then completes some practice exercises. . . .

. . . Flexible Choice Time

Now it's time for the daily CONNECT hour. Cal struggled in literacy yesterday afternoon while working on a narrative writing piece for his Future City project, so he pulls up a digital spreadsheet to check when and where his literacy facilitator will be available to provide some coaching on his work today. Seeing that she's available now, he heads off to meet with her and gets her feedback on crafting a stronger narrative piece that will grab the reader's attention with some descriptive voice. Now feeling more confident, he decides to upload the piece of writing to his portfolio. He then heads off to eat lunch with his friends. He realizes he has not yet listened to the daily announcements, so he pulls up a YouTube video and watches as fellow students share coming events and opportunities to connect within the community. . . .

. . . A Garden Project

Science is an exciting class for Cal—there's a buzz of conversation between him and a group of his peers as they transition from CONNECT time and head outside to look at their raised garden bed and compost stations. They then come back inside and pull up Google Classroom on their devices to record progress on their gardening project, which involves growing produce that they will sell at the local farmers' market. The science teacher facilitating the class stops by and asks if they would like to meet, so Cal and his group pull some chairs in a circle to confer about the observations they made from the garden bed and compost station, as well as the costs of the produce and logistics for moving the food to the farmers' market.[60]

And on this "personalized learning" spectrum where Brooklyn, New York, and Waukesha, Wisconsin, students reside, there is yet even a third category located in the middle of the spectrum between competency-based learning and project-based instruction where district and school administrators and teachers pick and choose from both sides of the continuum to create hybrids.[61]

No surprise, then, that these various categories of technology-driven "personalized learning" have given this catchphrase a gaggle of different meanings. Is it updated "competency-based learning"? Or "individualized learning" redecorated? "Blended learning," "project-based teaching," and "21st Century skills" are a few recent bumper stickers that have generated many meanings as they get converted by policy makers, marketeers, researchers, wannabe reformers, and, yes, teachers into daily lessons. Such proliferation of school reforms into slogans is as familiar to observers of US school reforms as photos of sunsets.

With a glance at the rearview mirror, however, one can easily see in this spectrum of three categories how the past is alive in the present. The current language used to describe the "next new thing" resurrects "efficiency engineers" and pedagogical Progressives from yesteryear in their competing views of "success." And as in the previous century, the resurrected quantifiers who capture what can be measured won again. In their victory, they have appropriated the language of the "whole child" and "learning by doing" and applied the words to a technocratic and behaviorist view of content and skills.

Imbued with visions of students being prepared for a world where adults change jobs a half-dozen times in a lifetime, these efficiency-minded reformers tout schools that have tailored lessons (both online and offline) to individual students, teachers have turned into coaches, and students collaborate with one another, thus reflecting the changed workplace of the twenty-first century. Efficiency-minded reformers' victorious capture of the vocabulary of "personalized learning" has made parsing the present-day world of school policies aimed at making classrooms havens of "personalized learning" confusing to those unfamiliar with century-old struggles over similar issues. Yet baffled or not, what continues to determine institutional "success" and "failure" for today's "personalized learning" champions remains student performance as measured by test scores, high school graduation rate, admission to college, and similar outcomes.

So as the turn from school inputs to outputs shifted between the early to late twentieth century, and the continuing popularity of both efficiency and effectiveness as markers of organizational "success" and "failure, a question arises about the sources for these notions. From where did educational policy elites, then and now, get these competing concepts of institutional and individual criteria for judging "success" and "failure"? Chapter 2 answers that question.

– CHAPTER 2 –

FROM WHERE DO THESE IDEAS OF "SUCCESS" AND "FAILURE" COME?

[T]he average Americans' ideal vision of being successful [in 2018] is when they are married with two children, and earning $147,000 from their stay-at-home job that only makes them work up to 31 hours a week and rewards them with five weeks of vacation. Although only 31 percent of respondents worked from home, more than half of them said they wanted to be working remotely in their successful futures. The average respondent's commute took 17 minutes and they wanted it to be shaved down to ten minutes to consider themselves as more successful.

—MONICA TORRES[1]

[In addition], 67 percent of survey takers said that, "money was the major missing part of their equation for success."
[To the question:] how much would your home and vehicle be worth if you "made it"? About $461,000 and $41,986 respectively.

—JEFF DESJARDINS[2]

Although there is no objective definition of "success" or "failure" that everyone can nod in agreement to, informal ways have arisen to quantify what the terms mean in America. The above survey is one way to take high-blown rhetoric about "The American Dream" and being "successful" and applying it to the present. Yet in doing so, sorting out an institutional definition of "success"—school effectiveness in raising student test scores and graduation rates—from an individual definition—making money, buying a home, and feeling personally confident—is essential.

"Success" in contemporary America can be translated into individual earnings, property purchased, and time spent with family. Money is the personal currency of "success" in a market-driven economy. The connection to public schools is the way that the quantification of "success" that occurs daily in American life spills over to numbers being used to judge how "successful" schools are and have been as an institution. This chapter describes and analyzes the history of that connection between organizational and individual numbers, American notions of "success" and "failure," and how both have competed with one another over the past century in public schools.

■ ■ ■

Ideas of "success" and "failure" in public schools are anchored in a market-driven economy that seventeenth- and eighteenth-century colonists brought from Europe. Or as historian Carl Degler put it, "capitalism came in the first ships." Within that capitalist DNA and evolving democratic governance, Americans held core beliefs and values that have matured and remained constant since then: individualism, community, and equal opportunity. And within those prized societal values, particularly individualism, emerged ideas of what constituted "success" and "failure" in American society.[3]

These core beliefs and values grew in strength among Americans over subsequent centuries as the United States expanded across a continent and became economically and militarily powerful. From these core beliefs embedded in a property-based, market-driven economy fastened to individual competition and government protection of that property, ideas of personal "success" and "failure" in American society—avoiding being a pauper and becoming rich—inexorably flowed into and across US institutions including tax-supported public schools.

In 1931, a historian captured these beliefs:

> The American dream . . . has lured tens of million of all nation to our shores in the past century. . . . It is not a dream of motor cars and high wages merely but a dream of a social order in which each man and woman shall be able to attain to the fullest stature of which they are innately capable, and be recognized by others for what they are.[4]

A decade later, a Swedish sociologist and his team identified these beliefs and values as the "American Creed," embedded in principles drawn from the founders of the nation, the Declaration of Independence, the US Constitution, and continuing through Abraham Lincoln, Frederick Douglass, Franklin Delano Roosevelt, and Martin Luther King Jr.[5]

These beliefs in individualism, community, and equal opportunity—espoused in the Dream and the Creed and concretized in capitalism and democratic governance—are the basic ingredients welded together decade after decade to define "success" and "failure" often measured in dollars earned and property owned. This melding of dissonant values into popular views of what "success" and "failure" mean occurred in an ever-changing America that moved from predominately farming to an industrialized economy and now to an increasingly information- and service-driven one yet retaining through all of these economic changes individual aspirations—counted in dollars and status—to become noticed, recognized, approved, and rich.

Democratic governance also changed over time as voting rights initially for white males extended to other Americans and the rule of law became fixed in local and national practice. Just as unlikely ingredients put into a soup that over time dissolve into a palatable dish, these beliefs and values, often in tension with one another since they emerged in the American consciousness, have been incorporated into a highly diverse society, including tax-supported public schools.

CORE BELIEFS AND VALUES CONFLICT

Individualism means that Americans seek (and have sought) to achieve personal economic success in a highly competitive, market-oriented system embedded in a democratic, highly decentralized government. The epigraph captures the beliefs of Americans that amount of money equates to personal "success." In pursuing their economic interests and passions, Americans wanted the freedom to choose, excuse the cliché, come hell or high water. And even if they chose unwisely and fail, so be it.

As a team of sociologists who studied the American character in the 1980s put it:

> [W]e are united . . . in at least one core belief, even across lines of color, religion, region, and occupation: the belief that economic success or misfortune is the individual's responsibility and his or hers alone.[6]

This growth of individualism appeared in the earliest years of the nation where abundant land greeted land-starved English farmers and was available for the taking (once they forcibly removed indigenous peoples). Puritan minister Cotton Mather preached the following sermon to his Massachusetts congregants in 1701:

> A Christian should follow his Occupation with INDUSTRY [sic]. . . . It seems a man Slothful in Business, is not a man Serving the Lord. By Slothfulness men bring upon themselves, What? But Poverty, but misery, but all sorts of Confusion. . . .
>
> On the other Side, . . . A Diligent man is very rarely an Indigent man. . . . I tell you, With Diligence a man may do marvelous things. Young man, Work hard while you are Young: You'll Reap the effects of it, when you are Old. . . .[7]

Benjamin Franklin, the colonial archetype who praised individual success, promoted diligence and hard work as virtues in the "The Way to Wealth":

> Sloth makes all things difficult, but industry all easy. He that riseth late must trot all day, and shall scarce overtake his business at night; while Laziness travels so slowly, that Poverty soon overtakes him. Drive thy business, let not that drive thee; and Early to bed, and early to rise, makes a man healthy, wealthy, and wise. . . .[8]

Over a half-century later, French aristocrat Alexis De Tocqueville toured the United States, and in *Democracy in America* he commented about individualism as an American character trait:

> As social conditions become more equal, the number of persons increases who, although they are neither rich nor powerful enough to exercise any great influence over their fellows, have nevertheless acquired or retained sufficient education and fortune to satisfy their own wants. They owe nothing to any man, they expect nothing from any man; they acquire the habit of always considering themselves as standing alone, and they are apt to imagine that their whole destiny is in their own hands.[9]

And a decade after Tocqueville, a born-and-bred New Englander, Harvard graduate, poet, and lecturer Ralph Waldo Emerson wrote in his journal in 1842: "The merchant evidently believes the State Street [Boston] proverb that nobody fails who ought not to fail. There is always a reason, *in the man* [original emphasis], for his good or bad fortune, and so in the making of money."[10]

Fast-forward to 1999 and Andy Grove, longtime CEO of Intel who extolled individualism in managing one's career:

> Your career is literally your business. You own it as a sole proprietor. You have one employee: yourself. You are in competition with millions of similar businesses: millions of other employees all over the world. You need to accept ownership of your career, your skills and the timing of your moves. It is your responsibility to protect this personal business of yours from harm and to position it to benefit from the changes in the environment. Nobody else can do that for you.[11]

And here is thirteen-year-old Sally Avach in 2018 who says: "Right now, if you put your mind to it, you can do it. You want to be an astronaut? You can do it. As long as you work hard enough, no one's going to stop you."[12]

But how did Americans know they were "successful"? Within an economic system where owning land and striving for profits, where being a "business man" in the nineteenth century was equivalent to being an upstanding citizen, accumulating land and money became clear markers of "success." Numbers mattered. Acres could be totaled; dollars could be counted. Time to make a profit could be measured.

Or as historian Jill Lepore pointed out:

> The quantification of time led to the quantification of everything else: the counting of people, the measurement of their labor, and the calculation of profit as a function of time. Keeping time and accumulating wealth earned a certain equivalency. "Time is money," Benjamin Franklin used to say.[13]

Beginning in the seventeenth century, as Americans added, subtracted, and multiplied numbers at home, on the farm, and in the general store, as they kept time with clocks and calendars, such figures became scorecards determining individual "success" and, of course, "failure."[14]

And what mattered was property and cash. Those with little or none "failed." They became the "misfits of capitalism," with popular labels being "born losers," "deadbeats," and "good-for-nothings." Such individuals were seen as inveterate loafers, their failure due to character flaws, not as the result of circumstances. The poor were poor because they didn't work hard enough. Failure was personalized. Ignored for the most part were economic and social structures such as an unstable bank system, unfair tax policies, racial discrimination, and lack of government oversight.[15]

The self-made man (and much later, woman) became a common trope in the genre of subsequent rags-to-riches stories read by both adults and schoolchildren. Either "success" or "failure" comes from actions individuals take (or fail to take), not the situation within which individuals find themselves such as economic depressions that threw millions out of work, failed banks that lost depositors' savings, epidemic diseases and wars that killed hundreds of thousands, or government inaction. What mattered were the person's character, actions, and results—especially those that could be counted.

With "success" and "failure" made personal and quantified by land deeds and money in banks or hidden under mattresses, the basic lesson American fathers and mothers have taught their sons and daughters for generations is: work hard. Make smart choices. Beat out the next person in whatever you do. Merit counts. And rewards will come. American child-rearing practices and nineteenth-century one-room schools aimed at making children into independent adults who could take care of themselves, compete fiercely, and make wise choices. The popular nineteenth-century school textbook, *McGuffey's Second Eclectic Reader*, contained quotations about gaining success that boys and girls memorized:

Once or twice though you should fail,
    Try, Try Again;
If you would, at last prevail,
    Try, Try Again;

If we strive, 'tis no disgrace,

Though we may not win the race;

What should you do in that case?

> Try, Try Again. . . .[16]

Cotton Mather, Benjamin Franklin, Alexis de Tocqueville, Ralph Waldo Emerson, Andy Grove, and Sally Avach would nod in agreement.

The sharp focus on an individual's merit, drive, and persistence to acquire land and material goods promised by an economic system became as intense as the public prizing of the self-made man and the ideology of unchecked competition. Or as Herbert Hoover in 1928, the Republican Party nominee for President, said: "The American system . . . is founded upon the conception that only through ordered liberty, freedom and equal opportunity to the individual will his initiative and enterprise spur on the march of progress. . . . [It is] a system of rugged individualism."[17]

Why is this clasp of individualism in business, government, and tax-supported schools so American?

Cultural historian Scott Sandage's answer is that Americans

[e]mbraced business as the dominant model for our outer and inner lives. Ours is an ideology of achieved identity; obligatory striving is its method, and failure and success are its outcomes. We reckon our incomes once a year but audit ourselves daily. . . .[18]

No surprise, then, in a nation where individual rights and choices are highly prized; where competition is constant; where material "success" is gauged in dollars, net profits, and acquired property, the word "self" gets used often. In America, the young child, the grade-school student, and newcomer hear often such words: self-interest, self-reliance, self-sufficiency, self-help, self-discipline, self-made, self-educated, self-absorbed, self-actualization, self-esteem and, yes, in the moment of smart phones, selfies.[19]

Yet the total focus on the individual "making it" by avoiding "slothfulness," being "diligent," and becoming a financial "success" neglects the historic presence of the value of and belief in community where individuals meld into a larger whole, weaving a web of relationships that give meaning to the lives of ambitious individuals straining endlessly to achieve personal "success."

Community

The search for money and property is not enough for most Americans. They want also to help their immediate and extended families while competing in a market-based economy. Inescapably, they need others—family, friends, school chums, and neighbors—to look out for them when they stumble and require help. Feeling solidarity with others gives meaning to how individuals live and what they live for. Belonging to family, neighborhood school, and community groups can give individual strivers a sense of belonging in their struggle for "success."

Tocqueville, for example, noted that while Americans prized individual pursuit of property and personal gain, Americans in the early nineteenth century were also joiners:

> Americans of all ages, all stations of life, and all types of dispositions are forever forming associations. There are not only commercial and industrial associations in which all take part, but others of a thousand different types—religious, moral, serious, futile, very general and very limited, immensely large and very minute. . . .[20]

Over the centuries, Americans joined religious congregations, Rotary clubs, veteran groups, unions, and parent/teacher associations, while participating in sandlot sports and quilt-knitting groups. They started multigenerational family clubs and sought out like-minded hobbyists from stamp collectors to kite fliers.

Without interdependence and involvement in one or more communities, individuals often fail to gain a sense of belonging to something greater than me-me-me or weekly paychecks or vacation cottages. Communities mean a "we-ness."

As former President Bill Clinton put it:

> Take a penny from your pocket. On one side, next to Lincoln's portrait is a single word: "Liberty." On the other side is our national motto. It

says "E Pluribus Unum—Out of Many, One." It does not say "Every man for himself."[21]

The glue that holds a civil society together, that creates solidarity where "we" rather than "I" is used, is when individuals act to help one another and serve the community in which they live. Schools, neighborhood groups, natural disasters, and wars bring individuals together. Thus, there has been (and is) a constant tension among Americans between the time and energy spent in personal gain and pursuing what a family, group, or community desires.

Not too far from where I live, for example, after a recent accident maimed an eighty-year-old neighbor, residents called a city official to get a traffic signal on the corner where elderly neighbors and schoolchildren cross the intersection. City officials said there was no money available to add a light to that corner. The group met at a neighbor's home, drew up a petition, and gathered signatures from residents of nearby streets. Some members took time off their jobs and went to after-dinner meetings at neighbors' homes. And some did not do anything more than sign the petition. The ad hoc group delegated one neighbor to present the petition at the next city council meeting; the rest sat in the audience that evening. Time and energy strains exist between the freedom to pursue individual careers and dreams while working with others to improve life in a neighborhood. But becoming an active member of a community has larger meaning as well.

Consider public health. Community efforts to get safe drinking water and food, fire protection, and police safety supersede individual freedom to taint water supplies, sell rotting meat, avoid home smoke alarms, and rob citizens. Or, for that matter, vaccinating young children against contagious diseases.[22]

Also think about public schools. Past and present, every property owner pays taxes, a portion of which supports schools whether or not the taxpayer has children. Schooling the young to be literate, enter the workplace prepared, and engage in the community helps everyone. Educating the next generation preserves a government, bolsters an economy, and sustains a way of life. Schools are a public good.

Or as political journalist E. J. Dionne put it:

> A purely individualistic society cannot maintain the solidarity and so-
> cial cohesion that are a prerequisite for preserving freedom. Free men
> and women have to feel some sense of obligation to defend *each other's
> rights* [original italics].[23]

Such tensions between the beliefs and values of individualism and
community have often meant that Americans, past and present, shut-
tle back and forth between acquiring the accepted markers of personal
"success" and learning to make some sacrifice in time and dollars to help
others in a community in which they live. Philosopher Isaiah Berlin put
it this way:

> To avoid glaring inequality or widespread misery I am ready to sacri-
> fice some, or all, of my freedom. I may do so willingly and freely; but it
> is freedom that I am giving up for the sake of justice or equality or the
> love of my fellow men.[24]

Such tensions between liberty and justice reside in individuals,
schools, and the community especially when the strong belief in equal
opportunity comes into play.

Equal Opportunity

To Americans, each individual deserves an equal shot at success. Running a race to win prizes has to place everyone at the same starting line
ready to compete. Sure, there will be winners and losers, but the abiding belief is that each individual can not only compete but also make it
(acquire land, turn a profit in a small business, and become a reliable,
well-paid worker) if he or she sticks to goals, puts in the hours, has the
freedom to choose, and is treated fairly.

In 1860, Abraham Lincoln ran for president as the nation careened
toward dissolution. He promised

> [t]he humblest man an equal chance to get rich with everybody else.
> When one starts poor, as most do in the race of life, free society is such
> that he knows he can better his condition. I want every man to have the
> chance—and I believe a black man is entitled to it.[25]

Nearly all black men and women were slaves at this time, and not until the Emancipation Proclamation (1863) and only after the Civil War ended did the Thirteenth, Fourteenth, and Fifteenth Amendments free slaves, make them citizens, and enable them to become voters. The American Dream and Creed promised equal opportunity and now included a once-enslaved minority. But equal treatment lagged considerably even after laws were passed.

A half-century later, the notion of political equality expanded to women when the Nineteenth Amendment gave them the right to vote. Similarly, another half-century later, protest movements challenging rights and privileges heretofore held by white males succeeded in reaching other ethnic minorities (Hispanics) and Americans excluded from political, economic, social, and educational life—those with disabilities, and those gay, lesbian, bisexual, and transgender individuals barred from full participation in society. Laws fell as these previously excluded groups became full citizens. But laws expanding equal participation did not guarantee equal treatment.[26]

The view that even though people differ in their talents, needs, and attitudes, all must be treated equally before the law meant that Americans could choose freely and act individually as long as they abided by the rules of the game. This view is taught in kindergarten. US Supreme Court Justice Thurgood Marshall said: "Equal means getting the same thing, at the same time, and in the same place." Schoolchildren and youth across the nation would agree. By the early twenty-first century, the American Creed applied to all but still contained glitches where hidden bias and overt discriminatory actions persisted.[27]

There are, however, other views of equality held by Americans both then and now. Some Americans have believed that equality means not only opportunity and fair treatment but also the duty of the community and government to reduce inequities. If some Americans suffer injustice and endure miserable circumstances, then some private and public bodies must determine the degree of inequality (e.g., education, housing, social services) and then pursue remedial action. And it is here that these varying core beliefs within a market-friendly government and a competitive business sector cause friction.[28]

To eliminate economic inequality and inequitable justice for some Americans often means other Americans curtail their personal freedom (e.g., some pay higher taxes, previously discriminated groups receive benefits unavailable to others, legislators pass gun control laws) to do what they want in order for fellow Americans to gain full equality and a justice system color- and class-blind.

Over the past three centuries, each of these values and their permutations has politically and culturally risen to the surface and then sunk out of sight. Before the Great Depression of the 1930s, the dominant belief in "rugged individualism" undercut the value of community, but during those Depression years, President Franklin Delano Roosevelt and Congress acted to help banks and businesses re-open and create jobs in communities for families to survive. During the 1960s with the Civil Rights movement protesting political and social injustice, joining others seeking equal rights, belonging to antiwar groups raised issues among nonprotesting Americans who saw the extension of rights to groups previously excluded as their loss of personal freedom.

Keeping both individualism and community in sight, while attending to the fairness of equal opportunity amid constant competition for money and status, has challenged a nation then and now split between all stripes of political conservatives and liberals.[29]

The opening decades of the twenty-first century reveal anew those challenges, as tensions within those core values have arisen in increasing attacks on unrestrained capitalism, hyper-individualism undercutting community ties, and polarized governance unlike any seen since the Civil War.

Consider current criticism of an economic system unrestrained by governmental action where wages for most Americans have either declined or remained stagnant, and the enormous gap between the very rich and the middle and working classes is closer to an abyss than a crack in the pavement. Continuing inequality in the distribution of wealth damages the incentives that drive most Americans to take risks to succeed. Concentrated wealth and its political influence tilt policies to benefit the rich rather than the middle class, further eroding trust in democratic institutions, including schools, the historic up-escalator for individuals to earn decent wages. Local, state, and federal policy makers are expected to restrain (and regulate) markets and avoid the dangers of the very rich influencing public officials. As political journalist Michael Tomasky put it: "Democracy can't flourish in a context of grotesque concentration of wealth." Greed trumps community and equality of opportunity.[30]

Even as critiques of capitalism have multiplied in contemporary years, since the colonial era these core beliefs and values of individualism, community, and equal opportunity, contested as they have been and in conflict with one another, continue to be the DNA of the American character.

HOW DID THESE CORE VALUES TAKE HOLD AMONG AMERICANS?

Identifying core values is one thing, but figuring out how they took hold over hundreds of years among Americans located in cities, suburbs, and rural villages inhabiting a land stretching 3,000 miles east to west and over 1,500 miles north to south is another thing.

I begin with the taken-for-granted economic structures that historically have been central to the American experience for nearly a half-millennia. The ideas and practices of a capitalist economy accompanied the first English settlers to the Atlantic coastline of North America in the seventeenth century. These ideas and practices were rooted in the individual's right to own private property, establish a farm or a business, use the newest technology of the time, set prices for customers, pay wages to employees, and have access to credit. Such a market-based economic system prizes individual action, competition, risk taking, and innovation without interference from government. The belief, expressed in Adam Smith's *Wealth of Nations* (1776), is that such an economic system where millions of self-interested individuals engaged in trading and exchanging goods and service make decisions to benefit themselves and also thereby benefit society. Unobserved market forces—the "Invisible Hand"—create a balance between supply and demand of goods, which comes from self-interested individuals not only producing a larger economic pie but also building social cohesion and amity. Believers in this economic dogma saw market-based capitalism, not the government, as the answer to political and social problems.[31]

The legal and civil systems, also imported from England, were anchored in the sanctity of contracts, individual rights to own property (including slaves), and the consent of the governed. Political thinker John Locke summed up the trinity of values that later found its way into the Declaration of Independence at the end of the eighteenth century: "life, liberty, and the pursuit of property." Entrepreneurs, relishing competition to succeed in whatever market they entered, were present among colonists who settled along the Atlantic seaboard and dotted the American landscape in every century since.[32]

The growth of capitalism as an economic system based on individual competition, unrestrained trade, increasing productivity, the strength of markets, and the hidden control of the "Invisible Hand" to improve the lives of all Americans became and has stayed the prevailing ideology, including defining individual "success" and "failure." In 2019, eighty-eight-year-old investor Warren Buffet told reporters at the annual meeting of Berkshire Hathaway stockholders in Omaha, Nebraska, that he was a "card-carrying capitalist." He said: "I believe we wouldn't be sitting here [at the 2019 annual meeting] except for the market system."[33]

Throughout the eighteenth and nineteenth centuries, strong social beliefs that individuals can be a "success" by acquiring land, getting jobs in factories, starting businesses, and competing in markets free from government oversight permeated the thinking of merchants, workers, ex-slaves, and immigrants. These beliefs were deeply embedded in these imported economic and legal structures and became so grounded in the American experience that they were then hardly noticed and simply taken for granted.

Challenges to these deeply embedded beliefs arose during the nineteenth century when periodic economic "panics" led to failed banks with depositors losing savings, credit drying up, businesses closing, and unemployment mushrooming (there were ten such "panics" in the nineteenth century and at least two more in the early twentieth century before a Federal Reserve system was established). That economic instability—no longer called "panics" but "recessions"—often lasting for a few years at a time occurred before and after the Great Depression (1929–1941). There were ten recessions between World War II and the 2008 Great Recession.[34]

Thus, the boom-and-bust economic cycle, an evitable feature of market capitalism, has yet to come to grips with the inherent tension between "glorification of individual autonomy above the collective needs of the community" and "how best to balance the [individual's] economic gains against the social costs" as these recessions tore at the national fabric.[35]

The Great Recession of 2008 brought to the fore how much economic inequality in the distribution of wealth (e.g., homes, cars, savings, investments, personal valuables) over the past half-century had occurred. That recession and growing awareness of such inequalities have created deep divisions in American society. Americans see fairness and equal opportunity violated when the top 1 percent of fellow citizens controls nearly 40 percent of all wealth. Faith in working hard, following the rules, doing well in school, and trusting government to keep a level playing field become harder to believe and pass on to the next generation.

The Congressional Budget Office concluded that between 1989 and 2013:

> [T]he difference in wealth held by families at the 90th percentile and the wealth of those in the middle widened from $532,000 to $861,000 over the period (in 2013 dollars). The share of wealth held by families in the top 10 percent of the wealth distribution increased from 67 percent to 76 percent, whereas the share of wealth held by families in the bottom half of the distribution declined from 3 percent to 1 percent.[36]

This skewing of the wealth distribution has created a hollowed-out middle class—the one percenters and the rest of Americans—and raised serious doubts about the American Dream. In 2015, Donald Trump became a candidate for the presidency announcing that "The American

Dream is dead. . . . But if I am elected president, I will bring it back big-
ger and better and stronger than ever before, and we will make America great again." The spillover from growing fears of inequality raised
doubts about the political structures in place for two centuries, including tax-supported public schools, that fostered the growth of economic
inequality.[37]

Still amid past and current economic inequality, significant changes
had accrued over the decades. Those who governed initially were only
white male property owners. They voted. They got elected. They sat on juries. And they governed in the colonial and post–Revolutionary War years.
Because colonists were fearful of concentrated power as experienced under British rule for 150 years, a federal system of governance came directly
from the Declaration of Independence (1776), the short-lived Articles of
Confederation (1781), and the US Constitution (1787).[38]

That document separating the powers of the executive, legislative,
and judicial and dividing authority between the federal, state, and local
governments—checks and balances—and protecting individual's rights
in the first ten amendments to the Constitution (1789) continues to be
the source of democratic rule for the United States in 2019, the longest
lasting constitutional democracy in the world. While the Constitution
sets the legal framework for democracy, it is the process of making decisions with others—voting, serving on juries, joining associations, and
following rules in debating issues—that has over the years become the
heartbeat of democracy. No surprise then that a *Pocket Manual of Rules of
Order for Deliberative Assemblies*—a guide later called *Robert's Rules of Order*
that gave instructions for holding meetings, electing officers, conduct-
ing discussions, and making decisions—came out in 1876. This primer
of the democratic process sold more than a half-million copies by World
War I. As one Boston newspaper put it, "[The Manual is] as indispens-
able as was the Catechism in more ecclesiastical times."[39]

These habits of governing, choosing leaders, debating issues, making rules while adhering to majority rule, and protecting minority opinions—that no person is above the law—are learned by children, youth,
and adults largely in voluntary associations (e.g., playgrounds, boys
and girls clubs, religious groups, unions) in neighborhoods, towns, and

cities involving hundreds of thousands and later millions of Americans. As historian Arthur Schlesinger Jr. put it in 1944:

> [Voluntary associations] provided the people with their greatest school of self-government. . . . Rubbing minds as well as elbows, they have been trained from youth to take common counsel, choose leaders, harmonize differences, and obey the expressed will of the majority. In mastering the associative way they have mastered the democratic way.[40]

Yet self-government and a capitalist economy at the birth of a nation were married to the enslavement of black men and women. The Declaration of Independence and later the Constitution promised the end of slavery in the former but embedded it deeply in the latter. The Three-Fifths Compromise worked out between southern states and the rest of the infant nation (a slave would be counted for representation, but not taxation, as 60 percent of a person) nestled in the Constitution and lasted until the end of the Civil War.

Ex-slave and abolitionist Frederick Douglass eloquently summed up the contradictions (and yes, the hypocrisy) between these founding documents and enslaving black people in an 1852 speech:

> What, to the American slave, is your 4th of July? I answer a day that reveals to him . . . the gross injustice and cruelty to which he is the constant victim. To him, your celebration is a sham . . . your shouts of liberty and equality, hollow mock; your prayers and hymns, your sermons and thanksgivings . . . are to him mere bombast, fraud, deception, impiety, and hypocrisy—a thin veil to cover up crimes which would disgrace a nation of savages. . . . There is not a nation on the earth guilty of practices, more shocking and bloody, than are the people of these United States, at this very hour.[41]

Social and political protests against deeply embedded undemocratic economic and political structures arose from rank-and-file Americans starting in the late eighteenth century with abolitionists in northern states (e.g., Benjamin Franklin, Quaker leaders) and white and black abolitionists in the mid-nineteenth century (e.g., William Lloyd Garrison, Frederick Douglass) seeking the end of slavery. Then in post–Civil War decades, religious leaders in the social gospel movement sought an end to poverty and urban slums. The growth of labor unions and the upswelling of Progressives in the late nineteenth and early twentieth centuries fought corporate excesses and advocated women's suffrage. Decades later, the Civil Rights movement led to expanded freedom for racial, ethnic, and gendered minorities in the late twentieth and early twenty-first centuries.

And in the present moment, the awareness of pervasive economic inequality, the rise of extreme wealth and the weakening of a strong middle class by loss of manufacturing, outsourcing of jobs to other nations, accelerated automation, and the growth of national policies enhancing the fortunes of wealthy Americans have raised grave questions about how fair democratic governance is to its citizens. The election of two presidents in the twenty-first century who got fewer popular votes than the other candidates and the use of "dark money" to get legislators to enact tax and banking policies congenial to wealthy contributors have caused Americans to ask whether the system is rigged against them.[42]

Yet too many Americans have forgotten the gradual, meandering, and highly contested path that the nation has trod to spread equality and justice to its citizenry. Too many Americans overlook the incremental progress amid a painful journey that slaves, immigrants, women, and others have experienced in the past. The individual's right to cast votes and become a full-fledged citizen, for example, expanded to nonproperty owners, ex-slaves, women, and ethnic, racial, and gendered minorities including American Indians, Hispanics, and gay individuals.

Propelling that bumpy trek to more equality and justice has been an unalloyed faith in reason. Operating within a set of larger social beliefs about the sources of knowledge and truth beyond what religion can supply, the importance of reason in making decisions in both public and private venues became the bedrock of American life.[43]

Look back to the impact of British and French thinkers on the rule of law and their influence on the American War of Independence (1775–1783) and the forming of a constitution that split power among three branches of government (1787–1789). All of this occurred during the European Enlightenment, sometimes called the "Age of Reason," when ideas of Continental political philosophers gained ascendancy among political elites both in Europe and in the American colonies. These ideas of humans as rational individuals who could make decisions based on factual evidence and reason (rather than on religious teaching or tradition) permeated the beginnings of democratic government and capitalism in the United States.[44]

Concepts of rationally establishing political, economic, and social goals and striving for efficiency and effectiveness in reaching those goals through science, technology, collection of statistics, and nimble wits began early. Think of the list of colonial grievances justifying a Declaration of Independence from Britain in 1776. Recall how numbers, arithmetic, and early statistics were critical in Benjamin Franklin calculating costs in printing a newspaper and comparing figures before and after his experiments; Thomas Jefferson tracking expenses for seeds, equipment, upkeep for slaves; merchants totaling up net profits after deducting expenditures; and Constitutional Convention delegates figuring out how to count people including slaves in the newly created states for representation in the first US Congress.

Consider further that the US Congress authorized the first federal census for 1790, counting how many people resided in the thirteen states. And do not forget that the federal government established the first armory to produce weapons for the US Army in 1797 paving the way for the creation of the assembly line and mass production of goods a century later. Using reason to solve problems, using numbers to calculate representation, and using a proto-typical assembly line were early signs of a government using facts and numbers—rational means—in seeking both efficiency and effectiveness.[45]

Rational decision-making based on factual evidence to solve daily problems, make policy, render professional judgments, and discover new knowledge has different names such as technical rationality, clinical reasoning, legal thinking, the scientific method, and engineering solutions. Such names dominate American organizational life in defining institutional and individual "success" and "failure."[46]

Yet in the past half-century, social science researchers have made apparent the limits to rational thinking by revealing biases that influence such thinking and the inexorable influence of emotion in making decisions. Buying a pair of shoes, for example, for an upcoming wedding is not an easy, rational choice to make when comfort, cost, style, and other values come into play. States gerrymandering districts to ensure that the ruling political party continues its dominance in electing its members displays bias in the face of a constitutional direction on allotting equal numbers of persons in each district.[47]

Deep-seated beliefs in rationality in human affairs and the importance of science in making public and private decisions have created and sustained American legal, economic, and political structures over the centuries. So the answer to the chapter question is that these beliefs were baked into these structures within which colonists, pioneers, immigrants, and native-born Americans operated as they earned a living, had families, worshipped God, engaged neighbors in their communities, and participated in local government. What emerged over time were both individual and institutional definitions of "success" and "failure."

Even more, these beliefs in rationality and numbers gave Americans committed to the core values of individualism, community, and equal opportunity a basis for determining "success" and "failure" in everything that Americans did from farming, starting businesses, competing in sports, and yes, sending children to tax-supported schools.

How, then, were (and are) these beliefs and values in American society transmitted to Americans? Chapter 3 answers that question.

- CHAPTER 3 -

HOW WERE THESE IDEAS AND VALUES TRANSMITTED TO AMERICANS THEN AND NOW?

W ithin these larger intertwined economic and political structures, these core ideas and values of individualism, community, and equal opportunity touched Americans in the past and continue to do so now. They were transmitted both formally and informally through various democratic institutions such as political parties, the workplace, sports, religious groups, cultural institutions (e.g., media, pop music, comedy, fashion), families, and, of course, schooling. All of these institutions shaped the entry, flow, and exercise of these values for young, middle-aged, and old Americans. I chose three institutions as exemplars of how these ideas and definitions of "success" and "failure" permeated Americans' daily lives: businesses, sports, and public schools.

BUSINESS

We live at a time when almost everything can be bought and sold. Over the past three decades, markets—and market values—have come to govern our lives as never before. We did not arrive at this condition through any deliberate choice. It is almost as if it came upon us.

—MICHAEL SANDEL, 2012[1]

United Airlines merges with Continental Airlines. Amazon engages in price wars with Walmart. Hundreds of thousands of shares are bought and sold in a nanosecond on the New York Stock Exchange. Thirty-second ads run during the Super Bowl, costing companies millions of dollars. Media owner Ted Turner owns two million acres in the United States, one of the largest landowners in the U.S. Many believe that these examples illustrate American capitalism. But business in the United States is more than corporate mergers, ads, and mega-landowners.[2]

Capitalism is also Safeway, McDonald's, In-and-Out Burgers, the nearby Starbucks, and the family-owned dry cleaner down the street. Also capitalism lies within the American home.

If I hire gardeners to weed, prune, and care for the shrubs I have, I pay them for their work. I did not compel or coerce them to do the job. Similarly, the Sunday farmers' market in my neighborhood brings sellers and buyers together to exchange money for fruit, vegetables, and breads. Paying a gardener and crew and buying lettuce and peaches at a farmers' market—just as factory or office workers punch time cards and receive weekly wages—are at the heart of the market system as much as Google selling ads, Toyota turning out Camry hybrids, teenagers taking orders at Jack in the Box, and brown-clad drivers delivering packages for UPS.

A market-based economy is dependent upon producers supplying goods and services and consumers buying those products. Such an economy means owning property, starting businesses, paying wages, and securing credit—what has occurred in the nation's history for over four centuries. But a market-based economy is also entangled with government.

Government has historically been involved in the market system. How best to grow an economy is a question that Americans have debated for centuries. To Alexander Hamilton—the nation's first secretary of the treasury—an "energetic" government that builds canals and roads, establishes a national banking system, taxes foreign goods competing with American ones, and gives direct help to those who made products would grow and protect the economy of the young nation while making it a strong competitor in overseas trade.[3]

To Thomas Jefferson, however, such government involvement would deprive Americans of their personal liberty to do what they think best economically for their family. Such government activity in a market system through improved transportation and communication, subsidies for particular manufacturers, and tariffs on imported and exported goods would lead to greedy speculators buying and selling land, harm farmers who tilled the soil and brought products to market, and create cities inhabited by the poor.

These rival ideas of how best to grow a strong economy in a place with seemingly unlimited land and minerals and peopled by generation after generation of immigrants have competed with one another for over two centuries. Debates over the role of government in a market-driven society continue to this day for the simple reason that both Hamiltonian and Jeffersonian ideas persist as political parties joust with one another to expand or trim back government regulation.

Recall Theodore Roosevelt and his trust-busting efforts to break up monopolies in the decades before and after the beginning of the twentieth century. The laissez-faire attitudes of subsequent presidents toward stock market speculation, increased indebtedness, and refusal to rein in excesses of business leaders led to Black Tuesday, October 29, 1929, when the New York Stock Exchange's collapse led to the worst depression the United States had ever experienced. And what occurred during the Great Depression and since have been a series of efforts to regulate certain economic activities to curb "rugged individualism" and untrammeled profit taking.[4]

What has emerged is a capitalist democracy where government and business are enmeshed and dependent upon one another. Within this form of democratic capitalism, rules and regulations (e.g., antitrust laws; bans on insider trading of stocks) are put into place and jiggered continually to keep the market system working fairly for both producers and consumers.[5]

Political and legal structures evolved over centuries to coordinate buying and selling in this form of market capitalism while helping individuals gain wealth through protecting property ownership, establishing businesses and corporations, joining unions, and becoming professionals. Not until the late nineteenth and early twentieth centuries did government intervene to protect workers and consumers—middle- and working-class Americans—from greedy monopolists gouging the public and corporations exploiting workers (e.g., Federal Food and Drug Act, National Labor Relations Act). In the depth of the Great Depression, government intervention in the banking system and the creation of federal alphabet agencies (e.g., CCC, AAA, WPA, TVA) were responsible for helping those out of work, farmers, and youth. And then during the Cold War, federal funding launched new technologies in Silicon Valley where once rural California orchards grew peaches, plums, and oranges. A system of federal and state rules and infusion of funds to jump-start new industries sanded the rough edges of market capitalism and illustrated the entanglement of a market economy with democratic governance.[6]

Consider that market capitalism came to an America rich in resources and vast stretches of forested and fertile plains—a land of abundance. As early as the 1780s and then after the Civil War, the federal government gave away land to individuals. Eager Americans had to stake a claim to land and then get 160 acres free of charge under the Homestead Act of 1862. Northern and western European immigrants homesteaded the Midwest while those from eastern and southeastern Europe came to cities to find work, start businesses, and raise families. Both wealth and poverty accumulated as many homesteaders (and speculators) acquired acreage that was once inhabited by the American Indian. Government provided roads and railroad tracks to get harvests to market while other immigrants, overcome by bad weather, failed crops, and unpaid mortgages, left. Just as there were individual winners and losers before the Civil War in making money, so there were in the decades after Appomattox.[7]

As post–Civil War America became industrialized, corporations in steel, mining, manufacturing, clothes, and food products grew dramatically in size and reach to employ blue-collar workers drawn from European immigrants and rural American migrants. Factories and mills located in and near cities drew those eager to earn higher wages than they could ever have earned in their native land or on the farm.[8]

In 1914, for example, Henry Ford shocked his competitors and the nation when he doubled the minimum wage for workers on his "continuous motion" assembly line to $5 for an eight-hour day. Ford told a reporter:

> The owner, the employees, and the buying public are all one and the same, and unless an industry can so manage itself as to keep wages high and prices low it destroys itself, for otherwise it limits the number of its customers. One's own employees ought to be one's own best customers.[9]

As startling as the $5 daily wage was, most Americans had to get along on much less. Many newly arrived immigrants found themselves year after year stuck in poverty from low-paying jobs that barely put food on the table or a room for a family to live in. There was the searing, abiding poverty in the rural South where most black tenant farmers were mired in crushing debts owed to white landowners. Poverty was as much inherent to market-driven capitalism as were a growing middle class and millionaire industrialists and businessmen. Inequality in the distribution of wealth ebbed and flowed in the United States—at its highest in the years at the turn of the twentieth century and the present day and at its lowest during the Great Depression in the 1930s and in the three decades following World War II. Economic inequality is part and parcel of America's democratic capitalism.[10]

While urban slums expanded and rural poverty persisted, the movement of working-class families into the middle class of first- and second-generation Americans occurred. With money in their purses and wallets, these Americans acquired homes, indoor plumbing, and stoves, and bought fashionable products in neighborhood businesses and later in emerging department stores that dotted cities beginning in the late nineteenth and early twentieth centuries.[11]

The growth of consumer spending tracked the spread of big and small businesses providing goods and services to Americans. And it is consumer spending—individuals buying products—that is central to the growth (and shrinking) of the US economy. By 2018, over two-thirds of the American economy (the gross domestic product, or GDP) depended upon Americans buying homes, food, clothing, cars, and services.[12]

Consumer spending is another way of saying that Americans exercised individual choice in deciding what to buy with the money they had. It is also the historic expression of personal "success." And that democratizing of spending on individual needs expanded dramatically since the 1920s with the growing availability of credit and the spread of advertising in newspapers, radio, and then television. By the 1960s, there were dozens of television channels, scores of cereals in supermarkets, hundreds of car models in dealerships, and seasonally fashionable clothes for sale in department stores to upper-, middle-, and working-class Americans. And it is, as historian David Potter concluded, "advertising now [he was writing in the early 1960s] compares with such long standing institutions as the church and the school in the magnitude of its social influence."[13]

In past and present ads, including the half-time commercials run during the annual National Football League's Super Bowl championship, observers can see tangibly how the core values of individualism, community, and equal opportunity embedded in the American Creed and Dream get transmitted to the reading and viewing public.

Americans buy advertised products to bolster their individual health (e.g., prescriptions for everything from constipation to multiple sclerosis), enhance physical appearance (e.g., skin creams that rid facial wrinkles and grow hair on bald pates), appeal to different tastes in entertainment (e.g., vampire and horror flicks to Bambi and sitcoms) and increased social status (e.g., moving from a studio apartment to a two-bedroom house). Buying merchandise is the retail definition of individual "success."

And anyone over the age of twelve has noted that ads asking consumers to buy particular products have become racially, ethnically, and sexually diverse in recent decades. Black, Latino, Asian, and gay adults announce the most recent drug for diabetes, most popular hair shampoo, which beer to drink, and what automobile to buy. Ads having interracial couples and families display that they are equal opportunity vendors who relish a diverse America.[14]

The annual Super Bowl draws tens of million eyeballs to watch commercials. Ads for cars, beer, electronics, and other products cost at least $5 million for a 30-second spot in 2017. One memorable Coke ad—"It's Beautiful"—ran in 2014 and 2017. The ad had the patriotic song "America the Beautiful" sung in English, Spanish, Hindi, Hebrew, and French to mark the many immigrants who have become Americans.[15]

If most ads cater to individuals' tastes, health, looks, entertainment preferences, and social status while illustrating inclusivity, there are also ads that ring consumer bells to engage with their community. The restaurant chain Chili's, for example, ran a clutch of ads a few years ago showing fathers and daughters talking over burgers, a family party welcoming a returning soldier, and neighbors helping strangers after a natural disaster.[16]

But it is not only media ads. Television networks and cable shows reveal these deeply embedded American values. Take the plethora of reality shows over the past decades that focus on individual achievements and competition. Popular programs like *Survivor* with diverse ethnic and gendered contestants blend fierce competition among the half-dozen or so individuals placed on an island. They form a community that is riven by fierce competition to be the last person not to be voted out of the conflict-ridden community. Or *The Apprentice*, where a palette of diverse job seekers compete for a high-level job. Contestants dreaded the moment when real estate mogul Donald Trump would say, "You're fired." Such reality shows added to the constant stream of media commercials not only enshrines the core values and beliefs of Americans but also makes money for network and cable companies. As do sports in the United States.

SPORTS

Think about Little League, pick-up soccer games, boxing, tennis matches, golf tournaments, and professional baseball where individuals shine as all-stars and others stumble into errors, where some teams are victorious and others collapse. Competition and cooperation are the meat-and-potatoes of sport novices, amateurs, and professionals in America. Yet there is always a winner and a loser in baseball's World Series, tennis's National Open, and football's Super Bowl.

Sports mirror the core American values of individualism, community, and equal opportunity every summer day that ten-year-old boys and girls play baseball or middle-aged men compete at soccer on fall weekends, and indoor gym pick-up basketball games pit tall, short, skinny, and fat teenagers. Then on TV screens dynamically graceful professional basketball players float to the basket rim as millions watch National Basketball Association (NBA) games. Tennis stars grunt as they slam aces past their opponents, and a golf great putts a 15-footer into the cup for an eagle. Amateur and pro, men and women, both individuals and teams play every day of the year. Sports are ubiquitous.

Since the integration of professional sports after World War II, individual merit counts far more than race, ethnicity, religion, geography, or who one knows. From all-white professional leagues in the major sports, minority athletes have increased their numbers. In 2012, for example, black athletes made up over 66 percent of all players in the National Football League (NFL), 76 percent of NBA athletes, and just over 8 percent of Major League Baseball (MLB) players.[17]

Working together in competitive sports to lead the NFL in victories or sweep the finals of the NBA championship teams requires constant cooperation among players to learn and execute plays. Team success is easy to recognize in league standings. Yet individual playing and teamwork go together as when two basketball players do a pick-and-roll to make a three-pointer or a short stop scoops up a grounder and throws to the second baseman, who rifles it to first for a double play to end the inning. Individuals cooperate for a team to win a game.[18]

And when a team from Cleveland, Boston, New York, Pittsburgh, or Dallas wins the national championship—be it in baseball, basketball, or football—the city comes together to celebrate and display its pride and joy in the victory.

Yet parents and sports fans worry about individuals using dope to enhance their performance in, for example, professional football, baseball, and competitive bicycling. Then there are concerns over individuals and teams cheating to throw matches, especially when gambling stakes are high. For nonprofessional sports in school and college—more than 60 percent of Americans say that they are involved in sports-related activities—many participants and parents like the excitement of Friday night football and children's participation in Saturday Little League games. Still other parents and players worry over pressure to win at all costs, thereby harming both players and fans.[19]

In both individual and team competition, as both spectators and participants winning a game, match, or championship, American children, youth, and adults daily enact these values of individualism, community, and equal opportunity. Sports permeate American life now as they have done for the past century. And through athletic competition, these values get displayed and reinforced daily.

Take baseball, "the national pastime." As one writer put it, the popularity of baseball can be seen in the

> [M]illions of boys and girls who join thousands of youth, scholastic, collegiate and American Legion baseball teams, along with the men and women who play baseball and softball in industrial and semiprofessional urban and rural leagues, and the continuing interest in the history and cultural meaning of baseball, as measured by the sale of baseball books, the popularity of baseball films like *The Natural* and *Field of Dreams*, and the public's continuing fascination with the origins of the sport.[20]

That baseball was (and is) popular and that it echoed core American values was picked up by Mark Twain when he said: baseball was "the very symbol, the outward and visible expression of the drive, and push, and rush and struggle of the raging, tearing, booming nineteenth century!"[21]

Ditto for football. Professional sports have become gold mines from which club owners extract profits year after year while cities compete with one another to erect large stadiums, often with taxpayer support. The popularity of professional football among Americans, for example, has turned players (as in other major sports) into celebrities from whom children beg for autographs and that US presidents admire.

President Richard Nixon was one such admirer. At a 1971 White House conference on drug abuse that drew nationally recognized researchers and celebrities, Nixon walked into the meeting late and saw Chicago Bears star Gale Sayers. He beckoned Sayers and then walked out of the conference, taking him to the Oval Office to talk football. Or the time that Nixon spoke at a Wisconsin reception for Bart Starr, then the Green Bay Packers' quarterback, and said the following:

> A word about your Secretary of Defense [Wisconsin native, Melvin Laird]. I think it is only proper to speak of him in this room where all of us who follow football—and I guess presidents have no secrets but it is no secret that I am a football fan—that we know that the defense is essential if you are going to be able to win the game.

I remember two Super Bowl games. I think Bart Starr will agree that the defense played as much of a role in winning those games as the offense—the defense against the Chiefs and the Raiders. And I think, too, as we look at the United States of America today, we look at the defense of America [war in Vietnam] which Mel Laird, a great son of Wisconsin, now has responsibility for.[22]

Or consider Vince Lombardi, coach of the Green Bay Packers, once a losing team that went on to win five National Football League championships and two Super Bowl victories in nine years. Nixon admired Lombardi, especially after the coach came to Washington, DC, in 1969 to turn around the Redskins, a perennial loser. Nixon was the first sitting president to attend a regular-season NFL football game. After the game in which the Redskins lost, Lombardi said: "I'm just sorry we couldn't play a better game for him."[23]

Vince Lombardi was quoted continually on what he believed to be crucial to his success. His words appeared across the nation then and are repeated often today:

- Winning isn't everything, but wanting to win is.
- Football is like life—it requires perseverance, self-denial, hard work, sacrifice, dedication and respect for authority.
- If it doesn't matter who wins or loses, then why do they keep score?
- Individual commitment to a group effort—that is what makes a team work, a company work, a society work, a civilization work.[24]

Individual and group competition, teamwork, and equal opportunity are at the heart of professional sports and illustrate, if not enact, American beliefs and core values.

As do tax-supported public schools. They enter the picture as another social institution reflecting not only the larger culture but also as a public organization with teachers and administrators who are expected to directly and indirectly instill in the next generation beliefs in following rules and norms, competing to win, cooperating with others, and working hard. Students displaying these beliefs in daily behavior will be recognized and rewarded in school, the workplace, and community.

INSTILLING CORE VALUES IN STUDENTS

Why do teachers scold students? Because the student has given the wrong answer? Because, try as he might, he fails to grasp the intricacies of long division? Not usually. Rather, students are commonly scolded for coming into the room late or for making too much noise or for not listening to the teacher's directions. . . .

—PHILIP JACKSON[25]

A "hidden curriculum" existed [in these teachers' classrooms] . . . consisting in certain rules that were embodied in management-type behavior. Children were expected to internalize these rules in every classroom:

1. Do what the teacher says.
2. Live up to teacher expectations for proper behavior.
3. Keep busy.
4. Keep quiet and don't move too much.
5. Stick to the schedule.

—MARGARET LECOMPTE[26]

How does society transmit and instill core values of individualism, community, and equal opportunity into the next generation? Of course, in the family, these values are taught explicitly and absorbed from mothers, fathers, grandparents, uncles, aunts, cousins, and neighbors. Sure, children compete for both physical and psychological resources within families, but emotional ties soften winner-take-all competitiveness. Historically, outside of the family, private and public schools, peers, religious groups, and the workplace—be it a farm, a store or, later, a factory—account for learning the practical aspects of these values. Schools, then, as do the workplace and sports, socialize these values into the next generation.

Families surely begin the process of children becoming literate, but nineteenth-century farm families and those living in villages and towns saw that the world outside the home required more than what a family could provide in educating children and youth. They had to become literate to read the Bible; sign documents; write wills and letters; and add, subtract, and multiply numbers. And be ready to enter the workplace and do what citizens are supposed to do. Sociologists call these the "manifest" or "intended" functions of schools. There are also "latent" or "unintended" functions of schools. What sociologist Robert Merton called "unanticipated consequences of purposive social action."[27]

Here is where core values enter the picture. After all, the intended functions of schooling described above seldom appear in teachers' lessons or tests. Students say little publicly about the importance of individualism, community, and equality of opportunity in their daily lives. Nor do teachers instruct students in how to bend bureaucratic rules or get the highest grade point average in high school. Nor do teachers teach students to appear obedient while gaming the system to gain the few awards and benefits that schools offer. Absorbing these value-laden behaviors and attitudes in schools, absent from the intended curriculum or teacher lesson plans, is what young children learn throughout their thirteen-year career as students.[28]

These collateral learnings—including the core values—became the "hidden curriculum" embedded within an educational innovation imported in the late 1840s—the age-graded school.

STANDARDIZATION AND THE "GRAMMAR OF SCHOOLING"

The birth and slow growth of tax-supported public schools in the colonial era, Revolutionary decades, and early nineteenth-century years offered more than literacy to the young. Schooling also socialized students into a community and nation while preparing them to do more than work on the family farm. The vehicle that enacted these educational, political, and economic purposes for tax-supported public schools was the innovation reformers imported from Prussia called the age-graded school, a way to organize schooling the young that slowly replaced the familiar one-room schoolhouse.[29]

The physical structure of the age-graded school at that time contained eight separate classrooms with students of a certain age and one teacher assigned to each room who was responsible for covering one chunk of the curriculum tailored to that age group. This major change—a structural reform that has lasted until now—from one-room schools to graded schools is the beginning of the standardized classroom and what has been labeled as the "grammar of schooling."[30]

The mid-nineteenth-century eight-grade school housing six- to fifteen-year-olds has become an unquestioned institutional "success" by continuing into the twenty-first century. The first age-graded structure appeared in Boston in the late 1840s. Consider that the four-story Dwight School built in 1856 had fourteen classrooms, with each having sixty-three individual stationary desks. The school could hold nearly nine-hundred students grouped by age. As cities multiplied in the post–Civil War decades, age-graded schools spread. In rural areas, one-room schoolhouses eventually consolidated into age-graded schools by the first half of the twentieth century.[31]

Or consider efficiency and effectiveness. The age-graded school has processed millions of students over the past century and a half, sorted out achievers from nonachievers, able from disabled, and now graduates over 80 percent of those entering high school.

Or adaptability. The age-graded school exists in Europe, Asia, Africa, Latin America, and North America, covering rural, urban, and suburban districts. By these criteria, this school organization has been an unrivaled "success."

In creating the structure of the age-graded school, reform-minded policy makers sought uniformity in how schools should be built, operated, and—within classrooms—what content and skills teachers should teach and how they should teach both. To policy makers, establishing uniformity in schooling meant both efficiency (saving taxpayer dollars) and effectiveness (achieving multiple goals). Thus, the structure of the age-graded school made it possible to devise over time standardized furniture, curriculum, ways of teaching, norms for children behavior, and socially acceptable ways of competing with others in every classroom.

Between the late nineteenth and early twentieth centuries, then, consistency in schooling spread across the nation. Architectural designs of school buildings standardized the size of classrooms, the number of windows in them, the arrangement of student and teacher desks, the circulation of air, and heating. All became similar as school reformers sought uniformity across schools (except for those children of color who went to segregated, dilapidated, underfunded schools in these decades and children with disabilities excluded from public schools).[32]

Late nineteenth-century age-graded schools promoted students from one grade to another who recited lessons, passed tests, and listened to teachers. There were, however, increasing numbers of students who failed to recite lessons correctly, did poorly on tests, and only occasionally obeyed teachers. Such students were held back and lagged behind their classmates for one or more years. Many teachers would have to teach older students who "flunked," keeping thirteen-year-olds with nine-year-olds in the third grade. Educators of the day saw repeaters, called "laggards," as inevitable products of the age-graded school. Attrition then (now called dropouts) ran extraordinarily high. Or as one astute observer put it: "[r]etardation is a symptom of good schools."[33]

Seeking consistency in buildings, policy makers also sought common standards for who taught and what was taught. States raised qualifications for who became teachers to meet minimum standards of knowledge and skills to teach. Moreover, standards for the physical dimensions of the school and the curriculum also promised equal treatment to those who attended tax-supported public schools.

Take the standardization of the physical design of classrooms and what that meant in practice for both students and teachers over the past century.

- For decades, classrooms contained rows of bolted-down desks facing a slate blackboard and a teacher desk. Walls and closets held stacks of textbooks for each academic subject. Such furniture and instructional tools communicated to those who inhabit that space who is in charge, who asks questions and does most of the talking, and who must answer those questions and do most of the listening.
- Wall clocks signal keeping to a schedule of classes (e.g., forty-five-minute to hour-long lessons in secondary schools) with bells telling students that the lesson is over. Schedules are important because school is seen as a preparation for the adult work world where white- and blue-collar employees punched time cards to

begin the workday. Clocks also mean that learning is measured by how long students attend classes during the school year, and credentials awarded on the amount of time students spent in school.

- The American flag and the daily reciting of the Pledge of Allegiance were clear signs that pride in and loyalty to the nation were primary obligations.

All of these standardized artifacts appearing in classrooms over the past century have become part of the "hidden curriculum" for transmitting to the next generation cultural values of obeying authority, adhering to institutional rules, the importance of time in the workplace, patriotism, and pride in country. Academics called these taken-for-granted ways of organizing classrooms and schools the political, economic, and cultural socialization of the young. Historians of education increasingly came to call it the "grammar of schooling."[34]

What about classrooms in the 1950s? 1970s? Now? Have schools and classrooms changed over the past century? Yes, they have.[35]

- Because a minority of students could not keep up with peers, classifying students as "slow," "average," and "gifted" by their ability (e.g., I.Q. tests) and performance (e.g., achievement tests) became organizational mainstays.[36]
- By the 1930s, movable chairs, desks, and tables had replaced bolted-down desks in many urban and suburban districts.
- Most elementary school teachers moved from depending upon whole-group instruction to working with small groups of children and individual study during the school day.
- Secondary schools offered electives (e.g., Advanced Placement, career academies, ethnic studies), giving students choices beyond required courses.
- Schools provided space for after-school student and community activities (e.g., drama, music, science, athletics, social services).

These few examples of organizational and instructional changes offer evidence to rebut those who say schools have remained the same over decades. Such changes, however, did not erase the school's "hidden curriculum," those latent functions of instilling cultural values, prizing individual and team competitiveness, and seeking workplace compliance and civic competence. Beneath the noise of moving desks around during lessons to form small groups, establishing different tracks separating students by ability and performance, offering students exciting elective courses, and students clicking away on computer keyboards—the "grammar of schooling" persisted.

More specifically, the age-graded school's definition of normal progress—children of a certain age complete the content and skills for that grade in so many months or be held back for another school year—created "laggards" and dropouts as well as special classes targeted to low performing students (e.g., business math rather than algebra) to keep students in school. Moral lessons taught explicitly and implicitly to build character, competition for higher grades, and end-of-year achievement tests continued to socialize the young into accepting competitive rankings of performance and abiding by rules.

In elementary schools, quizzes and class contests appeared often in language arts, math, science, social studies, foreign language, art, and physical education classes. In secondary schools organized by academic departments, the content of these subjects was more complex and harder to learn. Yet similar individual and group competition occurred as students vied for high grades.

"Success" and "failure" were tied to grade point averages, test scores, and graduation. Every year, a certain percentage of students dropped out of school—the failures. And a certain percentage of students became valedictorians—the successes. And other students with disabilities or not yet attaining fluency in English were in the gray area between success and failure. The grading system of A to F (or use of percentages) identified mediocre students as ones receiving Cs and Ds or just passing with 60 percent. Winners and losers remained easy to spot in age-graded schools.

"Success" in school, then, had both institutional and individual features. What ties the individual to institutional definitions of "success" and "failure" together is three links.

First, there are public and private goals for tax-supported public schools. Schools are now judged "successes" if public goals of graduates being literate, being prepared for the workplace, and contributing to the community are achieved. But parents also evaluate schools if they see their individual sons and daughters become financially comfortable and rise in social status—a private goal.

Second, there is the "grammar of schooling." The regularities of age-graded schooling not only allow both individual and institutional definitions of "success" and "failure" (e.g., each student's grade point average and school graduation rate) but also maintain both definitions with rules for when and how many tests individual students take, when and how students get promoted or retained, what letter grades each student receives in negotiating a chunk of the age-graded curriculum annually, and under what conditions individual students graduate high school. Gathering those individual student outcomes into collective test scores and numbers of graduates makes possible institutional judgments of "success" and "failure."

Third, numbers are crucial. In judging institutional and individual "success," statistics rule. Stories and anecdotes make vivid instances, but in a culture where quantification has been around for centuries to judge individual and institutional merit, figures matter (see Chapter 1). Monthly or yearly earnings, the price of a home, and the ability to keep an accurate checkbook register or pay promptly bills online are important markers of individual worth. Numbers are also critical in determining institutional "success" insofar as school test scores, seniors graduating, and how many will attend college.

Multiple goals, the "grammar of schooling," and dependence upon numbers, then, tie together individual and institutional definitions of "success." Those institutional and individual definitions are anchored in the age-graded school, a societal vehicle for making the next generation into adults who learn to compete while absorbing American core values of individualism, community, and equal opportunity.

CRITIQUES OF STANDARDIZED SCHOOLING

While there have been criticisms of this organizational form in the past— many readers have heard often the dismissive contemporary epithet describing age-graded schools as the "factory model of schooling"—few of these critiques or the reforms they inspired have altered the basic structure of the age-graded school or diminished their institutional definition of "success."[37]

Efforts to create nongraded schools or multi-age teams of children in schools have occurred but either soon disappeared or remained marginal to mainstream practices. Reforms geared to individualizing teaching and learning within the age-graded organization have a long checkered history with the most recent push to "personalize" learning through use of technology.[38]

Why have most current school reformers and educational entrepreneurs been reluctant to examine, much less overhaul, an organization that now influences daily behavior of nearly four million adults and well over fifty million children?

The primary reason is that most parents and educators have a picture in their heads of what a "real" school is. A "real" school is where children learn to read in first grade, get promoted every year and move into secondary school, and finally graduate with a diploma. In a "real" school students have textbooks, do homework, take notes, and receive report cards. In a "real" school students behave respectfully and strive for academic and extracurricular honors.

Sure, occasional reformers create private nongraded schools such as AltSchool and the Khan Lab Schools. In public schools, nongraded schools appeared now and then but were outliers. Social beliefs in the age-graded school with its manifest and latent functions are steadfast. Even with parents having options to send their children to private schools, 90 percent of all children attend tax-supported public schools (of which, 6 percent enroll in publically funded charter schools).[39]

Another reason is that over time, external constraints allied to these dominant social beliefs have constricted reformers' maneuverability in altering school structures. Consider that state-mandated standards, college entrance requirements, and the federal No Child Left Behind (now Every Student Succeeds Act) regulations, such as testing in various grades with attached accountability rules, are wedded to the historic age-graded structures.

And then there is the undeniable fact that tax-supported public schools are basically political institutions geared to socializing the young into exercising their civic duties, doing well in the workplace, and riding the social escalator into the middle and upper-middle classes. Moreover, the age-graded school has been the primary mechanism for processing millions of Americans through thirteen years of a standardized education. Politically, schools serve the larger society. Again and again, American political, business, and civic leaders faced national and local social, political, and economic problems that they found too hard to directly solve. Instead, these leaders often turned to schools to indirectly solve pressing problems by having the next generation work on those problems.

Public concerns, for example, over too much alcohol, tobacco, and drug use outside of school in early twentieth-century schools morphed into mandated courses for students to learn to drink moderately, smoke less, and avoid addictive drugs. Too many deaths from car accidents on highways turned into schools establishing driver education classes throughout most of the twentieth century. Too few American mathematicians and scientists after the Soviet Union put Sputnik in the sky led to pumped-up graduation requirements in these subjects.[40]

And since the late 1970s, a floundering economy with a shrinking pool of skilled workers for a postindustrial workplace and automated technologies reducing industrial jobs led to increased vocationalism in the nation's schools—everyone goes to college or enters a career, the slogans ran. Again and again, top civic and business leaders handed the baton to schools to solve the nation's problems. US problems became "educationalized."[41]

Finally, most policy makers believe that the age-graded school, with all of its shortcomings, has still succeeded for nearly two centuries in absorbing, assimilating, and graduating immigrants and native-born American children and youth. No, the age-graded school is hardly perfect, but even with institutional imperfections, standardized schooling has worked. Decision-makers ask: why dump it?

So age-graded schools in mirroring the contents and discontents of the larger society ever since the mid-1800s have also had the primary task of socializing the young in the core values of American society:

individualism, community, and equal opportunity. Schools receive much help from other social institutions such as corporate advertising, sports, summer camps for children to learn about entrepreneurship, organized religion, and the workplace in reinforcing these beliefs and values. Also multiple school goals, familiar school structures, and classroom lessons that contain within them institutional and individual definitions of "success" and "failure" combine to make the age-graded school and its "grammar of schooling" an incontrovertible fact.[42]

In short, "success" and "failure"—along with thoughts of fulfilling the American Dream—are baked into the democratic, market-driven society called America. Within the private family and public institutions such as business, sports, and schools, these beliefs and values are transmitted daily into homes, the workplace, and, with social media, any time an American opens a smart phone or laptop.

Of course, the strength and vigor of these values play out differently among Americans depending on geography, social class, ethnicity, race, religion, and personal preferences. But they remain lodged in the American character and institutions.

Yet who are the chefs and bakers that do the "cooking" of these values, and exactly how does the heating and simmering occur? Chapter 4 answers these questions.

CHAPTER 4

WHO DECIDES (AND HOW)
WHETHER SCHOOLS "SUCCEED" AND "FAIL"?

[We] should try to lead the world in access to high quality pre-kindergarten. We're like 28th. We're not close. Second, we were able to get high school graduation rates to an all-time high of 84 percent, which we were very proud of but obviously that's nowhere near high enough. . . . Third, we should make sure that 100 percent of those high school graduates are college ready, with higher standards. And then fourth, we should try and lead the world again in college completion. That's four-year universities, that's two-year community colleges, it's trade, technical and vocational training.

   Those are goals that keep high-wage, high-skill jobs in our country. Those are jobs that grow the middle class, those are jobs that keep our civic democracy healthy.

—ARNE DUNCAN[1]

WHO DECIDES?

In the above quote from an interview in 2018 with former US Secretary of Education Arne Duncan, the problem is the mismatch between traditional schooling and a workplace where jobs are exported to other countries, a shrinking middle class, and a democracy riven by conflict. The statistics Duncan used show the breadth and depth of the problem that he and others framed as a top priority to solve. These ideas and statistics had been around for many years and are variations of the template laid down in 1983 with *A Nation at Risk*. That the economy had just tanked in the Great Recession of 2007–2008 provided a window of opportunity for policy entrepreneurs and elite officials to make the case anew that schools are a lever to strengthen both the economy and democracy.[2]

   Using ample federal resources available in the American Recovery and Reinvestment Act (2009), President Obama and Secretary Duncan, through direct grants and a newly designed Race to the Top competition, solidified policy elites' agenda for national school reform (including donor initiatives from the Gates, Broad, and Walton Foundations). That agenda saw schools as primary instruments of reducing societal inequalities and strengthening the economic system. The thinking went—and continues to this day—that by increasing educational opportunities for low-income and minority students, human capital essential for a market-driven economy expands.[3]

A century ago, similar thinking among those who wielded influence and power became ascendant. In the early 1900s, business, civic, and philanthropic leaders supported educational Progressives who sought to bring greater efficiency to schooling masses of children. Three-quarters of a century later, business and civic leaders (including donors) wholeheartedly supported reformers who took the 1983 *A Nation at Risk* report—released after an economic recession in the early 1980s battered the American people—and used it as a guide to reform schools in the early twenty-first century. Then and now, these policy elites, representing different interests, framed what the problem was, put it on national and state reform agendas, suggested how to solve those problems, and included what metrics would show institutional "success" or "failure." For the past century, then, these policy elites, time and again, grabbed national attention, pressed for particular school reforms, fashioned compromises among conflicting economic and political interests, and mobilized media and popular support for their reforms.

POLICY ELITES JUDGE INSTITUTIONAL "SUCCESS" AND "FAILURE" NOW

Drawn from civic, business, and philanthropic leaders, policy elites (e.g., top federal and state education officials, the Business Roundtable, the Bill and Melinda Gates and Broad Foundations) and surrounded by cadres of policy analysts and academic researchers (e.g., American Enterprise Institute and Brookings Institution), these political and business leaders heavily influence direction of school reform. Highly educated, upper middle class, even wealthy, these elites usually have elevated social status as groups and individuals. They are both Democrats and Republicans although they bend conservative on issues of parental choice (more), unions (fewer), and taxes (less). They are biased toward goal-driven districts and schools as rational organizations whose top officials exert command-and-control decision-making through bureaucratic structures. Overall, policy elites tilt toward doing "good" by making incremental improvements without shaking the larger economic, social, and political structures that keep tax-supported public schools and inbred inequalities in place.[4]

These high-status leaders juggle values of equity, efficiency, and excellence to get re-elected, appointed, or receive federal subsidies. Because they are partial toward test scores and accountability (e.g., holding school officials, teachers, and students responsible for school outcomes) as key markers of institutional "success," they are also especially sensitive to gaining public support for such indicators of quality schools. And since the world they inhabit is one of running organizations and doing "good," their authority and access to mainstream and social media give them the leverage to spread their views and shape popular conceptions of what the primary problems are, the solutions that need to be put into practice, and what constitutes organizational "success."

Although within policy elites' vested interests and attitudes toward schools there is much overlap, they are hardly monolithic in what they want from K–12 schools. Even as wealthy donors have recently exerted outside influence on policy, as David Callahan points out, "the wealthy are also more divided than ever" on policy direction; "their clout," he continues, "is rarely directed in any one, uniform direction. . . ."[5]

Differences exist among donors. Some value efficiency highest, some value equity as most important, and others seek academic excellence while even others want combinations of these values to appear on reform to-do lists for "failed" public schools. While there is no interlocking directorate among education policy elites, the overlap in seeking particular values does produce fleeting convergences in reform agendas, strategies, and tactics as events unfold and the larger political and economic environment shifts.[6]

Some critics allege that these national policy elites engage in either conspiracies to end tax-supported public schools or subvert their mission. Critics call changes endorsed by policy elites "privatization," "neoliberal," or "corporate school reform," terms unintended as compliments.

Under the umbrella of "corporate school reform" are proposals and programs such as increasing the number of voucher programs and charter schools, implementing Common Core curriculum standards, evaluating schools and teachers using student test scores, and weakening teacher tenure and seniority rights.[7]

From veteran teacher and writer Stanley Karp:

> These policies undermine public education and facilitate its replacement by a market-based system that would do for schooling what the market has done for health care, housing, and employment: produce fabulous profits and opportunities for a few and unequal outcomes and access for the many. . . ."[8]

From educational historian, blogger, and critic, Diane Ravitch:

> The corporate reformers have done a good job of persuading the media that our public schools are failing because they are overrun by bad teachers, and these bad teachers have lifetime tenure because of their powerful unions.[9]

I have tried to avoid such terms because, in my opinion, they are both pejorative and inaccurate. They imply absolute certainty about these reformers' motives, smell of conspiratorial decision-making, and ignore the unvarnished embrace of market-driven capitalism and business practices that has swept across all US institutions, including schools, in the past quarter-century. Consider the following points:

- While the current generation of national civic and business leaders, donors, and elected federal officials believe in the crucial importance of schooling spurring economic growth and believe in market forces advancing equal opportunity and democracy, such convergence in beliefs does not a conspiracy make.
- Both national and local policy elites (see below) have varied, not uniform, motives (e.g., create competitive markets among schools, increase academic excellence and equal opportunity for poor and minority children and youth, expand parental choice, enlarge individual liberty, hold schools accountable for student results on

tests). These varied and contradictory motives and strategies make cabals difficult to sustain, much less take united action.

- National policy elites drawn from overlapping but distinct spheres of influence (e.g., CEOs, donors, elected officials, think tank analysts) are seldom organized enough to maintain secrecy, control the flow of information, and follow through with timely decisions. But they can and do move in a certain direction even if they occasionally stumble.

- Policy elites are pragmatic decision-makers. Policies often evolve out of practical decisions made under political and economic conditions that require action to advance an overall agenda (e.g., abandon small schools as a reform strategy and embrace pay-for-performance plans as best ways to improve minority and poor schools as the Bill and Melinda Gates Foundation did within a few years of each other).

How do I know this? Much of this comes from direct but limited experience with national and local policy elites and what I have learned as a historian of education. It is no secret, for example, that since the collapse of the Soviet Union in the early 1990s, market-based ideas have swept across US institutions. After nearly seventy-five years, democratic capitalism defeated state-managed socialism. The notion that the market solves public and private problems better than government gained widespread acceptance. Ideas, language, and practices drawn from the private sector have seeped into military planning and operations, government agencies, health-care institutions, and churches. School leaders are hardly alone in importing business practices, seeing education as a commodity, and adopting the vocabulary of market-driven capitalism.[10]

I also have learned about policy elites from direct experience.

In Washington, DC, schools in the 1960s, I was a district-based reformer but not a member of any policy elite. I met and worked with national and local policy leaders of the day in developing new models for training teachers, creating curricula for urban youth, and tying together community and schools. What struck me in the years I worked in urban schools and with these opinion-shapers was a mélange of their intensely held beliefs about reducing social inequalities, doing what was best for children and youth, struggling internally over both the ends and means, and constantly tripping over one another in getting things done.

Then I became a district superintendent in the 1970s and early 1980s. As an educational decision-maker, the school board and I—members of the local policy elite—were determined to improve the district schools. As superintendent in the metropolitan Washington, DC, educational community, I attended many business and social meetings where I saw national policy elites belonging to both political parties define problems, propose solutions, and make decisions. By this time the national and local elite members I had known years earlier had been replaced by another generation of smart, agile, influential leaders in their respective fields. Again, I was a marginal player, but I watched what transpired. Those two experiences in the Washington, DC, area left a strong impression on me about how smart, influential, and pragmatic individuals with similar beliefs converge and diverge as issues arise and evaporate. Cooperation between individuals and groups was episodic and transient.

I also served on a board of trustees for a charter school network of four high schools in the San Francisco Bay area. Half of the directors were local entrepreneurs and high-tech executives in start-up companies. They (I include myself) were clearly dedicated to the mission of getting 1,500 low-income minority students enrolled in their high schools into college. My colleagues on the board used their business experience to raise money, monitor budgets, find efficiencies, and expand innovations. Again, I was struck by the intensity of the beliefs, mix of motives, and variation in interests among these very smart and committed reformers.[11]

I raise these points to make clear that I avoid such phrases as "neoliberalism" and "corporate reformers" because they suggest far more coherence and concerted action than occurs in the real world of politics and elite policy making. I do understand how politically progressive critics can see profit-driven conspiracies to destroy public schools in the words and actions of deep-pocketed donors, federal officials, and test company executives who attack teacher unions and praise the release of data to rid districts of ineffective teachers. But my experiences and research see no conspiracies to destroy public schools or bash teachers; I do see differences in political beliefs and the weight given to values of excellence, efficiency, and equity over the direction public schools should take in an ever-changing global economy, one in which business, government, and donor leaders have been and are continually entangled in making decisions.

No surprise, then, as to whose criteria determine institutional quality within K–12 organizations. National and local coalitions of elected leaders and top civic and business figures often take innovations directed at school improvement, package the reform agenda (e.g., more accountability for teachers, new curriculum, innovative instruction, school reorganization) to educational policy makers and donors who, in turn, put their fingerprints on the proposals, and shove them downward into schools and classrooms through official policies and procedures. While there are other ways for reforms to enter schools such as from the local school community, neighborhood organizations, and teachers and principals—from the bottom up—the top-down framing of a problem has been the dominant pattern in the history of school reform.[12]

The national and local policy elites of this generation seeking overhaul of "failing" public schools described above have continued a tradition that policy elites a century earlier followed in seeking school reform.

POLICY ELITES WHO JUDGED INSTITUTIONAL "SUCCESS" AND "FAILURE" A CENTURY AGO

Push the "rewind" button and return to early twentieth-century Progressive leaders—the national policy elites of the day—who saw politically partisan influence in schools as a serious problem in need of a solution. City school board members took bribes from companies building, furnishing, and equipping schools; they appointed family members and supporters to become teachers and principals. Getting a contract or job in big city districts meant buying it from particular school officials or political party bosses. Such political influence corrupted the mission of schools to educate Americans to fulfill their civic responsibilities and be prepared for the workplace.[13]

These early twentieth-century policy elites joined by the donors of the day, including a dollop of academic entrepreneurs—they were then called "administrative Progressives"—saw "successful" schools, first, as politically free of partisanship and patronage; that is, qualifications for a job and merit determined who became teachers and administrators, not party bosses in a city or county. The solution was to end corrupt practices through legislation. The top-down reform agenda particularly in big cities increasingly took hold in getting partisan politics and crooked practices out of districts as a first step in making schools do what they were supposed to do.

City after city legislated that school boards had to be appointed by blue-ribbon commissions or elected by eligible voters. By the 1920s, political partisanship in appointing urban school board members and party boss–driven patronage systems had largely disappeared. And the evidence was there in numbers of big city school boards being elected and media watch-guards reporting when political bosses dispensed bribes and jobs.[14]

These administrative Progressives, active during the years that manufacturing, food production and distribution, transportation, and mining companies became Goliaths, saw the widespread adoption of Frederick Winslow Taylor's practices of "scientific management" in industry after industry. This was a window of opportunity that educational entrepreneurs climbed through. Copying corporate managers, these Progressives sought efficiency in operating schools. Using limited resources for the right purposes and reducing waste became goals that administrative Progressives sought.

Freed from patronage systems—the removal of partisan politics—only meant that school leaders could now act politically within their organizations in shaping agendas, defining problems, and proposing solutions without outside intervention. Driven by a growing sense of professionalism, district school boards and superintendents hired cadres of "educational engineers" to conduct systemwide surveys. These outside experts would determine if buildings had classrooms with the correct amount of light, adequate heat in winter time, and sufficient space for children—all designed and bought at the least possible cost. Increased efficiency also meant that teachers and principals acquired additional education and credentials to become professionals pursuing the best practices of the day. Since boards of education depended upon local voters for monies raised by tax levies on property, such school surveys and emerging professionalism could be used to drum up public support for raising additional monies and putting bond referenda on the ballot.[15]

One "efficiency expert" created a scorecard based upon one thousand points to measure building design, equipment, sanitation, and ventilation that was published and used by similar "educational engineers" in districts across the nation. Scores were added up to judge where a building was on the scale running from "excellent" to "obsolete." When schools scored high on efficiency measures, they were considered "successful." When they fell short, they became "mediocre" or "failing" schools.[16]

All of these top-down efficiency measures a century ago required numbers to sort out the best schools from the worst. Comparisons within the district and across districts became possible in constructing measures of district efficiency and performance. Experts measured what could be counted. If it could not be counted (e.g., effectiveness of teaching individuals, students' well-being, school and district culture), it was seldom quantified except when proxies could be found such as spelling and arithmetic tests and teacher credentials.

Academic experts conducted city school surveys to determine district efficiency from Portland to New York to Denver to Baltimore beginning in 1910 and running through the 1930s. Leonard Ayres's survey of Cleveland public schools, for example, hired twenty-two education experts to interview, observe, and measure what went on in the district administration and schools.[17]

But measures of district and school efficiency—the then trademark of school quality—shifted over time so that the numbers used before World War I through the 1960s—morphed later into quantifying student outcomes as measures of organizational effectiveness and school quality.

CONTEMPORARY POLICY ELITES SHIFT CRITERIA FOR
INSTITUTIONAL "SUCCESS" AND "FAILURE"

By the mid-1960s, amid the Civil Rights movement, cultural changes, and the war in Vietnam, a new criterion for judging organizational "success" had emerged with the passage of the federal Elementary and Secondary Education Act (ESEA) in 1965. The standard shifted from "efficiency" measures such as per-pupil expenditure, building quality, existing laboratory equipment, and teacher credentials to "effectiveness" metrics, that is, an arsenal of student outcome measures (e.g., student test scores, graduation rates, number of dropouts, college admissions). Federal and state policy makers, as well as donors and policy entrepreneurs—new national policy elites—wanted to see if school results matched the intended goals of a reform.

A half-century later, the dominant standard to judge district and school success remains *effectiveness*. The primary questions national and local policy elites asked are: What is the evidence that the policy has produced the desired outcomes? Have districts and schools achieved what officials said they were going to do? Where's the evidence? In a society where corporate "bottom lines," Dow Jones averages, Super Bowl victories, and vote counts matter, quantifiable results now determine the degree to which districts and schools are viewed as effective.

For example, in the late 1970s top business and civic leaders joined by policy entrepreneurs concluded that public schools had declined because scholastic aptitude test (SAT) scores had plunged downward. Even though test-makers and researchers repeatedly stated that such claims were false, falling SAT scores fueled public support for states raising academic requirements in the 1980s and adding standardized tests to determine organizational success. *A Nation at Risk* (1983) presented a list of economic problems that had to be solved by educational leaders and communities. The report advanced a top-down reform agenda consistent with the claims that the then national policy elite had made about the linkage of education and the economy. In the ensuing decades, states raised graduation requirements and created curriculum frameworks liberally dotted with adjectives like "rigorous" and "demanding."[18]

With the federal No Child Left Behind Act (2001–2015), test scores embedded in state accountability systems rewarded and penalized districts and schools. But continuing and virulent criticism of NCLB over the heavy hand of the US Department of Education labeling schools as institutional "failures" and prescribing solutions, the US Congress passed the Every Student Succeeds Act (2015), which President Obama signed, thereby shifting responsibility for choosing the best standardized test and accountability measures to the states rather than federal officials.

Did national and local policy elites' agenda for improving poor performance of US students on international and domestic standardized tests and yawning achievement gaps between white and minority students lead to solutions that have solved these problems? Sporadic improvements, "yes," but passage of ESSA says "no" to federal regulation of schools (and yes to continuing state oversight). Underlying gaps in academic achievement and inequalities in schools remained unresolved in the midst of an economic boom since 2008, raising serious questions about policy elites' search for both excellence and equity and wedding public school improvement to a strong economy.[19]

OTHER CRITERIA FOR JUDGING INSTITUTIONAL "SUCCESS" AND "FAILURE" IN REFORM AND SCHOOL QUALITY

Yet even using test results as a primary criterion in determining "success" of districts, schools, and individual teachers proved disappointing. Consider the mid-1960s' evaluations of Title I of the Elementary and Secondary Education Act (ESEA). They revealed little improvement in low-income children's academic performance, thereby jeopardizing congressional renewal of the program. Such evidence gave critics hostile to federal initiatives reasons to brand President Lyndon Johnson's War on Poverty programs as failures.[20]

Nonetheless, the program's political attractiveness to constituents and legislators overcame ambiguous and weak test scores. Following Johnson, each successive US president and Congress, Republican or Democrat, has used that popularity as a basis for allocating Title I funds to needy students in schools across the nation, including No Child Left Behind (2001) and its successor, Every Student Succeeds Act (2015). Thus, Title I of ESEA sent $15 billion to states and districts in 2016 serving over fifty-six thousand public schools (well over half the total of US schools) and more than twenty-six million students, again over half of the enrollment in public schools—regardless of how well or poorly students scored on tests.[21]

Popularity, then, is a second standard that policy elites, especially public officials, use in evaluating institutional "success." The spread of an innovation and its hold on voters' imagination and wallets has meant that attractiveness to parents, communities, and legislators, not necessarily test scores, easily translated into long-term political support for a particular reform. Without the political support of parents and teachers, few innovations and reforms could fly even short distances.

The diffusion of kindergarten and preschool, special education, bilingual education, accountability testing, charter schools, and electronic technologies across schools over the past half-century are instances of innovations that lacked solid evidence of effectiveness, yet long exposure in schools captured the attention of practitioners, parents, communities, and taxpayers. Few educators or public officials questioned large and sustained outlays of public funds for these popular reforms because they were perceived as resounding organizational "successes." And they have lasted for decades.[22]

Longevity, then, is a first cousin to the popularity criterion. How long a school reform has lasted becomes a sign not only of its political approval but also of its presumed effectiveness. For example, age-graded schools, a mid-nineteenth-century innovation, slowly spread across the country replacing one-room schoolhouses as the nation became urbanized. It has become a taken-for-granted institution in mass schooling. Even private schools and publically funded charter schools, both released from adhering to regular school policies and procedures, still retain the age-graded school organization. Because of its longevity, the age-graded school is presumed to be the best way to organize schools. Thus, popularity and longevity have become political proxies for effectiveness.

Another standard comes from researchers who judge institutional success by the *fidelity* standard. This criterion assesses the fit between the initial design, the formal policy, the subsequent program, and the degree to which it is faithfully put into school and classroom practice.

Consider the boom in Effective Schools that spread swiftly across urban districts in the 1980s. By the end of that decade, however, many researchers had pronounced the Effective Schools research seriously flawed in theory, design, and implementation although a few did point out redeeming qualities in that literature. This researchers' standard has been selectively used by policy elites including donors and practitioners in making judgments about Effective Schools programs or any of its subsequent incarnations since the 1990s, such as the Coalition of Essential Schools, Knowledge Is Power Program (KIPP), and charter schools.[23]

Champions of the *fidelity* standard ask: How can anyone determine actual effectiveness if the implemented reform departs from the original design? If federal, state, or district policy makers, for example, adopt and fund a new reading program because it has proved to be effective elsewhere, teachers and principals must follow the blueprint as they put it into practice; otherwise, the desired outcomes will go unfulfilled (e.g., Success For All). When practitioners add, adapt, or even omit features of the original design, then those in favor of fidelity say that the policy and program cannot be determined effective because of these changes. Policy adaptability—what teachers often seek—undercuts fidelity.[24]

And that very adaptability is another standard that practitioners use in assessing institutional and individual quality of their performance and that of students. School-based practitioners judge a reform by its flexibility in being tailored to their ways of teaching and whether it will benefit their students.

Can teachers adapt the innovation, say, a new way of teaching reading that uses both phonics and whole word instruction, to fit their students? If teachers say "yes," then such modifications occur once they close their doors and begin lessons. If a district adopts, for example, Open Court reading, classroom revisions inexorably occur within a school and across schools. Sure, the criterion of fidelity is abridged, but individual lessons taught by teachers are often beyond the surveillance of other teachers, principals, researchers, and district office administrators. Thus, the freedom to tailor innovations to the contours of their students is what teachers prize when asked to put into practice a particular curriculum, a technological device delivered to their classroom, or a mandate to shift to problem-based learning.[25]

But where do these dominant standards of *effectiveness* and *popularity/longevity*, and lesser used criteria of researchers' *fidelity* and teachers' *adaptability* come from?

DIFFERENT WAYS OF SEEING ORGANIZATIONS

Policy elites derive the criteria of *effectiveness* and *fidelity* from viewing organizations as rational tools for achieving desired goals. Defining the problem clearly, framing one or more solutions, crafting policies that will put the solution into practice, and then evaluating the results in light of the initial problem are at the heart of a rational organization. Through top-down decisions, formal bureaucratic structures, clearly specified roles and procedures, and technical expertise, administrators and practitioners get the job done. Such a view, however, is only one way of describing how organizations are and should be.[26]

Within organizations where rational decision-making and control are prized, policy makers ask: Have the prescribed procedures been followed (*fidelity*), i.e., put into practice, and have the goals been achieved (*effectiveness*)? Hence, in judging reforms, those who propose solutions to the identified problem and those who carry out the changes must be faithful to the design before the standard of effectiveness in achieving goals can be invoked.

With the growth of social science research beginning in the late-nineteenth century and spreading in subsequent decades through the professions and organizations in the private and public sectors, these beliefs in rational organizations and use of rigorous research gained support and the cachet of legitimacy. Programs in corporate training and university professional education programs adopted this perspective throughout the twentieth century. Donald Schon called this view "technical rationality." Rather than favoring practitioner expertise derived from school and classroom experience, public officials and researchers use this scientifically grounded "technical rationality" to evaluate the degree to which reforms are implemented and judged effective.[27]

Contrary to the *effectiveness* and *fidelity* standards, *popularity* and its cousin, *longevity*, derive from the political nature of schools as public institutions and policy elites' astute use of symbols (e.g., American flags in classrooms, test scores, computers) to convey core American values. Schools, for example, are totally dependent on the financial and political support of local communities and the state. Taxpayer backing for, or opposition to, bond referenda or school board initiatives is often converted into political capital at election time. Whether innovations spread (e.g., charters, classroom laptops) and capture public and practitioner attention over decades becomes a strong basis for evaluating its success.[28]

Now consider a seldom-mentioned criterion that practitioners use: *adaptability*. Can the mandated policy be tailored to school and classroom conditions? For practitioners, pliable policies can be more easily put into practice than ones that have inflexible requirements and sanctions accompanying them. Such policies have a strong claim on teachers' attention.

Adaptability as a criterion derives from a set of assumptions about organizations different from the ones dominating mainstream policy thinking. Practitioner-based assumptions find organizations less rational; more loosely coupled to policy mandates allowing teacher autonomy; and shaped more by external political, social, and demographic factors.

Unpredictable events (e.g., economic recession, demographic changes, political shifts) and a web of larger social beliefs (e.g., unregulated markets and entrepreneurial risk taking are better than governmental intervention) intersect with an informal side of the organization—networks of who talks to whom, the stories that people tell—to fashion workplace behavior, often producing unintended consequences for rationally inspired policies. In educational organizations, there are often loose ties between, say, school board goals, district procedures, school activities, and classroom lessons. As policies travel from one organizational level to another, they accumulate fingerprints and changes by the time they reach classrooms. Teachers, then, close their doors and tailor policies to their views of what is best for students. Adaptations in roles and structures occur naturally and often as people within an organization cope with the inexorable range of external and internal problems that ebb and flow.[29]

However, policy elites often using a technical rational lens seldom consider practitioners' experience and the different assumptions that flow from other ways of seeing how organizations work. The question boils down to one of power and status.

WHOSE CRITERIA COUNT?

Even with these multiple standards available in making policy decisions, the answer to the question of *whose* criteria get used in making policy decisions is clear. Those with the most clout in making decisions, that is, policy elites then and now, have determined which of these standards to use in judging institutional "success."

When national, state, and district policy makers—holding technical-rational views of how organizations work, using research findings to bolster their decisions, and having access to media—place their weight behind reforms, political influence and organizational legitimacy in making changes rest with those at the top of the organization, not those at the bottom—researchers and practitioners—whose political power is thin and whose views, expertise, and values differ. Without the cachet of scientific evidence, access to top officials, or easy entree to mainstream media, individual teachers are stuck.

Collectively, many teachers have organized into unions and asserted their political clout through taking explicit positions on school reform. In 2018–2019, teachers in various states and big cities did go on strike for higher salaries, more funding for schools, smaller classes, better working conditions, fewer charter schools, and less testing.[30]

Yet in making policy and judging organizational success in a pro-business climate, unions play a limited role in enlarging the autonomy that teachers have when working in age-graded schools. Thus, when individual teachers do choose to make adaptations, they do so unobtrusively or, in some cases, engage in guerrilla warfare with administrators to do what they wish. What individual teachers have, thanks to the "grammar of schooling," is a self-contained classroom that has a door. Behind that door, teachers enact lessons that may or may not adhere to policy directives about what and how to teach. They have constrained autonomy.[31]

These practitioners in adapting policies to fit their students are just as interested in student outcomes as are policy makers, but the outcomes they seek go beyond what school boards and superintendents prize. Practitioners ask: What skills, content, and attitudes have students learned beyond what is tested? To what extent is the life lived in our classrooms and schools safe, democratic, and caring? Can reform-driven programs, curricula, and technologies be bent to our purposes? Such questions, however, are seldom heard by policy elites who possess far larger megaphones. Seeking broader student outcomes than measured by test scores and job preparation leads many practitioners to adapt policies to fit the topography of their classroom and students' lives.

So multiple standards for judging school "success" are available. Practitioner- and researcher-derived standards have occasionally surfaced and received erratic attention from policy elites. But the strong, powerful alliance of policy makers, civic and business elites, and allies in the corporate, foundation, and media worlds relies heavily on standards of effectiveness, fidelity, popularity, and longevity. They continue to dominate public debate, school reform agendas, and determinations of institutional "success" and "failure."

Now, here is the spot where I should say which of these standards for judging organizational "success" of reforms is best and should be used. I won't do that. Why? Because while I prefer a mix of standards driven by practitioner, researcher, and policy maker values, the current dominance of policy elites in focusing upon test-driven, accountability-rich criteria in judging reform reflects the abiding fact that public schools have been shaped by political decisions since their founding nearly two centuries ago. Yes, I want a broader mix of criteria to judge quality of reform and individual schools and districts than exist now. But the unassailable fact remains that who decides what criteria to apply to schools is a political decision, and the public arena is where such decisions in a democracy are (and have been) made.

In a democracy, whose standards dominate decisions on institutional success are politically determined. And for nearly forty years (*A Nation at Risk* was published in 1983), a coalition of business-influenced reformers, civic and corporate leaders, educational policy makers, and donors has been politically skillful in initially framing and then shaping national and state reform agendas. Recall that for two decades, both Republican and Democratic presidents and Congresses supported major legislation (Bill Clinton's Goals 2000: Educate America Act; George W. Bush's No Child Left Behind; Barack Obama's Race to the Top and establishment of Common Core state standards). In all of these instances, the political coalition drawn from both national parties, divided by competing interests, nonetheless held together and supported legislation that pressed for uniform curriculum standards, state and local accountability regimes, more testing, increasing numbers of charter schools, and cash incentives for states and districts to do all of the above.[32]

Why? Because the coalition's dominant belief was that tax-supported public schools exist to prepare workers for an information-driven economy—everyone goes to college or enters a career after graduation. This was (and continues to be) the first commandment in the policy elites' playbook of school reform.

But the "first commandment" can change. Historically, it is well to remember that earlier policy elites had different purposes. In the mid-nineteenth century, Common School crusaders such as Horace Mann and a cadre of like-minded reformers established tax-supported schools that would prepare literate citizens to vote, serve on juries, engage in democratic practices, enter the workplace able to earn a living, and be decent members of a community. A later generation of policy elites advanced a Progressive agenda of expanded schools with playgrounds, lunchrooms, medical suites, social workers, and other professionals serving the whole child while being "socially efficient" in connecting to the larger society. The Progressive era in schooling lasted at least a half-century, spanning the late nineteenth to mid-twentieth centuries.

The current reform era of nearly four decades of tying individual so-cial mobility to job preparation with civic duties pulling up the rear can shift again as it has in the past.

Opposition to the current top-down reforms has arisen (e.g., parent boycotts of standardized tests, political conservatives criticizing Com-mon Core standards, teacher strikes to reduce spread of charter schools, researcher protests to using student scores to evaluate teachers); none-theless, the prevailing coalition pushing an economic purpose for schooling and parents seeing their children acquiring educational cre-dentials as the road to individual "success" remain largely intact. With-out a collective political effort to change contemporary policy elites' standards of *effectiveness, fidelity, popularity*, and *longevity*, these dominant criteria will remain defining what institutional "success" is. And alterna-tives to those standards will continue to be marginalized.[33]

Current and widespread definitions of institutional "success" and "failure" become clear in the following example.

The Bill and Melinda Gates Foundation's Intensive Partnerships for Effective Teaching (IPET) aimed at identifying the behaviors of effective teachers who raise students' test scores, giving minority and poor stu-dents access to such teachers, and creating new ways of evaluating teach-ers. I give this example without denigrating the content or worth of the initiative but more to illustrate how well-endowed members of policy elites exert their influence at every step of the policy process: framing problems to be solved, proposing top-down solutions, doing (or not do-ing) research, and making requisite policy changes that ripple through the entire decentralized system of US schooling.[34]

INTENSIVE PARTNERSHIPS FOR EFFECTIVE TEACHING

Between 2009 and 2016, three school districts (Hillsborough County, Florida; Memphis City Schools, Tennessee; Pittsburgh Public Schools, Pennsylvania) and four charter networks (California-based charter net-works—Alliance College-Ready Public Schools, Aspire, Green Dot, and Partnerships to Uplift Communities) spent over a half-billion dollars of which the Bill and Melinda Gates Foundation contributed $213 million in creating policies that would identify, recruit, train, and evaluate effective teachers while giving low-income minority children and youth access to those effective teachers. Giving access to children heretofore excluded from having the best teachers would offer equal opportunity to children and youth, one goal of the project.[35]

Teachers would learn how to do peer evaluations, collaborate with colleagues, receive professional development, and earn bonuses if their students scored well on tests. Finally, the project would determine whether student test scores, graduation rates, and attendance in college improved as a result of these policies. Note how this richly funded project combines an implicit economic purpose—students gain credentials for entry into the workplace—to American core values of competitive individualism, collaboration with peers, and equal opportunity for children and youth.

Consider, for example, pay schemes linked to teachers who are judged highly effective. Bonuses and salary increases go to those teachers who meet the criteria (i.e., student test score gains, highest ratings from peer and supervisor observations). Such economic incentives in sync with market capitalism spur many individual teachers to secure the highest ratings from evaluators. That such programs also encourage collaboration through collegial evaluation, that is, teachers learning together how to judge fellow teachers while offering every teacher the chance to participate in such efforts, reveals the core values embedded in the process of determining "successful" teachers.[36]

These years, then, brought together national policy makers and donors to push ahead on programs that policy elites determined were the best levers to improve the performance of US public schools and strengthen the economy. Even prior to this, the Bill and Melinda Gates Foundation had funded research to identify valid measures of effective teaching that were then incorporated into proposed policies the participating districts and charter networks could put into practice.[37]

In the first decade of the twenty-first century, then, there was a convergence of the largest US foundation investing in both research on effective teaching and Common Core curriculum standards intersecting with President Obama's educational policies including the competitive

Race to the Top program, and policy elites' passion for accountability by using student test scores to evaluate teachers' performance. The dollar-infused partnership of districts and charter networks fueled by sponsored research into effective teaching was a top-down initiative that national and state policy makers enthusiastically endorsed. To assess this massive effort, the Gates Foundation paid the RAND corporation to independently evaluate the reform.

A brief look at the largest partner in the project, Florida's Hillsborough County district, over the span of the grant documents the early exhilaration over the project to later stumbles over rising program costs that had to be absorbed by the district's regular budget, followed by key district and school staff's growing disillusion over the project's direction and disappointing results for both teachers and students. Consider what the *Tampa Bay Times* found in 2015 after a lengthy investigation:

- The Gates-funded program—which required Hillsborough to raise its own $100 million—ballooned beyond the district's ability to afford it, creating a new bureaucracy of mentors and "peer evaluators" who no longer work with students.
- Nearly 3,000 employees got one-year raises of more than $8,000. Some were as high as $15,000, or 25 percent.
- Raises went to a wider group than envisioned, including close to 500 people who don't work in the classroom full time, if at all.
- The greatest share of large raises went to veteran teachers in stable suburban schools, despite the program's stated goal of channeling better and better-paid teachers into high-needs schools.
- More than $23 million of the Gates money went to consultants.
- The program's total cost has risen from $202 million to $271 million when related projects are factored in, with some of the money coming from private foundations in addition to Gates. The district's share now comes to $124 million.
- Millions of dollars were pledged to parts of the program that educators now doubt. After investing in an elaborate system of peer evaluations to improve teaching, district leaders

are considering a retreat from that model. And Gates is with-
holding $20 million after deciding it does not, after all, favor
the idea of teacher performance bonuses—a major change in
philosophy.

- The end product—results in the classroom—is a mixed bag.

  Hillsborough's graduation rate still lags behind other large
  school districts. Racial and economic achievement gaps remain pronounced, especially in middle school.

  And poor schools still wind up with the newest, greenest
  teachers.[38]

Not a pretty picture. RAND's formal evaluation covering the life of
the grant and across the three districts and four charter networks used
less judgmental language but reached a similar conclusion:

> Overall, the initiative did not achieve its stated goals for students, par-
> ticularly LIM [low-income minority] students. By the end of 2014–
> 2015, student outcomes were not dramatically better than outcomes in
> similar sites that did not participate in the . . . initiative. Furthermore,
> in the sites where these analyses could be conducted, we did not find
> improvement in the effectiveness of newly hired teachers relative to ex-
> perienced teachers; we found very few instances of improvement in the
> effectiveness of the teaching force overall; we found no evidence that
> LIM students had greater access than non-LIM students to effective
> teaching; and we found no increase in the retention of effective teach-
> ers, although we did find declines in the retention of ineffective teach-
> ers in most sites.[39]

As with the history of such innovative projects in public schools over
the past century, RAND evaluators found that districts and charter
school networks fell short in achieving IPET goals because of uneven
implementation of the program.[40]

> We also examined variation in implementation and outcomes across
> sites. Although sites varied in context and in the ways in which they
> approached the levers, these differences did not translate into differ-
> ences in ultimate outcomes. Although the sites implemented the same

levers, they gave different degrees of emphasis to different levers, and none of the sites achieved strong implementation or outcomes across the board.[41]

But any absolutist judgment of organizational "failure" in achieving aims of this donor-funded initiative hides the ripple effects flowing from this effort to reform teaching and learning in these districts and charter networks.

Consider the subsequent political "success" of the reform. Over forty states and the District of Columbia had adopted plans to evaluate teachers on the basis of student test scores. How much student test scores should weigh in the overall determination of a teacher's effectiveness varies by state and local districts, as does the autonomy local districts have in putting into practice state requirements for evaluating teachers. For example, how much weight to give to test scores in judging a teacher's effectiveness varies from half of the total teacher evaluation to one-third or one-fourth. Even as testing experts and academic evaluators have raised significant flags about the instability, inaccuracy, and unfairness of such district and state policies being put into practice, they remain on the books and have been implemented in various districts. Because time is such an important factor in putting these policies into practice, states and districts will go through trial and error as they implement these policies, possibly leading to more (or less) political acceptance from teachers and principals, key participants in the venture.[42]

One serious unanticipated outcome to this reform, however, is concentrating on the teacher rather than other factors. While there has been a noticeable dulling of the reform glow for evaluating teachers on the basis of student performance—note how the Gates Foundation pulled back on its use in evaluating teachers as part of the half-billion dollar Intensive Partnerships for Effective Teaching—the rise and fall in enthusiasm for using test scores, intentionally or unintentionally, has focused policy discussions on teachers as the source of school "failure" and inequalities among students. In pressing for teachers to be held accountable, policy elites have largely ignored other significant factors influencing both teacher and student performance that are deeply connected to economic and social inequalities outside the school, such as neighborhood poverty and crime, discriminatory labor and housing practices, and increased funding as ways of improving schools.

By donors helping to frame an agenda for turning around "failing" US schools or, more generously, improving equal opportunity for children and youth, these philanthropists—unaccountable to anyone—as members of policy elites spotlight teachers as both the problem and solution to school improvement. Surely, teachers are the most important in-school factor—perhaps 10 percent of the variation in student achievement. Yet over 60 percent of the variation in student academic performance is attributed to out-of-school factors such as family income and neighborhood.[43]

This Gates-funded Intensive Partnerships for Effective Teaching is an example, then, of policy elites successfully shaping a reform agenda for the nation's schools using teacher effectiveness as a primary criterion and having enormous direct and indirect influence in advocating and enacting other pet reforms.

Did IPET "fail"? If the criterion of *effectiveness* is used—were the desired goals of improving academic achievement and providing equal access for poor and minority students to the best teachers achieved?—the answer is yes. Two separate sources (a newspaper investigation and independent evaluator) pointed out the failed venture.

If popularity and longevity criteria are applied, school districts either scaled back their efforts when donor money dried up or dispensed with the initiative. Yet many states adopted similar accountability plans. If the criterion of fidelity is invoked, the RAND judgment about uneven, fragmentary implementation across the three districts and four charter networks gets marked as another sign of "failure."

What about criteria like adaptiveness used by teachers to judge institutional and individual "success" and "failure"?

Were researchers to go to individual district schools and charters to interview teachers and observe lessons—I have yet to find such a study—chances are that residue of the Gates initiative would be found in certain district and school practices. Adaptations, I would guess, have occurred.

Would such debris from a reform constitute organizational "success" and refute the judgment of "failure"? No, it would not.

Within the business world, the bottom line of profit and loss is clear. Applied to schools, such bottom-line thinking largely equates to test scores and other quantitative indicators of academic achievement such as high school graduation rates and college admissions. *Effectiveness* remains a primary standard used to judge institutional "success" and "failure."

While I have noted donor-funded initiatives that have largely "failed" using the absolutist standard of effectiveness, the dominance of policy elites and transient partnerships that arise and disappear within the world of school reform persists. Think of state takeovers of troubled districts and results of Race to the Top as instances when applying these criteria also resulted in a judgment of "failure."

Yet there is cause for a mixed verdict or at least one that might be deferred rather than the bold red strikeover of institutional "failure." Consider the three strands of policy described in the Introduction: the process of defining the policy problem, designing a solution, and getting it adopted; the program itself; and the politics of implementation.[44]

With Gates funding of research on measures of teaching effectiveness, support of the Obama administration, and school districts and charter networks eager to take the money and put these ideas into practice, the process part of IPET policy making was clearly a political "success." IPET mobilized federal, state, and local officials to consider the project and then adopt it, even adding money to what the foundation gave.

For the program strand of the policy, it is clear that the federally funded Race to the Top's inclusion of teachers being evaluated through test scores and the Gates grant for IPET persuaded many states to pass legislation, prod local districts, and provide resources for school systems to alter their traditional ways of evaluating teachers. Over forty states, varying as they do in their evaluation requirements, still put these programs on the radar screens of local districts, and these districts, over time, have worked out varied ways of enacting different forms of teacher evaluation. A fair person could conclude that such fallout from the initiative makes IPET a precarious "success" teetering on the edge of "failure." Since data continue to come in from states and districts on what is occurring in schools, what may be down the road insofar as teacher evaluation remains unclear.[45]

Finally, there is the political strand. Grasping multiple threads that make up policy, influential and richly funded coalitions came together to support government intervention to ensure teacher accountability for student outcomes. States and districts adopted and implemented particular policies. Repercussions rippled through school districts where teachers and principals were expected to implement these policies while outside schools, parents and community organizations sought and acquired private resources to press teachers to be held responsible for student performance. All of these are political actions following in the wake of adopting teacher evaluation polices relying on student test scores. These political facts cannot be avoided or side-stepped because they do not neatly fit into the technical-rational model many policy analysts and elites would prefer to use. Surely ITEP was politically successful in corralling three districts and four charter networks to adopt policies to overhaul district and school ways of evaluating teachers and providing access to poor and minority students to identified effective teachers.

In handling the angry response from teachers who opposed the use of student test scores to evaluate their classroom performance, pushback from professional associations and unions, and academic critiques that pointed out the inevitable outcomes of such unreliable and invalid evaluations, ITEP and various states fiddled with their goals and programs to accommodate the rising tide of criticism. Political consequences piled up in the wake of ITEP.

Districts, however, scrambled to gain teacher support by having multiple measures, including principal observation and peer evaluation. Toward the end of Race to the Top and IPET, this political thread of policy making was seriously frayed.[46]

So in considering the political repercussions of IPET and state-driven teacher-accountability reforms, the picture is not one of unvarnished institutional "failure" but a mixed one. Partial "successes" salted with visible "failures" don't fit neatly into a binary decision of "success" or "failure."

What is far better, as Allan McConnell suggests, is a spectrum that runs from "resilient success," "conflicted success," and "precarious success." Few desired program outcomes were achieved for the target group, and the presence of substantial opposition to the program resulted in a mixed picture. IPET is an instance of one of the embedded contradictions in determining "success" and "failure" in school reform and program quality. There can be a successful political process of adopting an innovative program—as Gates dollars and school board support illustrated—but it turns out that the program failed because in this instance, primary program goals were unachieved and substantial political opposition to IPET arose inside and outside the district. IPET vanished.[47]

In short, making judgments is untidy rather than neat when it comes to policy being put into practice and the rippling political consequences of implementing programs. IPET is an example of that untidiness in deciding institutional "success" and "failure."

What also comes through in discussing IPET and the subsequent state laws on teacher evaluation is the embeddedness of American core values: individualism, community, and equal opportunity.

Consider that within IPET, teachers were not drafted to participate as peer evaluators or mentors. Each teacher decided whether to go for a bonus, train to become a peer evaluator, or join the initiative in other ways. The value of individual choice, protecting one's liberty to decide, was built into the reform.

Similarly, efforts to build a community among participating teachers and administrators occurred in the creation of peer evaluators and mentors. Collaboration among individuals normally isolated by the age-graded school organization within which they worked slowly unfolded in the project. Intentions to build community led to like-minded groups pursuing IPET objectives.

As for equal opportunity, project goals announced that the initiative would identify highly effective teachers who would end up teaching poor and minority children who heretofore were often assigned inexperienced and substitute teachers.

Although using policy elites' dominant criterion of *effectiveness* ends up judging IPET as a "failure," while applying less absolute, more realistic standards anchored in other criteria creates a mixed judgment of organizational "success" and "failure," the historic core values in American life remain evident in this well-funded, highly publicized school reform.

The next two chapters describe actual ongoing cases of school reform deemed by dominant criteria as institutionally "successful," yet these two schools also use individual student outcomes to broaden what organizational "success" means when judging school governance, curriculum, and instruction and student outcomes. In these two small high schools, I describe broader views of institutional "success" and "failure" that staff, parents, and students have while also examining the historic American core values as they played out within these schools.

– CHAPTER 5 –

WHAT DOES INSTITUTIONAL AND INDIVIDUAL "SUCCESS" AND "FAILURE" LOOK LIKE IN TWO CONTEMPORARY SCHOOLS?

This school [Social Justice Humanitas Academy] exists in the face of a bureaucracy [Los Angeles Unified School District] that doesn't want it to exist, not because they don't like us, but because we don't fit. Political activism . . . has to be ongoing: showing up and defying the odds every day in the face of so much apathy. And, given the current administration [President Donald Trump], it means embracing immigrants and becoming a sanctuary. I have to do it for my teachers, they have to do it for the students. And when we do it for the students, we realize they actually give it back to us. The students want us to be successful. I tell teachers: "Show up ready to go, make yourself vulnerable, and these kids will be rooting for you. You'll make a mistake and they'll forgive it. They want you to be successful because you're a human being, so present yourself as such."

–JOSE NAVARRO, principal and teacher founder
of Social Justice Humanitas Academy, 2017[1]

[In most high schools] you go to your different classes, turn in your homework and you go home. We actually have to think critically about what we're doing. . . . My satisfaction is in seeing my work in the community and affecting it. I felt grown. I felt independent and I like that feeling. . . . I didn't feel like any of the adults cared about how I did. Here, whether it's academic or personal, they care.

–PERLA CANTU, graduating senior,
MetWest High School, 2006[2]

In this chapter and the next one, I will describe and analyze two California public high schools that have expanded traditional definitions of "success" and "failure" beyond test scores, graduation rates, and college admissions. They are Social Justice Humanitas Academy (SJHA) in Los Angeles Unified School District and MetWest in Oakland Unified School District.

Neither school is a charter or magnet. They are regular public schools subject to their district's goals, policies, and regulations. Their staffs and students, however, are unique in how they collectively gained and used their autonomy to broaden the familiar definition of "success" in both school and classroom to include the well-being of individual students.

Yet in expanding what institutional "success" means, both schools pay careful attention to the dominant criteria district policy makers, practitioners, and parents use to judge school "success," such as test scores and graduation rates. They also pursue in their mission, school organization, and classroom lessons additional criteria for "success" that differ greatly from other schools in the state and across the United States. Moreover, these expanded definitions echo an earlier time in school reform movements that sought growth of individual children's self-knowledge, confident peacefulness, and connections to the community in which they lived, a point I take up in chapter 7.[3]

SOCIAL JUSTICE HUMANITAS ACADEMY (1980s–PRESENT)

Geological strata reveal historical periods of plant and animal life eons ago. Schools birthed in reform expose similar strata. Every district, every school in the United States, has historical layers of reform piled atop one another although the time frame is far less than an eon.

A case in point is the Social Justice Humanitas Academy. Consider the school's official statements:

Our mission is to achieve social justice through the development of the complete individual. In doing so, we increase our students' social capital and their humanity while creating a school worthy of our own children.[4]

In addition, there is the school's vision of what it aspires to:

At Social Justice Humanitas Academy, our vision is: **We will achieve self-actualization** *[original bold-faced]. The concept of self-actualization comes from Abraham Maslow, a leader in humanistic psychology, who understood a good life to be one in which an individual maximized their potential to become the very best version of who they are.*[5]

These mission and vision statements act "as a guide to all decision making" in selecting staff, arranging the daily schedule, organizing the curriculum, teaching classroom lessons, forming out-of-class ties between teachers and students, and engaging in community activities.

As the website declares:

> Our college-prep, interdisciplinary curriculum, advisory program, intervention systems, focus on social-emotional learning, parent engagement opportunities and community partnerships are all designed to understand the needs of each individual student and help them to realize their full potential.
>
> Our expectation that all Humanitas students will attend college stems from our belief that education is the best pathway for personal growth. Whatever path our students choose, we hope to start them on a life-long journey to realize their full potential. . . . We have established in our school a culture of academic excellence coupled with humanistic compassion. At SJHA, it is not enough to be a good student; you must also strive to be a good person. . . .[6]

Mission statements, of course, are often aspirational, offering the highest hopes of those working in and supporting the school. Those hopes also appear in hallway art and classroom posters.

From a rainbow-painted hallway mural in SJHA:

> *In Lak Ech*
> *You are my other me*
> *If I do Harm to you*
> *I do harm to myself*
> *If I love and respect you*
> *I love and respect myself*[7]

That mission of college for all, social activism, and growth in individual self-knowledge is tied closely to where the school is located in the city of San Fernando and the community in which it is embedded.

From painted words on a school wall:

> *Every Minute Is a Chance To Change the World*

From a hallway poster:

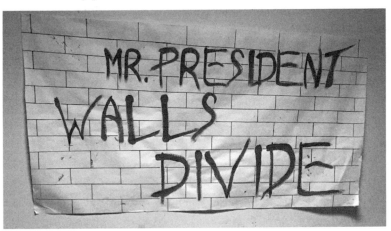

Formal, printed mission statements and hallway art give a sense of the school's aspirations and direction. Both are anchored in the community in which the school is located.

Consider the school's demographics and academic profile. Since SJHA opened, its student enrollments have stayed consistent. SJHA has 513 students (2019) enrolled in ninth through twelfth grades. On race and ethnicity (2015), 95 percent were Hispanic, 2 percent African American, and 1 percent each for Caucasian and Native American. Of that number 12 percent were English language learners. Special education students were 10 percent of enrollment. And 88 percent were eligible for free or reduced-price lunch (the poverty measure for LAUSD schools).[8]

And some of the academic results were sufficiently eye-catching to attract media attention.

- Graduation rates increased between 2011 and 2015 from 83 to 94 percent. Both exceed LAUSD and state rates of graduation.
- Ninety-six percent of students have an individual graduation plan.
- Seventy-five percent of students passed all college required courses.
- Suspensions sunk to 0.2 percent in 2014.

- Six Advanced Placement courses are offered (English language, English literature, analytic geometry/pre-calculus, macroeconomics, Spanish language, Spanish literature).[9]

From the main office:

Head shot photos of SJHA graduates and the year they graduated line three walls of the entire space housing secretaries and administrative offices. Most of these photographed students are the first in their families to graduate high school and attend college. When entering students, visitors, and parents waiting to see administrators sit on hard plastic chairs, their eyes invariably look up to the faces of SJHA graduates.

Yet work remains to be done in boosting academic achievement. Consider that in 2018, only one of four students in the eleventh grade tested proficient in math (the state average is 39 percent) although nearly two out of three students did so in English (the state average is 50 percent). Also, only 51 percent of Advanced Placement students passed one or more AP exams (the state average is 62 percent).[10]

Apart from the numbers, three features of SJHA give it a distinctive character unlike most public schools. Teachers have governed the school since its origins as a school-within-a-school in 2006. Second, the name of the school captures both its activist mission and the history of its founding. Finally, the goal of individual students (and teachers) knowing their values, beliefs, strengths, and weaknesses so that they can become authentic human beings may be an aspiration of many other public schools, but at SJHA it is embedded in the daily regimen.

Teachers Make Decisions

A group of teachers founded a school-within-a-school within an LAUSD high school that eventually through the organizational and political efforts of these teachers became a separate school in another location (see below). SJHA currently has a principal as required by LAUSD. Jose Navarro, a founding teacher, served between 2011 and 2018; his successor is another SJHA founding teacher, Jeff Austin, who assumed the post after Navarro left. Both Navarro and Austin made clear that SJHA teachers make key organizational, curricular, and instructional decisions for the school. The continuity in principals who were also founders of SJHA is one significant factor in what the school is today.[11]

For example, according to the 2015 self-study report seeking accreditation from the Western Association of Schools and Colleges, teachers decided to do the following:

> [E]very five weeks after grades are submitted the entire staff participates in Data Day, where teachers look at individual student data and all staff "adopt" three students to focus on for the next five week period. This includes developing an Individualized Pupil Education Plan (IPEP) for each adopted student. Through the adoption and IPEP process, teachers use data to identify students who are struggling and then meet regularly with the students for the next five weeks to make a plan for success with the student and then monitor the student's progress.[12]

Nor do teachers wait for an administrator to take an action they believe important for students. As one teacher-founder-turned-principal noted:

> Instead of waiting for an administrator to come up with a plan to do it, they just either do it or let us know. "I see this problem and I think I have a solution. Can I do this or can someone help me do this?" And it is just a matter of feeling empowered and understanding. That's why we have this model, so you don't have to wait for someone up the chain to give you approval.[13]

Called a teacher-powered school, it is part of a network of about 120 public and private teacher-run schools across the nation.[14]

Social Justice Mission

While the phrase "social justice," often interchangeable with "equity," has become common in 2019 among academics, practitioners, and activist parents who identify themselves as progressives, it has been associated with schools for well over a half-century. The phrase's recent popularity among practitioners and teacher educators—who can be against "equity" or "social justice"?—has increased the array of definitions and meanings to cover any school program from "restorative justice" to completing course requirements for entering college to mentoring students as instances of social justice in practice.[15]

If one turns to the classic definition of justice formulated by philosopher John Rawls, the efforts of SJHA to put its mission into practice does fall within Rawls's two principles:

1. Each person has an equal right to a fully adequate scheme of equal basic rights and liberties. . . .
2. Social and economic inequalities are to satisfy two conditions: first, they must be attached to offices and positions open to all under conditions of fair equality of opportunity; and second, they must be to the greatest benefit of the least advantaged members of society.

Fairness to those who have endured inequalities (and continue to) in a market-driven democracy is a must, according to Rawls. And it is not just a philosophical definition for those who stick to these principles. They must act politically and put those principles into practice. And that also is part of the SJHA story.[16]

As Robert Vega, SJHA social studies teacher put it in a video:

Social justice is a lived thing here. So to do that, you can't just teach history. You got to teach life lessons. What are the values we are talking about here? Where do you fit into this? . . . We want them to have AP [Advanced Placement] classes. We want them to have the highest GPA [grade point average] that they could possibly get, but we also want them to be the best version of themselves.[17]

In the same video, teacher Aseem Kelly talked to students directly about such issues:

My job as a math teacher is to remind the students that they have dignity. . . . [He looks at students in the class.] When you are in college, you are the only student that looks like you for a long way; it's going to be really helpful to be able to say, "Look, I need help." Self-advocating is absolutely a necessary skill and you can do it in a math class.[18]

Student Self-Knowledge

For SJHA to promote self-awareness, a school climate that encourages mutual trust among teachers and students is essential. That doesn't happen automatically. Specific school mechanisms are the gears that have been put into place to create such a school ethos.

For example, scheduled Advisory meetings between teachers and students, teachers mentoring students, students mentoring other students, and classroom nonacademic Council sessions compliment what occurs in daily lessons where content, skills, and personal knowledge are intentionally entwined.

Advisory classes meet four days a week. According to the 2014 Self-Study:

> Each day of Advisory has a different theme including college-readiness, character development, and academic support. Students receive a grade for participating in activities that support them in getting to and through college, such as college research projects or writing personal statements, as well as exploring their personal identity and values through councils and curriculum designed by *Facing History in Ourselves*. . . . In addition, Advisory days are used to collect student data through various assessments such as 50 Assets and multiple intelligence surveys as well as practice Common Core exams. Teachers then meet to analyze results to develop personalized learning plans based on this data.[19]

A classroom Council meeting is another vehicle for creating trust in one another and between youth and adults. A reporter described a Council meeting in 2018:

> It's a Tuesday morning on the Los Angeles campus of [SJHA] . . . and a classroom of upper-level high school students is standing in a large, inward-facing circle. Suddenly a wisp of a girl steps forward and, thrusting out her palms as if halting oncoming traffic, brings the gathering to a hushed silence. "I chose to honor myself this weekend by staying home and spending time with my family," she declaims confidently before rejoining the circle.[20]

At other times for the biweekly Council meetings in classrooms, students arrange their chairs in a circle and pass a stick or cushion to one another when wishing to speak. One student said about his reaction to Council. "When I first learned about Council, I was kind of scared because I had to share stuff about myself. Knowing that you have an accepting environment, knowing that people aren't going to judge you by the way they feel, it was really cool. . . ." Another student said. "You can't really excel in academics if you are not happy, not calm, and if you are not serene. That's why self-care is so important in this school."[21]

Or for another example, take the student mentoring program:

Our mentor program is a key component to our individualized intervention as well as an example of how our academy builds students' character and sense [of] community responsibility, not just their resumes. Our mentoring program consists of 30 mentors each in the 10th, 11th, 12th grade levels. Selected student mentors are those who have shown an ability and desire to help their classmates, have faced adversity, and are on track to graduate. These students serve their community every day by providing one-on-one assistance to struggling students, in addition to continuing their own academic success. Our mentors collectively assist hundreds of students providing one-on-one assistance to every student in our school.[22]

As one student says in a video: "Self-actualization means to be the person you want to be, your best self. At this school they push you to be that person."[23]

Beyond the anecdotal evidence from promotional videos, there is a University of California–Los Angeles study of SJHA students' responses to a survey on adults in the school. To the prompt, "Students at this school learn how to listen to respect each other," SJHA students (nearly 80 percent responded) strongly agreed with the statement (45 percent) and nearly 50 percent agreed. To the statement, "If students express concerns about a school policy, school leaders listen and respond," 45 percent strongly agreed and almost 50 percent agreed with the statement.[24]

SJHA embodies these principles in its press for every student—nearly all minority and poor—to graduate high school, enter college, help others in the community, and act well with other students and themselves. Hallway art, motivational posters, and college banners advertise both social activism and personal growth. School schedule, interdisciplinary curriculum, and classroom lessons tie in to SJHA aims. Student mentoring, teachers adopting struggling students, emphasis on student agency, and teacher decision-making are additional ways of putting these principles into practice. Thus, institutional "success" for SJHA as a school and individual "success" for students extend well beyond the familiar metrics used by the district and schools across the nation in 2019.

A school as complex as SJHA did not spring from the brow of a single-minded designer. Nor was it the work of a single organization. Over time, teachers, donors, district bureaucrats' decisions, and sheer luck came together to construct SJHA piece-by-piece.

THE HIDDEN GEOLOGY OF SOCIAL JUSTICE HUMANITAS ACADEMY

As in other urban districts across the country facing reforms aimed at improving student academic performance, different waves of reform deposited silt that over time hardened into strata noticeable to the trained eye. This occurred in LAUSD.

District changes spilled over SJHA prior to its becoming an Academy and in the subsequent decade after it became one of four academies in the Cesar Chavez complex located in the far northeast corner of the San Fernando Valley in 2011. LAUSD reforms going back to the early 1980s are as visible as strata in the Grand Canyon in SJHA's name, mission, and operation.

To fully appreciate the layered reforms producing this LAUSD school, one has to dig into its geological strata.

FIRST LAYER: HUMANITAS 1980s–1990s

In 1986, four Los Angeles foundations, the Los Angeles Education Partnership (LAEP), and LAUSD launched an interdisciplinary high school program combining literature and history, science, and art and other combinations of subjects to engage students in conceptual and critical thinking skills, writing, and other learning activities around themes that cut across disciplines. The program sought to engage both the minds and hearts of teenagers. As the *Los Angeles Times* reported in 1991:

> *At the heart of Humanitas are small teams of teachers who volunteer to work long hours together, creating interdisciplinary curricula aimed at making lessons relevant to students' daily lives. The approach creates small "communities" of teachers and students, providing a more personal, supportive environment for youngsters at very little added cost to the district.*
>
> *The themes—including the American Dream: From Rags to Riches; Women, Race and Social Protest, and the Protestant Ethic and the Spirit of Capitalism— are vehicles for coordinated instruction in English, social studies, art and sometimes science or math.*
>
> *Although the courses meet state and district curriculum requirements, many teachers chuck textbooks in favor of novels, biographies or writings in politics and philosophy, and substitute for standard classroom fare materials they pull together themselves. . . .*
>
> *Humanitas students, recruited with the help of school counselors, have many of the same classmates throughout high school, while their teachers share ideas and notes on their progress, lending hard-to-find continuity and intimacy to crowded urban campuses.*[25]

By 1991, Humanitas enrolled 3,500 students including English language learners and potential dropouts in twenty-nine of forty-nine LAUSD comprehensive high schools.[26]

A decade later at Sylmar High School in Northeast San Fernando Valley where mostly poor and Latino youth attended, a group of teachers designed a Humanitas program for a small number of students that slowly expanded. As Jose Navarro, one of the founding teachers, put it: *"Our job is to make these four walls magic . . . the reality is that education starts way before they enter my room. So we need this collaborative environment and not just on campus. It has to be in the community."*[27]

Another founding teacher, Jeff Austin, described the growth of the program within Sylmar to become a school-within-a-school and then the Humanitas teachers' decision to start elsewhere an entirely separate school:

This movement . . . started in 2000 when three teachers came together to start the Multimedia Academy at Sylmar High School. These teachers wanted to develop engaging interdisciplinary lessons to better support their students. By 2006, this group grew to become the Humanitas Academy, one of several Small Learning Communities at Sylmar. Humanitas included three teams that brought together a history teacher, an English teacher, and an art teacher working with students in grades 10–12.

We had incredible success with students who faced challenges in a community overrun by poverty, gangs, crime, and low expectations. We were doing a lot right. Our test scores were the highest in the school, our mentor program became a model schoolwide, and we introduced student-led conferences. Our students were getting accepted to universities. But it still wasn't enough. . . .

But our journey toward designing a better learning experience for our students had plenty of speed bumps. The further we pushed, the more we encountered people who didn't think a group of teachers could do all this. In 2009, we began to seek more independence, and we first learned about the pilot school model—a small school led by teachers who have autonomy over many of the school's operations. To get there, we would have to battle union politics, district policy, and a paradigm in which teachers didn't call the shots.[28]

The Humanitas program in LAUSD is the first layer of reform. It took root in Sylmar in the early aughts. After Humanitas became a school-within-a-school, the teachers wanted their own school.

SECOND LAYER: PILOT SCHOOL (2011–PRESENT)

In 2009, the LAUSD Board of Education approved a Public School Choice resolution to establish innovative programs designed to turn around low performing schools across the district. Teams of teachers, parents, community activists, and others drafted plans for new schools in each of four rounds that Public School Choice sponsored. The superintendent's review team critiqued proposals. In many cases, proposers revised and resubmitted their plans.[29]

At the same time, another LAUSD reform was underway called "Pilot Schools." The two streams of reform offering both parents and teachers more choice in schools converged as the teachers at Sylmar High School wanted a separate school and the autonomy that a "pilot school" had.

Copying Boston's Pilot Schools initiative, the LAUSD School Board and the teacher union, United Teachers Los Angeles (UTLA), agreed to stipulations laid out in a Memorandum of Understanding (MOU). After it was signed by both parties, LAUSD officials established pilot schools in 2007, putting a cap of ten pilot schools in the district.[30]

The MOU specifically allowed pilot schools to

- Select, replace, and reassign teaching staff (consistent with collective bargaining contract).
- Receive lump sum budget from district based on student enrollment. Students with special needs receive additional monies. Staff decides how to allocate resources.
- Design how school is to be governed through a council with increased decision-making powers over approving budget, principal selection and retention, discipline and attendance policies, and programs.
- Restructure their curriculum as long as revised curriculum is equal or better in rigor than District's.
- Adhere to state and federal requirements for testing but can adapt assessment practices that will prepare students for mandated tests. School can choose to opt-out of District tests as long as other tests are given equal to District ones to track student progress.
- Modify school calendar for both students and faculty consistent with their design of instructional program and state requirements for days of attendance minutes of instruction.
- Choose what content to cover and how to cover it free from central office mandates.
- Set promotion and graduation requirements equal to or higher than District's.[31]

After the LAUSD Board of Education had adopted Public School Choice in 2009, UTLA and other organizations lobbied the board to raise the cap of ten pilot schools by an additional twenty to allow greater parental and teacher involvement. By 2011, there were thirty-two pilots.[32]

In that year, the LAUSD superintendent recommended that SJHA's teacher-designed proposal become a separate pilot school. The board of education approved.

In September of 2011, SJHA moved into the brand-new Cesar Chavez Academies campus housing three other small schools and began their work with a mostly Latino population drawing from adjacent neighborhoods.

The Humanitas high school curriculum program, pilot schools, and Public School Choice were reform-embedded layers within LAUSD laid down over three decades from divergent streams of reform. Each district innovation was a tributary of a reform-filled river that twisted and meandered as years passed and as political coalitions, worried about low performing schools in largely poor minority neighborhoods, sought solutions. At times these streams unintentionally converged. A group of high school teachers working with district and foundation officials initially at Sylmar High School became over time the pilot school called SJHA located at 1001 Arroyo Avenue in the city of San Fernando.

But streams of reform pouring into a river of change did not cease flowing in LAUSD at a time when large urban districts searched for better ways to educate largely minority and poor students. Another tributary emptied into SJHA and later became another stratum of layered reform: community schools.

THIRD LAYER: COMMUNITY SCHOOL (2012–PRESENT)

Community schools are both academic and neighborhood institutions that through partnering with other agencies offer after-school programs, health clinics, mental health staff, and parent-support options becoming in the current phrase a school with "wraparound" services.[33]

LAEP, which has been involved with SJHA for years, funded Jennie Rosenbaum (nee Carey), a "community coordinator," shortly after SJHA became part of the Cesar Chavez Academy complex. Over the next few years, Rosenbaum, along with representatives of other agencies, and SJHA teachers built onto the existing program to include restorative justice; a focus on the "whole-child"; interdisciplinary teaching; family engagement; and on-campus supports filling student and community needs including physical and mental health, housing assistance, and legal support.[34]

In addition, SJHA launched other programs, described below.

Teachers "Adopt" Students

As mentioned earlier, teachers took on added responsibility for those students struggling academically and with family problems by meeting with them face to face and helping them cope with issues that get in the way of academic success.

One SJHA teacher described a ninth grader he "adopted" and how he was able to overcome the obstacles in his way. "I push him to make better decisions, he promises to do so, then messes up, and I talk to him again. And again. And again. He'll get there. I've seen my adopted kids do better in grades as well, but it's funny because I rarely get a chance to celebrate their victory because by then it's part of their DNA. They almost forget about who they were, and I usually try to forget so I can enjoy who they've become."[35]

Summer Bridge

Through Summer Bridge, a three-week program for ninth graders initially but now two weeks, these first-year students get to know one another, become familiar with the school's mission and curriculum, and develop relationships with classmates and teachers. Building a community prior to coming to school eases entry for those students into a new school.

For SJHA's work with students, parents, and neighborhood social services during and after school, the national Coalition of Community Schools recognized SJHA for its excellent work in 2015.[36]

Thus, one school called SJHA has a history in LAUSD. Over time, divergent streams of change extending back to the mid-1980s deposited reforms that established the current SJHA. Piled atop of one another, these strata illustrate how district reforms became layered on top of another and those layers are present in 2019 when one enters SJHA classrooms.[37]

CLASSROOM LESSONS

I come into the Ethnic Studies class just as Sasha Guzman, wearing a denim jacket over a T-shirt and jeans, is walking around the room checking on small groups of students at each table. The nineteen ninth graders wearing ID lanyards are tapping away on their Chromebook keyboards or reading screens. Guzman has taught for sixteen years in Los Angeles Unified School District, the last five at SJHA.

The period, which lasts one hour and fifty minutes, had begun a few minutes before I arrived, and students know what they are to do since their agenda is written on the side whiteboard:

Agenda	Homework
• Choose narrative	• Academic paragraph due 2/28 by midnight
• Write academic paragraph	

The spacious room has the obligatory clock and flag. There is also a printer sitting on a table in the back. College banners hang above the door and elsewhere in the room. Playing softly in the background are Mexican songs. Posters are on the four walls and door of the room. Above the door is one that says: "A Proud Member of the Facing History and Ourselves Schools Network." On the door is another that says: "Protect DACA." Propped against a wall nearby is a print of a woman with the inscription "Viva La Mujer."[38]

On another wall are two posters that hang in every SJHA classroom: the "Habits of Mind" poster contains ten statements that focus on using evidence to back up opinion, perseverance ("never giving up"), questioning and problem solving, interdependence ("collaboration"), service ("the desire to imagine and create a more just world"), and others.[39]

The other poster is "Common Core Mathematical Practice Standards" with statements such as "Make sense of problems and persevere in solving them," "Reason abstractly and quantitatively," and "Construct viable arguments & critique the reasoning of others."[40]

Three to five students sit at tables facing one another. The teacher's desk is in a corner at the front of the room. When students have questions, they address her as Ms. Guzman.

The teacher has loaded software content on their tablets about the current assignment. Students have to choose a story from political activist America Ferrera's *Americans Like Me*. Judith, a student sitting nearby, shows me which of the stories she has chosen (Carmen Carrera's "Letter to My Ten Year-Old Self") and the first few sentences of the "academic paragraph" she has to write. She answers confidently the questions I ask about who Carrera is and what she says in her letter.

I scan the class, and all students are clicking away or reading screens. After walking around and checking each table, Guzman goes to her desk and works on her laptop. After a few minutes, she gets up and walks among the tables, asking questions, making comments, and stilling a few talkative ninth graders. She then tells students: *"I don't know how much time you will have in Advisory [last period of the day]; I don't know how much time you have at home. Take advantage of the time you have in class."*

No one says anything and the clicking, small talk at each table, and on-task performance continues. Chatting students move off and on task, as Guzman cruises around class. She calls on Bernal, who has been nonstop talking to tablemates, to come and sit at a table in the rear of the room. Bernal stops talking, starts tapping away on his tablet. He stays put.

At one point, Sasha stops at my table and tells me about a new hire SJHA is making—a teacher committee interviews applicants and recommends a candidate to the principal—and the dilemma that this "teacher-powered" school faces. As she put it to me, SJHA looks for candidates who are very strong in their discipline (e.g., math, science, history) and cares for students. She tells me that SJHA has hired several new teachers over the years who were new to the classroom. Their content grasp needed to be coached, supported, and increased. However, she says, "An innate sense of caring and compassion for our kids cannot be coached; in the end, we require both content and caring."

After the teacher releases students for their next class—there are no bells that signal the end of the period except for first period of the day and lunch—I leave the room.

■   ■   ■

Brenda Arias teaches chemistry first period of the day—from 8:30 to 10:21 (most of the other periods in the day run about an hour and a half). This is her fifth year at SJHA. While she taught physics the first four years, she is now teaching chemistry.

The thirty-one students—the largest class I have observed at SJHA—mostly tenth graders are also having breakfast at the beginning of the first period of the day. Two students had gone to the cafeteria and brought back milk, juice, cereal, and egg sandwiches to class. Students picked what they wanted, and they spread out among lab tables to eat and talk. This occurs every morning at SJHA.

After breakfast, students toss trash in a can and pick up Chromebooks to take back to their lab tables. All tables holding two to three students face the whiteboard and teacher desk—also a lab table (see figure 5.2). As Arias takes roll, I look around the room and see the wall posters "Habits of Mind" and "Common Core Mathematical Practice Standards," college banners, and the obligatory Periodic Elements chart for a chemistry room. A teacher aide is in the room because there are a half-dozen students with disabilities who will need help with the lesson. He circulates and talks to particular students about the tasks they have to work on.

Arias tells the class what's due today and during the week. "I need you to look at me," she says. "I need you to focus." Most of the class will be taking a twenty-minute practice test for a later exam that will improve their low scores over the first time they took the test. All of the practice questions and answers are loaded on the Chromebook, and students begin working. Some students work with partners and others in small groups or alone at different tables. A nearby student shows me the questions and correct answers on her screen as Arias walks around the room

FIGURE 5.2 Lab tables in classroom

checking students' work and answering questions. I scan the class and see everyone clicking away on their devices.

Arias then asks the class to close the Chromebooks and return to their seats. She tells the class that they must have the practice test completed by Thursday or "you get. . . . " She pauses and a number of students say, "A zero."

She then segues to the next part of the lesson. "Ladies and gentlemen, we are going over 4.3 homework. Log on to 4.3 and we will go over 7, 10, and 11 because I made mistakes and want to correct them." A loud hum arises in class. Arias says, "Everyone calm down. If you didn't do homework, what will you get?" The class responds: "A zero." Students also know that the teacher gives them three chances to do homework correctly. The number (4.3) the teacher calls out corresponds to a text chapter on gases and solids and worksheets that are loaded on the Chromebooks and assigned as homework.

She goes over the incorrect answers on the whiteboard at the front of the room and asks the class to correct them. On one of the corrections about the temperature of a gas compared to a solid, she says, "My knucklehead move was the wrong answer." She says, "I'm sorry. Everyone makes mistakes."

Arias asks students to pair up and make corrections. As they do, they complete homework on the Chromebooks. The students I observe in the class pay attention to what the teacher says and respond to her requests. I see no students with their heads on desks, students playing with devices, or whispered conversations among the tenth graders. I leave the chemistry class after an hour there to go to another lesson.

■　■　■

With shaved pate and wearing a white shirt, blue tie, and gray slacks, English teacher Robert Martinez immediately turns to the white board as the period begins right after lunch. He directs the twenty-four ninth graders' attention to what he has written on it: "Community Cultural Wealth: A Review."

The students, sitting two to four at a table facing one another, look at the whiteboard as Martinez launches a whole group discussion through a series of slides on Community Cultural Wealth. From time to time, he calls on students to read a slide by addressing the student as Ms. Soto or Mr. Montero.

Earlier lessons have dealt with fixed and growth mindsets, grit, and three forms of capital: "Aspirational Capital, Familial Capital, and Navigational Capital." Martinez says, "I use these capitals to resist and overcome oppression." Then he asks the class what is "oppression." A few students answer. He then defines the word and refers to the book they are currently reading, *Always Running* (the full title is *Always Running: La Vida Loca: Gang Days in LA* by Luis Rodriguez).

Whole group discussion continues as the teacher moves through slides and students read about Aspirational Capital (hopes and dreams) and Navigational Capital (the different communities beyond family that each student interacts with). On the slide for Aspirational Capital, Martinez points out the upcoming trip to California colleges as an experience they will have that looks to their dreams—many are the first in their family to consider college.

Martinez intersperses reading of slides and occasional questions from students with comments such as "Ultimately, this (different forms of capital) is for you to see yourself what mindset you have. Make the jump and get out of your comfort zone," he says. To one student who reads a slide correctly, the teacher compliments her: "College level, girl."

As I look around the room, I see that about half of the class has notebooks out and are taking notes.

A phone on the desk rings and the teacher answers. He hangs up and directs a student to go to office. The teacher returns to definitions of different forms of capital. On Familial Capital, Martinez states: "You know the people who hold you back. You may be in a toxic relationship and have to ask yourself, 'Do these people have my back?'"

Some students yell out questions and statements after the teacher makes comments about a slide. When he asks for students to calm down, the class responds immediately and gets quiet.

After completing the slides on different forms of capital, Martinez shifts to the next part of the lesson when he divides the class into groups of four to six students to read chapters 7 and 8 of *Always Running*. He chooses which students will be in one group and tells them to read chapter 7 and does the same for the other group, asking them to read chapter 8.

He directs both groups to fill out worksheets on each form of capital. He passes out the worksheets and asks students to jot down what transpired in each chapter and to link examples to different kinds of capital. Then he says he will reassemble both groups so that each group will present information on their chapter to the other group. Each specific example drawn from the chapter and written on the worksheet will get one point, he says. He then announces: "Read for twenty minutes and complete chapter."

Groups turn to the task of reading and completing worksheets. I scan the classroom and see that individual students in each group are reading. Martinez walks around monitoring students reading. At this point, I exit the classroom to see another teacher.

■ ■ ■

I enter the classroom and look at the whiteboard. On it is written:

Monday, February 25
World Lit
Hamlet, Act IV
Advisory: Black History Lesson[41]

Marcella DeBoer presides over this group of fifteen senior students in World Literature. Arrayed in rows of desks facing the whiteboard, I see the "Habits of Mind" and "Common Core Mathematical Practice Standards" posters. Tacked to one part of the whiteboard is the poster: "The Only Place SUCCESS comes before WORK is in the dictionary." On a side whiteboard is written:

Act IV
Scenes 1–6

King	Fortinbras
Queen	Captain Horatio
Hamlet	Ophelia
Guildenstern	Messenger
Rosencrantz	Laertes
Gentleman	Sailor

Wearing a blue sweater over jeans and tennis shoes, DeBoer asks students to finish gluing the handouts that she gave them into their notebooks on Hamlet. She reminds the class of a homework assignment, pointing out that it can be done again. She points to a section of the whiteboard listing her office hours and invites students to come in. DeBoer then passes back marked-up homework students had turned in and she says: "You can do a make-up of this assignment." One student asks: "How many points?" The teacher answers: "Thirty." Half of the class raise their hands to get a make-up sheet.

DeBoer then directs the class to turn to page 25 of the play and review a prediction they made about Hamlet's relationship with Ophelia. "Get an elbow partner and review your prediction." She gives the partners two minutes to discuss their predictions and walks around the room listening to conversations.

After time has elapsed, she says, "I love to hear your predictions." Instead of calling on students who have raised their hands as occurs in most classrooms, DeBoer uses a random name generator on her smart phone for which students to call on. She then says, "OK, Christian, what was your prediction?"

He gives his prediction of trouble looming between the couple. DeBoer asks for clarification but makes no evaluative comment. The teacher generates other student names, and they offer their predictions from the couple living happily ever after to increasing stress on the relationship. The noise level rises as students cross-examine one another's prediction. DeBoer raises her arm, and students slowly quiet down as they recognize the teacher's signal.

The teacher then asks: "Will Claudius repent?" Again, names pop up on DeBoer's phone, and she calls on those students but also recognizes some students who have raised their hands because they want to chime in as well.

After five minutes, DeBoer moves to the next part of the lesson on Act IV. She asks the class to turn to page 26 in their notebook where key questions on the play are listed and page 100 of the play itself for students to read parts. She then asks for volunteers to read (see the above roles listed on the whiteboard). Individual students call out whose role they will read, and DeBoer marks down their names on the whiteboard.

DeBoer then asks the class to keep this question in mind as they read: What does Gertrude reveal to Claudius?

Students begin reading their parts. I scan the room and see that students are following text as each classmate says the lines. After the couplets are read, DeBoer asks: "Do you think Gertrude leans toward Hamlet or Claudius? Does Hamlet show remorse over killing Polonius?"

As the whole group discussion unfolds, some students are writing in their notebooks as classmates answer the teacher's questions. Students reading their parts continue as I exit the lesson.

■   ■   ■

These vignettes of teacher lessons across social studies, chemistry, and English give a snapshot of what I observed at SJHA. But as any teacher knows, there is far more to schooling than classroom lessons.

A whole school assembly celebrating Black History month had occurred the previous afternoon. Advisories meet weekly. Students talk personally in their Council circles during classroom sessions. Student mentors see their mentees. Teachers meet with "adopted" students. Two-day trips to college campuses occur. Community members gather in school.

And grade groups of teachers meet during the week to discuss individual students, arrangements for upcoming events, and how each teacher is feeling about the week. They decide on policies affecting their students, lessons, and the essential work surrounding college applications due during the spring. Such grade-level meetings reveal the unnoticed mechanics of working in a teacher-run school. I attended a ninety-minute after-school meeting of a group of twelfth-grade teachers.

Ranging in age from mid-twenties to mid-fifties, six experienced teachers, including a counselor, meet in Marcella DeBoer's World Literature classroom. We arrange movable desks into a circle. Coffee mugs, water bottles, and shared snacks are evident. Rachel Lewis, the counselor, manages the agenda, getting the meeting started by asking each teacher to "check in." One says she is very tired from the day of lessons and student conferences; another says she caught a cold from her nephew and has been "feeling sick"; another mentions that she was finally accepted into a "clinical trial" for cancer patients and was tired from the treatment. And one teacher says that the previous afternoon's assembly on Black History had upset her.

After making their comments, each teacher says, "I'm in," meaning "I am present and will participate." There is an easygoing rapport and supportiveness between and among the six teachers that I, an outsider, notice.

The next fifteen minutes are spent on teachers discussing their "adoptees" and where each of them is academically and psychologically. All of the teachers know the individual seniors they are discussing since they had these students in their classes.

Lewis then moves the group to the next agenda item, which is to plan a lesson together for the Advisory period on Friday and Monday and the upcoming field trip to Mission College. Each teacher contributes ideas for the joint lesson as they also record dates in their laptop or phone calendars and search for ideas. Cross-discussion among the six teachers flows easily as ideas for the lesson and college visit spill out. While the teachers look tired after a full day of interacting with students in and out of class, I do not sense any reluctance to participate in discussing ideas, evaluating suggestions, or disagreeing with a peer's point. Pronouns "we" and "ours" are often used when discussing next actions and programs. I notice no clock-watching or glances at wristwatches, no surreptitious looks at smart phones. My scanning of the group shows full involvement even at this time of day—it is after 4:30.

The group agrees that the upcoming Advisory meeting should deal with the Black History assembly that had just taken place. One teacher says that two of her Latino students had said the N-word loud enough for others to hear. She suggests that a lesson could be built around the power of words and their effects on people. One teacher begins describing her growing up in a family where the N-word was banned. Other teachers offer instances when the epithet was used in their class and what they did. One had stopped the lesson she was teaching and addressed the use of the N-word. Others said that students had to feel safe in a room where such a discussion occurs. There is nodding of heads that such a lesson should occur in Advisory.

Lewis takes up the next agenda item on which seniors should receive awards. A teacher says that two students have had 100 percent attendance at SJHA. The group discusses an appropriate amount for the award and reaches agreement that it should be $400.

By this time, it is nearly 5:00 p.m. and all agenda items have been covered. Lewis asks for any other points that the group wants to raise. There is no response as teachers pack up and leave for the day.

"SUCCESS" AND "FAILURE" AT SJHA

Divergent streams of school reform over nearly four decades converged to make Social Justice Humanitas Academy a metaphor for geological strata. Imaginative and determined teachers used varied district reforms over the years as opportunities to create a school that is heavily invested in both individual growth and social activism. Thriving in a larger political environment where the metrics of institutional "success" are drawn from decades of business influence on school reform is no easy task.

"Success" in schooling is not a binary judgment or a single number but a many- splendored phenomenon of improvisational policy making. And, given the school's dual mission of institutional and individual "success," most difficult to measure.

Listen to founding teacher and first principal, Jose Navarro:

> I . . . look at how many of our kids apply to college when no one in their family has gone to college before—and I feel successful because it's scary to be a trailblazer. I look at our high graduation rate and high . . . completion rates [for college prep courses]. I look at our 98 percent student attendance rate—people don't come to school when they don't feel comfortable or feel like it's not relevant.
>
> I feel successful when our students go off and they write me five or six years later that what they learned at my school helped them get through college—not just to college, but through it. I feel successful when I look at my kids and see how far they made it, especially when many of those kids are homeless, are foster children, and are living in poverty. These kids are resilient, they're resourceful, they're hustlers, they know how to squeeze two nickels and make a dollar. They're going to be successful, and I feel really blessed to be a part of that.[42]

Yet there are the constant messages from LAUSD officials, driven by conventional views of institutional "success," that expect principals and teachers to increase students' performance on state reading and math tests, raise graduation rates, and reduce suspension and dropout rates. Because SJHA is part of the larger state system and district organization, these numbers matter since state officials, LAUSD School Board members, the superintendent, district administrators, parents, and ever-present donors and reformers watch closely the school's statistics. So SJHA staff have to pay attention. They do, as principal Jeff Austin points out:

> While standards-based accountability is not our focus, we also know that we are working within a system that values it. As we tell students, sometimes you've got to hustle and play the game. In that interest, we do work with students on skills that will support them in meeting standards-based objectives while giving a higher focus on skills that we feel are relevant for our students.[43]

A wall mural (figure 5.3) in an SJHA hallway captures both the barriers and behaviors that students require to graduate.

Paying attention to SJHA's two-fold mission of justice and individual authenticity while simultaneously adhering to LAUSD demands for improved, quantifiable student outcomes is a balancing act that requires, at the minimum, political and organizational skills in finessing competing views of "success."

FIGURE 5.3 Wall mural in SJHA hall

IS SJHA A "SUCCESS"?

Media accounts have said SJHA is, indeed, a "successful" school. Students and teachers have said so repeatedly. External organizations have made awards to the school for its achievements. Because numbers matter, district officials' announcements and media use of graduation rates, college attendance, annual enrollment and attendance figures, test scores, and awards testify to the mainstream's deep-seated belief that institutional "success" and "failure" can be quantified and judged. By that definition, SJHA is considered "successful."

Yet, as I have argued in this book, there are historically multiple definitions of "success" and "failure," and they have changed over time. These definitions have deep roots in the democratic capitalism that has unfolded in America over the past four centuries and how those versions of institutional and individual "success" and "failure" have been quantified, permeating American life through everyday institutions like the workplace, commercial ads, amateur and professional sports, and schooling. Moreover, as I said earlier, there are degrees of institutional "success" and "failure." Unlike either/or judgments rendered in a court of law or a Super Bowl game, there are in-between evaluations that cover the launching, consolidating, and sustaining a school as complex as SJHA.

History, then, suggests that such judgments of "success" and "failure" are multifaceted, perhaps even many-splendored, not simple one-dimensional decisions. So in judging SJHA's "success," I need to look at more than the numbers compiled by policy makers and advertised in media accounts as well as testimonials from students, teachers, and parents.

In considering institutional "success," for example, recall from the Introduction how every policy aimed at solving a problem contains three basic pieces that demand attention prior to judging overall "success" and "failure."

First, there is the institutional *process* of adopting a policy. Then there are the *politics* necessary to put the policy into practice and, finally, the *programs* that enact the policy.[44]

Thus, there can be an organizational "success" across the three realms, but more often than not, there are temporary and partial "successes" leading to mixed judgments, such as the policy was a "success" in getting adopted but "failed" in achieving all of its goals or "failed" in securing sufficient political support from teachers and parents for classroom implementation. Furthermore, being "successful" in adopting a policy does not guarantee, much less assure, that the program will be implemented without conflict or that opposition will grow into a windstorm wiping it away. There are inexorable contradictions embedded in rendering a judgment, such as a program can be successful in achieving its goals, but political coalitions emerge later to sweep away the program. Hence, there can be early policy "successes" that end up as failed programs. Finally, there are degrees of "success" that can be identified such as "precarious," "conflicted," and "resilient."[45]

Recognizing that there is seldom one single goal for a policy, program, school, and district (in most cases there are multiple aims), these varied strands of policy making clarify that institutional "success" and "failure" are not binary judgments but multifaceted, contingent upon circumstances, and, the truth is, with contradictions and shades of gray between one and the other. Surely, it is far easier to have an "O" and "–" for the power switch on an electronic device, but individuals and organizations are far more multilayered when judging "success" of a classroom, school, and district.

Keep in mind that it took over two decades of meandering reform streams to create SJHA, a school that acquired a two-fold mission with multiple goals as varied LAUSD reforms tumbled forth over time.

So was the *process* of becoming SJHA "successful"?

In chapter 4, I described criteria used by policy elites and different groups to judge institutional "success": effectiveness, popularity, fidelity, and adaptability. The dominant criterion for the past century that policy elites applied to lessons, programs, schools, and districts has been *effectiveness* (and its kissing cousin, efficiency—see chapter 1).

Were the explicit goals achieved? When applied to educational ventures, the question in the twenty-first century requires quantifiable answers drawn from multiple metrics.

After all, historic and pervasive goals of literacy, workplace preparation, and civic engagement across US schools have to be reduced to proxies since no one can say with assurance that the gown-clad graduates standing on the stage prepared to receive their diplomas are literate in today's society, prepared for the workplace, ready to ascend the ladder of personal success with credentials in hand, much less being informed citizens contributing to the community. So surrogate measures for "success" offering the allure of objectivity are used as convenient shorthand to determine institutional "success," such as test scores, attendance rates, dropout figures, grade point averages, scholarship offers, and percentages of students attending college.

Policy elites, media mavens, and most practitioners use these proxy measures in judging educational effectiveness. No surprise, then, that state and federal laws for the past half-century (e.g., ESEA, NCLB, ESSA), local school boards, and parents have included test scores and other numerical measures as substitutes for determining institutional "success."

The other criteria—popularity, fidelity, and adaptability—come from those observers and participants in policy making who recognize that other factors play a large part in adopting and implementing reforms. Politically minded policy makers see the critical importance of voter and parent support for schools; researchers see that practitioners adhering to program design in putting ideas into practice is essential; and practitioners who appreciate policies and programs that they can fashion to benefit their students prize adaptability. These criteria, however, seldom get publicly used by policy elites.

I will use both the effectiveness and political criteria to determine institutional "success" since both my quarter-century of experiences as a teacher and administrator and two decades of research into the history of school reform provide evidence for these criteria.

I define institutional "success" as achieving goals leaders set for a policy, program, classroom, school, and district and attracting neither significant criticism nor loss of political support.[46]

Keep in mind that this definition is not an off/on light switch. The simple notion that there are (and may be) degrees of political and programmatic "success" and "failure" for a policy, program, classroom, school, and district mirrors how most people understand daily living in both the workplace and family. Adjectives are needed to precede "success." "Precarious," "conflicted," and "resilient" attached to the noun "success" at least offer a more accurate judgment about what has occurred. There are partial "successes" amid complete "failures" assuredly as there are minuscule "failures" among pronounced "successes." There are blurred areas where decisions about the outcome are uncertain and difficult to assess. To that off/on switch, a dimmer is needed.[47]

For the process that produced SJHA, the politics necessary to put the policy into practice and the programs that the school enacted, I will use the above definition.

Beginning in the early 1990s with the teacher-founded Humanitas program at Sylmar High School, teachers designed a proposal to become a pilot school. LAUSD officials accepted the proposal, leading to even more refinements when those teachers moved into a new building in 2011 as SJHA, one of four Cesar Chavez Academies. Shortly afterward, SJHA became a Community School, another LAUSD reform initiative that produced some modest alterations. Internal and external support for the school remained nearly universal.

While the above paragraph suggests a straight-line road to institutional "success," it was not the case. The lengthy *process* of becoming SJHA was in the end "successful" but hardly predictable. The path followed was closer to a butterfly than a bullet. There were times when the teacher founders teetered on the edge of "failure" yet with the help of many others and luck became a precarious "success." By the end of the process, events and actions added up to a "resilient success."[48]

Were SJHA Spanish teacher Lourdes Lizzarraga, one of the founding teachers, to reflect on two decades of becoming SJHA, she might marvel at all of the twists and turns that occurred, but the long process did indeed produce the school—with hardly any opposition from students, staff, parents, and district office administrators in which she now teaches. It is fair to say the *process* was an institutional "success."

Were the *politics* to put the programs into practice also a "success"? Yes.

Here again, political support from students, teachers, district administrators, donors, and intermediary organizations such as Los Angeles Education Partnership ebbed and flowed. Ample resources were eventually invested, but the timing was often erratic. Partial support from one part of LAUSD occurred simultaneously with indifference and outright hostility from other parts of the organization. Little could be counted on; nothing was certain.

Teacher founders of SJHA knew, for example, that the support of the teachers union, UTLA, was crucial in securing Pilot School status and negotiating the autonomy they would have in the joint LAUSD-UTLA Memorandum of Understanding. Jeff Austin told me of his and other teachers' efforts within UTLA's House of Representatives to have a "direct voice in that process and an actual vote" on the MOU when SJHA applied to become a pilot school.[49]

Now, the final question on "success": Were the programs SJHA put into place "successful" for individual students? Here notions of degrees of "success" and the gray cloud of uncertainty in judging student outcomes become most evident. An unambiguous yes or no is out of the question.

EFFECTIVENESS CRITERION APPLIED TO SCHOOL PROGRAMS

On achieving SJHA's mission, vision, and goals, there is both clarity and haziness:

> Our mission is to achieve social justice through the development of the complete individual. . . . At Social Justice Humanitas Academy, our vision is: We will achieve self-actualization [original boldface]. . . . [A] good life [is] one in which an individual maximized their potential to become the very best version of who they are.[50]

One specific way of achieving that mission, vision, and goals is for SJHA to prepare every student to attend college. And it does.

Academically, test scores on reading and math have increased, but much work remains to be done insofar as compared to LAUSD and state results.

Ninety-four percent of SJHA students graduating, a substantial increase and higher than district rates, and the nearly 100 percent of graduates who have met the California state and university requirements for higher education are evidence of reaching a school goal of getting students on track to the next rung of the educational ladder.

Then there is the haziness and uncertainty that clouds any judgment of effectiveness. How many graduates since 2011, for example, who attended colleges and universities have earned a bachelor's degree? How many have dropped out? In short, effectiveness also means that SJHA preparation was sufficient for students to negotiate college and earn a bachelor's degree within six years. Other data on low-income minority graduates, especially Latinos who are the first in their families to enter college, suggest that about half of those students complete their degree.[51]

I could not find systematic data collected on SJHA graduates who have entered colleges and universities beyond anecdotal reports of former students, staff recollections, and the head-shot photos in the school office. And what about those graduates who chose not to attend a college? I could find no data on those former students.

Even more difficult to pin down is exactly what "self-actualization" means in specific terms and how one knows that individual students have reached that state. Part of the official SJHA mission and one of the explicit goals of the school is for each student to "self-actualize" or be "authentic," that is, to reach the higher levels of Maslow's hierarchy. The school website has a picture of the Maslow pyramid to erase any doubt about the intent of shaping students' behavior to be the best persons they can be, in the words of many students and teachers featured in school promotional videos.[52]

The commitment to individual growth and agency shows up in classroom Council circles, lessons in academic subjects, mentoring conversations, and the easy give-and-take that characterize daily interactions among and between students and teachers. Programmatically, the school has instituted varied programs that seemingly enact this commitment to individual student growth and behavior.

But what does it mean when a student has indeed "self-actualized"? This is neither a petty nor persnickety question. The growth of each student into being a "good" person and one who is "self-actualized" I heard often from both staff and students. Founding principal Jose Navarro and successor Jeff Austin use the phrase in their describing what the school hopes to achieve with their students. What became obvious to me listening to students and staff and reading reports on the school was the diversity of meanings attributed to "self-actualization" and a reluctance to translate the concept into specific behaviors. The conflict in meanings arose for me when I realized that, as the mission says, being a "good" person does not necessarily mean that one is "self-actualized." So what does the phrase mean in specific terms for the direction and assessing the "success" of the school program? My answer is: I do not know.[53]

In looking at the literature on measuring Maslow's hierarchy of tiers leading to self-actualization, there are instruments that have been used in organizations and by individuals to determine whether such a state has been reached. In particular, Scott Kaufman has synthesized Maslow's hierarchy into ten characteristics of self-actualization (e.g., "continued freshness of appreciation," "acceptance," "authenticity") and given self-assessment surveys to groups. In this compilation and others, there are connections between being self-actualized and helping others, sharing, and becoming more humane (e.g., "I have a genuine desire to help the human race"). Self-actualization, then, does not necessarily encourage a hyper-individualism or personal self-growth seeking only personal fulfillment. SJHA may be able to connect self-actualization and social justice in its program, but as yet, the connection remains no more than a deep-seated belief seldom assessed in SJHA students or teachers.[54]

The other concern, again not fully detailed in the psychological literature, is that self-actualization may be developmental; that is, the older the person is, the chances of reaching that higher level are greater. Teenagers, then, have evolving selves. Their motivations and actions would differ from men or women in their thirties or fifties who have had many more life experiences in the workplace, family, and community. This caveat about age—after all, SJHA has fourteen-year-olds and eighteen-year-olds in classrooms and school activities—is recognized in the literature but not referred to by staff in their active quest for students to become self-actualized. The fact is that self-actualization is an ongoing process that is often unfinished in one's life.[55]

I have not found any documents that raise these issues—although I suspect that staff conversations have explored such points—nor have I encountered any assessments in or out of the school that have captured that desired outcome. Yet it remains a staple belief and core element of SJHA's mission. It is individual "success" that the school pursues.

Of course, just because students have not yet sat down and filled out answers to survey questions to determine their level of self-actualization at SJHA does not mean it does not exist. It is a pliable concept that is hard to grasp or specify when it is anchored in the very mission of a school. It eludes staff and student agreement and, for now, lacks proxy measures.

Yes, SJHA has "succeeded" institutionally in becoming what it is academically and as a school community. That is clear to me. In the long, meandering journey from Sylmar High School to the Cesar Chavez Academies, SJHA staff has used political savvy and contacts in LAUSD, donors, and partners to put into practice a rich mix of academic programs while providing personal support to students. SJHA has created a home away from home, a family in and of itself for most of its students. That is no easy task for a school and happens infrequently. Without experiencing any significant conflict or opposition, SJHA has, indeed, become a "resilient success."

My overall judgment of SJHA, however, is mixed. Creating an academic climate of achievement, personal support for students, and a complex of programs that entwine social justice and academic activities is tough to do and sustain. SJHA has done that.

What remains murky is the "self-actualization" part of the school's direction. The lack of tools that get at the concept evident in individual students suggests strongly that longitudinal studies of SJHA graduates including assessments of self-actualization are essential before any judgment can be rendered on the "success" of the school in helping individual students who have completed college, established careers, and have become "the best they can be."

Similar strengths and limitations at SJHA as an LAUSD small high school exist in a similar venue four hundred miles north. I turn to MetWest, in Oakland, California, another regular public high school that began nearly twenty years ago.

CHAPTER 6

METWEST HIGH SCHOOL IN OAKLAND, CALIFORNIA

It is a Monday, and the daily schedule calls for an 8:30–10 a.m. session with an advisor/teacher. I enter a spacious, well-lit room where eighteen ninth graders are sitting in a circle with Nick Palmquist. He is wearing black jeans, an untucked, button-down gray shirt, and dark tennis shoes. The assignment for these students had been to write down their goals for high school. I note that more than half of the students have a sheet of paper in hand.

Nick—students call him and every teacher in the school by their first names—begins by holding a multicolored cloth volleyball and stating what his goals have been for life and teaching. He then passes the ball to his left. That student doesn't say anything and passes the ball to another student who reads off his goals. As the ball goes from student to student in the circle, their goals fall into a familiar pattern of what most ninth graders in poor and nonpoor communities say: get good grades, graduate, and go to college. Two students say they want to get "good" jobs. After the ball travels around the circle and returns to Nick, he summarizes what most students said were their goals and says: "We are about to close the circle. Does anyone have 'any appreciation to share'?" He waits at least five seconds, no response. Nick then says, "Please return to your tables."

Students pick up their chairs and place them so that two students sit at each table. The tables and chairs are arranged in a horseshoe facing a front whiteboard with the open center space holding a small table upon which Nick's laptop and erasable markers rest. Students sitting at tables see classmates across the open space. On one side of the whiteboard is marked "Homework." Listed are the following:

- Semester goals + vision board/road map—due Tuesday AM
- Observation notes on my learning this week—due Monday AM
- Binder check Tuesday

Nick passes out a two-page worksheet from which the rest of the lesson unfolds. The worksheet lists "Lesson Targets": "I can explain and creatively portray my reflections on my first semester and how they connect to my goals for myself." Students answer the questions on the handout from information Nick gives them in a series of slides about the percentage of students in the nation who finish high school, go to college, and complete their degree; how much money high school and college graduates earn annually and over a lifetime; and similar information about educational outcomes. Included is a section on calculating grade point average. The handout ends with a long section on "Reflection and Goal Visioning," asking students to connect the goals they discussed in the circle to their current progress as MetWest ninth graders.

Over the next forty-five minutes, Nick and students go through a series of slides projected on the front whiteboard. One slide, for example, is marked "Show Me the $." It lists annual earnings of a high school dropout ($24,492), high school graduate ($33,904), and college graduate ($55,432). As he goes through the slides, Nick asks questions, usually choral ones with no student name attached. Some students respond. During whole group discussion of each slide, Nick also calls on particular students by name for a response. Student responses pick up considerably as the slide on money that one earns annually and over a lifetime gets absorbed. At one point, there is a great deal of student cross-talk; Nick pauses and waits for students to quiet down. They do. Nick continues with slides.

The slide on grade point average and Nick's calculation of it on a transcript of an anonymous student segues to getting these ninth graders to calculate their GPA. Nick passes out their actual transcripts and asks students to figure out their GPA. He then makes clear what students are to do for the remainder of the session: complete the blanks on the handout with headings such as "Semester 1 Reflection and Goal Visioning." Under that heading are questions with space for students to fill in:

> - What are your big, life goals? Write them, in one or two sentences, here.
> - Look at your report card grades. Do they reflect where you want to go? Be very specific.
> - What are your goals for your grades for the coming quarter and semester?
> - How will you actually achieve this? Do NOT write, "I'm gonna do my homework." Be more specific, and think about the reasons that will propel you to do this.

There is a section on the handout labeled "Advisor and Teacher Support." Nick asks:

> - How might I, as your advisor, support your learning more? Be as specific as possible! This is my job!
> - What types of learning activities will help you become more engaged and learn more next quarter. This is an opportunity to help shape how we learn! Really think about this!
> - We will be writing goals at our next internship visit. Think about at least two goals that you think are important for your continued growth in your internship.

I look around the room and see all twenty students (two more had entered the room) writing their answers to the questions in the handout. At that point, I have been there an hour and leave Nick's advisory group to see another class elsewhere in the building.

OAKLAND UNIFIED SCHOOL DISTRICT: METWEST HIGH SCHOOL

I spent time at MetWest High School in the Oakland Unified School District (OUSD). The school is neither a magnet nor a charter. Founded in 2002 as a Big Picture Learning school (more below), it is part of OUSD's decades-long effort to create small innovative, academically strong, and caring schools for children of color in a district that is largely low-income minority and low performing on state metrics of institutional "success." That small schools strategy begun in the early 1990s and expanded under Superintendent Tony Smith in 2011 with a community school initiative yielded many new schools yet strained a district budget subject to school board overspending, accounting errors, and poor projections. Oakland Unified's history of financial crises was well known in the Bay area, especially after a state takeover for fiscal mismanagement in 2003.[1]

OUSD has an average daily attendance of over 34,000 students distributed across 121 elementary, middle, and high schools (2018). Of the 121 schools, nearly one out of four is a charter. In addition to charter schools, OUSD has alternative schools, magnets, and thematic schools. The district has 87 of those schools with an average size of 412 students, prompting repeated public calls amid annual budget deficits to close the smallest of these schools.[2]

In 2019, OUSD faced a fiscal deficit, requiring substantial budget cuts, identifying schools to be closed, and provoking a week-long teacher strike that netted OUSD teachers significant salary increases, further adding to the deficit. Within a week, the Oakland school board made $20 million in cuts to programs and individual school budgets and laid off one hundred employees (mostly district office and clerical staff) in order to give teachers the raises they won in the strike settlement and balance the budget.[3]

Consider further that top district leadership has been a revolving door. Many observers have pointed out that reforming urban schools requires continuity in top leadership. Turnover among the nation's urban superintendents since the 1960s has been frequent; district leaders averaged over five years in office. Yet scholars of school reform estimate that it takes anywhere from five to ten years for school board and superintendent policies and programs aimed at improving district, school, and student performance to show positive outcomes.[4]

And the record of superintendent continuity in OUSD? Since 2000, the district has had seven superintendents, the most recent sworn in in 2017.

Not a picture of a school district displaying organizational stability or fiscal health, or on the road to higher academic performance. All of this with a half-billion dollar budget to spend effectively and efficiently.[5]

METWEST HIGH SCHOOL: A BIG PICTURE LEARNING SCHOOL

Within OUSD sits MetWest High School with 160 students. Of these students, 76 percent meet the measure of family poverty. Twenty-two percent are English language learners. On ethnicity and race, 61 percent are Latino, 19 percent African American, 7 percent Asian, and 7 percent white (less than 100 percent due to no reports and multiracial students).[6]

This small Oakland high school is nearly twenty years old. David Bromley and Matt Spengler, two former social studies teachers from Los Angeles Unified District, founded MetWest in 2002, one of a national network of Big Picture Learning schools. There are now sixty-five such schools in the United States, with others in Australia, the Netherlands, and elsewhere in the world.[7]

It is, of course, so easy to say that two teachers founded the school and leave it at that. What is missing is the grinding essential political work in the community that these teachers had to do with students and their parents, OUSD administrators, community activists, and the school board to simply get the mission of this small high school accepted and then get it up and running. The political spadework was constant and unrelenting in meeting people, locating resources, sharing the Big Picture Learning school design, and showing how MetWest would fit into the district plan for small, innovative schools.

And even after the school board formally adopted MetWest, the gritty work of finding a location for the school; acquiring staff; orienting parents, students, and faculty to its mission and design—all of these tasks were "musts" that involved serious negotiating and political tap dancing. But each step of the way was completed, and the small high school opened in 2002. Achieving the political basics of adopting and opening a new school was an institutional "success."[8]

MISSION AND LEARNER OUTCOMES

Reflecting the mission and design of Big Picture Learning schools, MetWest has revised its mission statement and goals for students a few times. The most recent statement I could find was its "Progress Report" prior to a visit from a committee from the Western Association of Schools and Colleges (WASC) in 2018:

> MetWest prepares young adults to recognize and take advantage of all resources to further their well-being and the well-being of their communities. Our graduates will have the skills, habits, knowledge, and networks to overcome obstacles to their success, access four-year colleges, engage in fulfilling work, and contribute positively to our world.[9]

The mission gets more specific with its statement of Expected School-wide Learning Results (ESLRs), which came about from preparation for a WASC visit in 2014. Prior to that, there were few specific curricular goals and objectives that the entire staff had agreed upon and enacted in their classrooms in a consistent way.

As one would imagine in small schools such as MetWest with its largely low-income enrollment and being part of the Big Picture Learning network, different literacies (e.g., reading, writing, math, and science) and "critical thinking" were expected as student outcomes. In addition, there were ESLRs that reflected BPL, such as "Real World Learning" ("Students will have the communication, independence, and self-advocacy skills . . . to follow their passions and successfully navigate professional and higher education environments"). Social and emotional intelligence was another ESLR. Finally, there was an ESLR for "Social Change Agents/ Promoters of Social Change," where students were to "understand the historical roots and current effects of oppression in society and affect social change in their communities and in themselves through conscious and liberatory actions."[10]

This combination of a range of student academic, personal, and activist outcomes echoes the Social Justice Humanitas Academy's mission and expected individual student growth. While SJHA had continuity in leadership and a coherence in linking its mission to daily school activities with two of the founding teachers who had been colleagues for years at a previous high school serving as principals since 2011, that has not been the case at MetWest.

SCHOOL LEADERSHIP

The founding teachers left MetWest in 2005, and since then there have been four principals who have adapted the Big Picture Learning design to the contours of OUSD and Oakland students. Eve Gordon, an advisor/teacher at the school, became principal in 2005 and stayed until 2010, when she took a post in the OUSD district office. Thus far, no principal has served five or more years.

Sean McClung succeeded Gordon in 2011. Coming from an assistant principal post in another OUSD small high school, the former Teach For America instructor left after two years for a principalship at Impact Academy of Arts and Technology in Hayward, twenty miles south of Oakland. Charlie Plant from the Big Picture Learning network arrived in 2014 and served four years. A former house painter and business owner, Plant turned to teaching and administration, becoming an advocate for youth who wanted to work in the trades. He returned to BPL to coordinate the Harbor Freight Fellows program that has high school students working in manufacturing and craft trades.[11]

Michelle Deiro is the fifth principal of the school. A former English teacher and department head in an East Bay district, Deiro came to MetWest in 2004. As an advisor/teacher, she spent nine years before getting her administrative credential and leaving MetWest for a string of posts in another district, with a charter school in the area, and a hospital. She returned to MetWest after Charlie Plant departed. She was named principal in 2018.[12]

Except for a commitment to the student internship experience, this instability in leadership exacted a price in pursuing consistently and coherently the school's mission and expected learner outcomes over the years.

From the founding teachers who served as coprincipals through Deiro, these principals had moved in and out of different locations in OUSD before entering a new building shared with an elementary school in 2014. Through these changes in facilities, site administrators remained attached to the design of a Big Picture Learning school. Even with principal instability, these administrators found the commitment to students working outside the school and integrating academics and work into daily lessons worthwhile enough to serve as MetWest leaders. Knowing the Big Picture design, then, is an important factor in understanding how this small high school expanded traditional notions of institutional "success" and "failure" in US schools.

THE BIG PICTURE LEARNING DESIGN

The Big Picture Learning vision, mission, goals, and program design are intimately tied together and mirror the intentions of MetWest staff over the years:

> It is our vision that all students live lives of their own design, supported by caring mentors and equitable opportunities to achieve their greatest potential. We move forward prepared to activate the power of schools, systems & education through student-directed, real-world learning. We are activists.[13]

The Big Picture Learning website is clear on how that mission is to occur. Under the title "How It Works," the design of the model becomes evident:

> Each student at a Big Picture Learning school is part of a small learning community of 15 students called an advisory.
>
> Each advisory is supported and led by an advisor, a teacher that works closely with the group of students and forms personalized relationships with each advisee.
>
> Each student works closely with his or her advisor to identify interests and personalize learning.

The student as the center of learning truly engages and challenges the student, and makes learning authentic and relevant.

Each student has an internship where he or she works closely with a mentor, learning in a real world setting.

Parents and families are actively involved in the learning process, helping to shape the student's learning plan and are enrolled as resources to the school community.

The result is a student-centered learning design, where students are actively invested in their learning and are challenged to pursue their interests by a supportive community of educators, professionals, and family members.[14]

But the Big Picture Learning schools are not like matching cupcakes sitting in a muffin pan. Although they follow the same design, there are differences that set apart MetWest in Oakland from The Met in Providence, Rhode Island, and others in its national network. While there is much that is common in the design and BPL wants it to be adhered to across the network, contexts differ, causing adjustments to be made.

Rural and urban BPL schools, for example, have different students and stakeholders. Community politics vary across settings. Some schools are in spanking-new buildings, others are in trailers and reopened old schools. Some BPL schools have stability in principal leadership, some do not. Then there is demography. Students coming to the Lafayette Big Picture High School in Onondaga County, New York, differ racially, ethnically, and academically from those arriving at MetWest in Oakland. Nonetheless, there is a common design with key features required in any Big Picture Learning school.[15]

ONE STUDENT AT A TIME—The entire learning experience is personalized to each student's interests, talents and needs. Personalization expands beyond mere academic work and involves looking at each student holistically.

ADVISORY STRUCTURE—Advisory is the core organizational and relational structure of a Big Picture Learning school, its heart and soul, often described as a "second family" by students. Students stay with an advisor and a group of fellow classmates for two to four years, building close personal relationships that last a lifetime.[16]

LEARNING THROUGH INTERESTS AND INTERNSHIPS (LTIS)—Real world learning is best accomplished in the real world. Big Picture students intern—often twice a week for an entire school day—with experts in their field of interest, completing authentic projects and gaining experience and exposure to how their interests intersect with the real world.

PARENT AND FAMILY ENGAGEMENT—Parents are welcome and valued members of the school community and play a proactive role in their children's learning, collaborating in the planning and assessment of student work. They use their assets to support the work of the school, and often play an integral role in building relationships with potential LTI mentors.

SCHOOL CULTURE—In Big Picture schools, there is palpable trust, respect and equality between and among students and adults. Students take leadership roles in the school, and teamwork defines the adult culture. Student voice is valued in the school decision making process and visitors are struck by the ease with which students interact with adults.

AUTHENTIC ASSESSMENT—Students are assessed not by tests, but by public displays of learning that track growth and progress in the student's area of interest. Assessment criteria are individualized to the student and the real world standards of a project. Students present multiple exhibitions each year and discuss their learning growth with staff, parents, peers, and mentors.

SCHOOL ORGANIZATION—Schools are organized around a culture of collaboration and communication. They are not bound by the structures of buildings, schedules, bells, or calendars. There is an interdependence between school and community.

LEADERSHIP—Leadership is shared and spread between a strong, visionary principal; a dedicated, responsible team of advisors and other staff; and students. The community functions as a democracy. A pervasive sense of shared ownership drives a positive culture dedicated to ongoing improvement.

POST-SECONDARY PLANNING—Students develop plans that contribute to their future success—be it through college, trades, schools, travel, the military, or the workforce.

PROFESSIONAL D EVELOPMENT—Regular advisor PD is conducted at each school by principals, other school staff, and BPL staff and coaches. A Big Picture School is a community of lifelong learners who embrace continuous improvement.[17]

Most of these features stem from the small school movement in which BPL participated, yet one key component missing from most small high schools founded in the 1990s and at the core of the BPL design—its "heart and soul"—is the internship. Students leave school twice weekly to work at a hospital, school, city agency, or business. That is central to BPL, as it is at MetWest.[18]

Nonetheless, there remains a tension between fidelity to the BPL design and the inevitable adaptations that occur in the different settings in which schools are located. Sticking to the elements of the design while tailoring those important pieces to fit a particular set of students amid changes in principals is a tightrope walk that each school, including MetWest, undertakes. BPL leadership acknowledges and encourages local adaptations as long as key design features are incorporated.

In what ways does MetWest vary from BPL design?

Neither a charter nor a magnet school, as a regular public school in OUSD, MetWest has carved out autonomy to meet BPL requirements for advisories, teachers staying four years with the same group of students, internships, a flexible schedule, focus on the humanities, and activism in the community by applying and receiving independent school status. Hence, MetWest conforms to the design, especially the role of advisor/teacher, internships, and connections with the community. Where it swerves from the design is due to the Oakland students entering the school.

For example, MetWest accepts many students whose prior experiences in school left them minimally prepared to succeed in high school academic subjects, meet college requirements, and graduate. To conform to the BPL design and deal with the wide variation in student academic knowledge and skills, MetWest needed to adjust to the diverse and demanding academic needs of its students. To do that, MetWest had to be free of many, but not all, OUSD policies and procedures.

To gain that essential autonomy and adjust key features of the BPL design, MetWest school founders applied for Independent Study status as a school. As an Independent Study school, MetWest had wide-ranging autonomy to have smaller classes, extra time in academic courses, teachers who doubled as advisors, afternoon internships, and, equally important, the discretion to design an infrastructure for staff growth in expertise and skills. Savvy political negotiations on the part of MetWest leaders to become an Independent Study school made possible the creation of a high school very different from others in the district while tweaking both OUSD and BPL requirements.[19]

Variation in design requirements occurred in the school's work to strengthen students' academic skills in reading, math, and writing. Elementary and middle school preparation left gaps in many students' academic portfolios. MetWest students in 2017, for example, did not score high on state reading and math tests; proficiency levels in math were very low (7 percent with the state average 39); in reading, it was 46 percent with the state average at 50. Moreover, students take few advanced courses and are ranked low in college-readiness factors even with a 95 percent graduation rate. Such metrics only confirm the amount of work that needed attention during these high school years for students, many of whom were the first in their families to consider college.[20]

For students to graduate and be prepared to enter college, much attention had to be paid in and out of class on sequencing of skills and knowledge from one course to another and one grade to another insofar as Expected Schoolwide Learning Results (ESLR). Additionally, a consistent strengthening of study, note-taking, and inquiry skills necessary for students to do well not only academically but also in their internships and planning for college had to be coherently planned across advisor/teachers.

MetWest's daily schedule reflects the increasing concentration on improving academic skills and meeting ESLRs. For example, while most BPL schools set aside two days a week for internships uninterrupted by in-school classes, MetWest's schedule calls for Tuesday and Thursday as Learning Through Internship (LTI), permitting students to leave for their worksites after 10:00 a.m. except for those students taking math and science classes each day. Those students leave around 11:30 a.m. In addition, there is an array of volunteer tutors, adult mentors, peer help, and daily coaching by advisors/teachers that supplements coursework, making MetWest more academic-focused upon strengthening subject matter and skills than other BPL schools. And the current principal sees even more tightening up of a coherent academic program necessary.[21]

FROM DESIGN TO CLASSROOM

A twenty-seven-year veteran of teaching in OUSD, Shannon Carey greets me at the door when I arrive at 8:30. She is wearing a UC Berkeley shirt (teachers that day wore clothes that advertised where they attended college) over jeans and dark ankle boots. The classroom furniture is arranged in a horseshoe shape with tables seating two tenth graders each facing one another across the open space in the middle of the horseshoe. There are two large couches in the rear of room. The walls at the front of the large classroom hold whiteboards with nearby easels showing assignments and homework. Posters adorn other walls.

The schedule for this period is listed on the front whiteboard:

Friday, February 1, 2019

I can reflect deeply on my strengths and weaknesses [Shannon mentions later in the lesson that this is the objective of the lesson]

8:30 Independent Reading

8:50–9:40 Non-Cognitive Variables: Self-Assessment and Interviews

Circles Today

HW [homework]

Gateway Project

    —self assessment

    —interview w/adult

    —interview w/peer

Due Friday

As I look around the room at 8:45, everyone is reading a book or article—no devices that I see. Three students are sitting on the well-cushioned couches in the rear of the room.

In the open space within the horseshoe sits Shannon with her laptop. Sixteen students are there that morning. They walk in, toss their cell phones in a box that Shannon holds [other teachers do the same at the beginning of class], and go immediately to their tables and take a book out of their backpack. The first half-hour is Independent Reading. Here is a sampling of what students are reading around me:

- Gillian Flynn, *Gone Girl*
- Suzanne Collins, *Mockingjay*
- Terence McKenna, *Food of the Gods*

As students are reading, Shannon, who is responsible for teaching English and social studies and managing her students' internships while integrating both into her Advisory role in helping students become college-ready, scans the classroom. She walks around and checks students' notebooks and assignments lying on table [students know this morning routine and have papers lying on tables]. She picks up and date stamps the students' "work samples" such as "Semester Reflections" and papers from other classes at MetWest. Shannon submits these to the OUSD department of Alternative Education for certification that students are in an Independent Study school.[22]

After a half-hour of silent reading, Shannon segues to the next part of the lesson. She asks students to put away their readings and says: "I need everyone's eyes on me." She then begins a whole group discussion of a handout on "Noncognitive Variables." She cautions Juan to stop playing with a stapler and Hunter to put away his book; he is sitting across from me and continues to read *Food of the Gods*.

The teacher asks: "Does anyone know a relative, adult, or friend who has gone to college?" Half of the students raise their hands. Shannon calls on students by name to tell about who they know and what they were told about college. A back-and-forth ensues between students and teacher on what they learned from those who have attended college.

Shannon then turns to the "Noncognitive Variables" handout. "Does anyone know," she asks, "what cognitive means?" A few students offer answers, and she builds on their responses. She summarizes a definition—"mental processes," writes it on the whiteboard, and then asks the class to write it down. Next Shannon asks a choral question: "How many of you know someone who is 'school smart'?" Students call out and raise their hands. "What else do you think you need besides school smarts?" A student says: "High test scores." Shannon replies, "High scores do not mean you succeed in college."

What unfolds is a whole-group discussion of noncognitive variables— what the teacher calls "people skills," "soft skills," and "social skills." She asks the class to take notes. As the teacher-led discussion proceeds with questions and responses from different students, Shannon's energy is obvious.

Calling it a mini-lecture, Shannon displays slides on the front whiteboard of noncognitive variables listed on the handout. She and the class enumerate each one with the teacher coaching students to define each one:

- Positive Self-Concept or Confidence
- Realistic Self-Appraisal
- Understands and Deals with Oppression
- Prefers Long-Range Goals to Short-Term or Immediate Needs
- Availability of Strong Support Person
- Successful Leadership Experience
- Demonstrated Community Service
- Knowledge Acquired in a Field

Shannon asks different students to read each variable, and the group defines it. The teacher asks students to put the variable in everyday language ("dumb it down," she says) and then directs the class to rate themselves on each variable on a four-point scale (e.g., 4 = "This really, totally, positively describes me" to 1 = "I do not think this describes me at all"). As the whole group discussion unfolds, the teacher constantly inspects the class for students who are inattentive, cautions them, and returns to Q&A discussion.

For the variable on "Oppression," a student wearing a head scarf talks about sexism she recognizes in and out of school. Other students chime in. Shannon uses the example of family discussions about immigration and fears about deportation. The teacher makes a point that it is less a personal problem and more of a systemic, social problem.

The class's progress through variables on the handout halts as three students enter the classroom and, with the teacher's permission, announce a new school tardy and absence policy. Also, they say that they are selling cookies and candies for Valentine's Day. They exit.

Shannon resumes the lesson and asks individual students to read variables. For some, she offers personal examples from her life and occasional students chime in with their experiences. She asks Mohammed to read the last variable and asks him for his "Knowledge of a Field." She reminds him and others about internships they are involved in and their passions about cosmetic make-up, video gaming, and working with animals at a veterinarian's office.

For the final part of the lesson, Shannon turns to questions listed in the handout such as "Which two variables do you feel you most demonstrate? Give TWO reasons why you think this." And "Which noncognitive variables did you score the lowest in?" As she eyes the class, she calls on Kevin to stop bothering the student at his table. She asks students to read these questions and assigns the class to answer them for Friday.

As time for the session comes to a close, Shannon passes out green detention slips for being tardy and walks around checking on students' completion of their assignments. Students begin packing up, picking up their cell phones, and waiting for the buzzer to sound.

Descriptions of Nick's and Shannon's classes are ones where social studies and English—called Humanities at the school—are integrated into the counseling, mentoring, and coaching roles that teachers have at MetWest. In most high schools, teachers are subject-specialists who do perform these other roles in varying degrees before and after school (and during lunch and preparation periods).

At MetWest (as well as Social Justice Humanitas Academy), teachers are expected to perform multiple and expanded roles that wrap into one bundle of academic, emotional, psychological, and social connections with students in class, outside school, and in internships. Close relationships between teachers and students evolve since advisors/teachers stay with the same group of students for two to four years. Of course, individual teachers vary in how they manage the social-emotional connections with students. Whatever the variation at MetWest, BPL and the principal expect advisors/teachers to display and enact a much larger emotional and social skill repertoire than teachers in regular high schools.[23]

Every MetWest teacher, however, is not an advisor. There are math and science teachers who teach and do not have formal Advisory duties with a group of students. At MetWest, these teachers are crucial to ensuring that all students meet university and college requirements in their subject areas and perform reasonably well on state tests, their Senior Thesis Project, and their final Exhibition. Consider this math class taught by a first-year teacher.

FROM THE CLASSROOM

After walking into the classroom, I sit down at a table with another student and wave hello to the young teacher. On the whiteboard are the objectives for the day:

Geometry
- Do Intro task now
- $$$$$$$
- exit slip

Lawrence Teng, wearing chinos and a plaid shirt, is a first-year teacher and graduate of the University of Michigan. One semester at MetWest under his belt, he collects cell phones from students and passes out the Introductory task—a slip of paper with three questions (e.g., what did you do over the weekend? How many blocks are missing from the rectangle?) for students to answer as they enter the classroom.

A slide on the whiteboard replicates what is on the Introductory task. It shows sixty-four blocks arranged in rows to form a rectangle with a large empty space in the middle of the rectangle. The nineteen students begin working on an answer to the question of how many blocks are missing from the rectangle.

The large classroom has a slowly whirling ceiling fan. Tables sitting two to three students each face the whiteboard and the teacher who is working in the front of the room with his laptop and document camera sitting on some cabinets (his desk is in the rear of the room). Lawrence uses the laptop to flash images onto the whiteboard. The room has a clock and phone.

After about five minutes, Lawrence asks the students to stop. He then turns to the question on the slip. "Anyone have any memories from the weekend?" One student responds about what his family did. No other responses. Then the teacher asks about the rectangle of sixty-four blocks and how to find the answer of how many are missing from the blank space in the middle without counting them. He calls on Bruce, who says his answer. Lawrence asks Bruce to come to the front of the class to explain his strategy in getting the answer he gave. Bruce tells the class each step of his thinking to reach his answer; Lawrence is at the whiteboard illustrating what Bruce said on the grid of sixty-four little blocks.

The teacher then says that there are many strategies to solve the problem, and Bruce returns to his table. He begins applauding Bruce and a few students join in. He then calls on Maurice, and he and Maurice go through the same routine of figuring out that there are fifty-six blocks with eight missing—all without physically counting them (as I did). Lawrence sums up the student answers and shows the different strategies of adding, subtracting, and multiplying to get the correct number of missing blocks. Wrapping up the opening exercise, Lawrence tells the class what assignment is due Friday.

I note that there are two other adults in the room. One is a volunteer (a retired math professor) who helps individual students when the class is doing independent work. The other adult is a resource teacher working with individuals who have been identified with special needs.

Then Lawrence turns to the item that was listed on his agenda for the day's geometry lesson: $$$$$$. He shows a brief video of an art exhibit at the Guggenheim exhibit of paper one-dollar bills pasted to the walls and columns of a room. After showing the short clip twice, he stops it at the dollar room.

As I scan the class, students are very attentive to the images of one-dollar bills in this museum exhibit. I do not see any students off-task.

He then asks the class to write down their questions and turn to a partner at the table and share questions with one another. Students do so. At one point, he says aloud that he is putting Angel's and Maurice's names on the whiteboard for playing around. No response from either student as the class works on questions.

Lawrence then asks students to tell him what their questions are and he will divide them into two categories: questions he can and cannot answer. "Can you grab money off the wall?" "No," Lawrence replies, "it is an art exhibit and there are security guards in the room." He calls on students by name and they reply with their questions.

One student question he pauses over: "How much money is on the walls of the room?" Lawrence asks students to guess at an answer to the student's question. Tables erupt into numbers yelled out, and there is much quizzical laughter throughout the class.

Lawrence lists the guesses on the whiteboard:

- $20 thousand
- $1,500
- $5,500
- $10,000

The teacher then directs students to tell their tablemates how they arrived at their guesses. Students actively engage with one another as I look around the room.

Lawrence quiets the class and asks: "To get the correct amount of money in the room, what information do you want or need from me?"

Students quickly yell out what they want from Lawrence.

- How big is the wall?
- What is size of a dollar bill?
- Are there layers of dollar bills or one each pasted to the wall?
- How many feet across is the wall?
- How tall is the wall?

At the table next to me, I ask the three students what question they came up with. One showed me what they wanted to know: "The area of wall and the area of dollar."

Lawrence then flashes on the whiteboard close-up photos of the money (students see that there are no layers of dollar bills) and then slides of the dimensions of the columns and walls. He hands out a two-page floor plan of the room with the surface area in meters and centimeters of both the columns and the walls. The handout also shows a photo of a dollar bill and its dimensions in centimeters. Further information on the handout states that there are 3,516 dollar bills on the North Column and the same for the South Column. The dimensions on the floor plan for the width, length, and height of the room are on the floor plan marked in meters and centimeters. He calls on one student to read out dimensions listed on the floor plan. Lawrence asks the class: "How do you find the area of one of the walls?" A few students respond by saying to look at the dimensions of the floor plan.

Lawrence then asks students to estimate how much money is on the walls and columns. A few students move to a file box near me and take out calculators and return to their seats. Students at each table (a "team," Lawrence calls them) get to work. A buzz of noise arises in the class as teams work at their tables.

Lawrence quiets the class, and before asking them what amount of money they came up with, he asks the class—a choral question—what strategy each team used in coming up with their answer. In the whole group discussion, a few students reply and list the steps.

Lawrence summarizes the strategies students used: divide the area of the walls by the area of the dollar bills. He goes over the steps to find the area of the rectangle (base multiplied by height). A few students near me comment aloud that their estimates resemble the problem of a rectangle of blocks that they looked at when class began.

A few minutes remain in the class—students look at the wall clock—and begin putting notebooks and papers in their backpacks and standing up. Lawrence tells them to fill out exit slips. Standing students sit down and write answers to three questions on the slips:

- How did you feel during lesson?
- Did your group work well together?
- Choose option that best describes you;
  I do not know what is going on.
  I know how to solve problem.
  I am done with problem.

Chimes sound and students drop off slips in a box on a table near me as they leave the room.

ASSESSMENT

The exit slip is a quickie assessment that many teachers use at the end of their lessons. MetWest teachers, like nearly all OUSD teachers, give classroom quizzes, multiple-choice tests, and written essays as ways of determining what and how much students have learned. But a BPL design feature requires forms of performance assessment that go beyond the familiar repertoire high school students experience. Recall the BPL's "authentic assessment" feature: "[P]ublic displays of learning that track growth and progress in the student's area of interest. Assessment criteria are individualized to the student and the real world standards of a project."

At MetWest, "authentic assessment" is a senior project and the end-of-the-year Exhibition. As in other Big Picture Learning schools, all MetWest twelfth graders must do a Senior Thesis Project (STP).[24]

Seniors present their projects to a group of advisors/teachers, administrators, and staff who judge the worth of the presentation and determine whether a student has passed or not. Each defense has to include an action project linked to their research and anchored in social justice. Each student gets three chances to pass. Most often the STP is anchored in the student's Learning Through Internship (LTI). Passing the STP prepares seniors for their final Exhibition, usually on the same subject, before an audience of students, teachers, family, and invited guests.

Each STP has a format in which a student presents slides to a jury of staff. Each project has to have a question, a way of answering the question, the theory behind an answer, evidence, analysis of data presented, and a conclusion. It is a format familiar in college and graduate work. The panel uses a rubric that MetWest teachers have created laced with specific examples to judge each student's presentation.

On March 11, 2019, I observed Brenda and Hugo make their first presentation to a panel of three teachers and the principal. Two ninth graders were there also to become familiar with the process.

Brenda is first. Interning at Oakland's Heritage Psychiatric Clinic, she asks, "Mass Shootings: Why White Males?" In a series of slides she describes the history and context of various shootings by white males such as Charles Whitman, the Texas Tower shooter (1966); Adam Lanza, the Sandy Hook Elementary School killer (2012); and Dylan Roof, who murdered nine people in a Charleston, South Carolina church (2015).

In a quiet voice, Brenda links the question to the psychiatric clinic in which she was interning. She reads through a series of slides about the question, such as the "Big Idea," her "Theory of Change" driving her action project (that professional development of certain staff would reduce patients' emotional volatility and improve their behavior), and her proposal. She elaborates on her action project, including the impact of the ideas she has on her design of the professional development workshop. She goes over rubric categories such as relevance, feasibility, and rigor of her proposal. She swiftly goes through the slides. They are in a small font, and observers lean forward to read them. Brenda ends up with a timeline of activities to execute the project. The group applauds at the end of her presentation. The staff exit to discuss her presentation.

After the staff return, Hugo presents his slides. Hugo interns at a nearby elementary school's fourth-grade class. His action project drew from the work of the Robert Moses Young People's Project and sought to improve these children's math skills and their mindset. His research question is: *"Why are low-income students of color not succeeding at math?"*[25]

In a series of slides, the senior lays out his theory of change:

> If I target elementary students at La Escuelita in East Oakland with educational workshops and inspirational quotes, then I can help them improve their math skills and help them increase their confidence.

His tactics were to use workshops on math skills that included a multiplication game and fourth graders parsing inspirational quotes. He wants to change the "mindset" of these ten-year-olds about math. He then describes No Child Left Behind and the Young People's Project to get at the history and context of low performance of minority and poor children in math.

To illustrate relevance of the action project, Hugo shows a photo of himself at age ten and tells of his own struggle with math in elementary school. Other slides get at rigor through a pre- and post-survey of these fourth graders' responses to workshops. He ends with an interview of the mentor teacher with whom he worked.

The group applauds. Teachers and the principal leave the room. I stay and listen to Brenda and Hugo express their nervousness over whether they passed or will have to present again later in the term. They are anxious. The two other students there cheer them up and compliment their presentations. The staff return.

One advisor/teacher gives the group's evaluation of Brenda. He says that the staff judged her project presentation to be below expectations, and she will have to do better next time in order to pass. He lists some strong points in Brenda's presentation, but overall there are a number of specifics such as little evidence that was collected and linking her question to the professional development workshop she designed. These issues need attention, he says, including the timeline. Brenda responds to the points and clarifies others. She is obviously disappointed. Another teacher says that the staff's comments on her presentation would be included in an email to Brenda.

For Hugo, another teacher presents the group's conclusion. Hugo approached expectations and had much that the staff felt was worthwhile, but improvements had to be made in providing evidence that fourth graders' did improve in math skills and showing how exactly inspirational quotes would alter the mindset of these ten-year-olds. He would have to return with an improved presentation. Again, the teacher says the staff's report would be emailed. Hugo asks a few questions and staff members respond.

The group applauds Brenda and Hugo just as chimes sound, ending the period.

After the assessment of two students' Senior Research Project Defense, I go out into the atrium of the school and see at least a half-dozen sheets tacked to the walls with the name of the advisor/teacher at the top and below a list of student names with their internship placement for the semester (see figures 6.1 and 6.2).

FIGURE 6.1   School atrium stairways

Name	LTI Site	Hours & Mentor Info
Marcos	BAY - PEACE	
Amir	OUSD	
Berenice	OUSD Talent Division	
Lauryn	Peralta CC	
Thomas	YPP	
Patrick	Laney Department of Athletics	
Adam	Maker Lab (TU)@McClymonds	
Perla	67 Sueños	
Francisco	67 Sueños	
Stephanie	67 Sueños (TU)/Rock Paper Scissors (TH)	
Amy	CHAMPS / Peralta CC	
Scedric	Young People's Project	
Alonzo		Riley Poign
Meelan		
Pedro	Precision Motors	
Sandra	Two Feet by Four	
Jonathan	BAY PEACE	
ili	CHAMPS / OUSD MetWest front office	
neera		
niel	Community Auto	
an	Reading Partners c Franklin Elementary	

FIGURE 6.2
Name-LTI
Site paper

While academic subjects to prepare for college are one pillar of Met-West, another is the internship, which is connected to both academic subjects and a possible workplace in which they may enter in a few years beyond the fast-food jobs and part-time work they had collected over the years.

INTERNSHIPS

Forty percent of the school week is devoted to Learning Through Internship (LTI). Every advisor/teacher, including Nick Palmquist and Shannon Carey, meets with students in and out of school to discuss the work done at the intern site, the on-site mentor, and any issues that have arisen.

As in all Big Picture Learning schools, MetWest has structured the academic year to have students search for and enter into unpaid internships two days a week during school hours. There is a coordinator that oversees the entire program, called Learning Through Internship. A former advisor/teacher, Mike Cellemme, heads this part of MetWest's program. He is the only staff member who has also worked as an advisor/teacher at the first Big Picture Learning school, The Met, in Providence, Rhode Island. He is responsible for finding sites for internships, interviewing potential mentors, making matches between individual students and mentors, and monitoring what goes on in the internship.

Local mentors take on the responsibility of helping a student acquire the work and social skills necessary to succeed in a business, a government agency, an educational or a health organization, and similar Oakland groups. From 2002 ,when MetWest opened, to 2010, the school had placed students with more than four hundred organizations, including local hospitals, radio stations, and restaurants to provide learning opportunities.[26]

Advisor/teacher Shannon Carey (see above) sees how the internship experience has made a huge difference for one of her former students, Kris McCoy. McCoy had struggled in school and had been in Oakland's juvenile hall for being involved in an armed robbery while in the eighth grade. When he arrived at MetWest, he got into several fights in the ninth grade.

Carey said, "He came with an ankle bracelet, and with visits from his parole officer." She continued: "And needing to be the alpha male and needing to show MetWest who he was and that he shouldn't be messed with. He was way more concerned with that than he was with his academics or his future career."

What happened was that McCoy began to trust Carey. He looked for an internship himself and found one at an auto repair shop. Edward Lam, his boss and mentor, gave him a chance and treated him like an employee, while teaching him many auto shop skills. Carey talked with McCoy's family about staying longer at this internship than usually occurred. They agreed, and McCoy stayed there for a few years, an unusual decision but one that helped the young man.

"For students, like Kris, who really struggle with positive adult relationships, I see no reason to interrupt that relationship," Carey said. "He can go deep in the content and he can go really deep in the really caring, trusting, loving relationship with adult men in his life."[27]

The theory of action behind Big Picture Learning schools such as MetWest using two-day-per-week internships is straightforward. By interning with mentors at a worksite, teenagers enter the world of adults beyond family and school. Working with adults and picking up different technical and social skills broaden and deepen learning by engaging their hands, hearts, and minds. That engagement is deepened when MetWest advisors/teachers and the LTI coordinator meet with worksite mentors and students. Such personal connections bridge the workplace and academic classes as teachers make curricular choices during the rest of the week in their daily lessons. Connected learning occurs also with Senior Thesis Projects (see above) and end-of-the-year Exhibitions most often growing out of internships.

Internships, then, lead to learning about how adults work in organizations and the repertoire of skills needed to succeed at a job while applying that learning to academics (and the reverse as well). Thus, through personal engagement between teachers, on-site mentors, and students, the two worlds of work and classroom come together to create deeper, more meaningful, and connected learning. That's the theory.

Internships, however, do not always work out for students. A few are fired for not showing up or being late. Some have to be retrained. Most students and worksite mentors, however, do fit together.

MetWest students go to their internships on Tuesdays and Thursdays. The advisors/teachers keep abreast of their students in their internships as well as in classrooms. Then there is the crucial LTI coordinator, Mike Cellemme. He works with students and teachers at MetWest on finding internships, working out problems with worksite mentors, and keeping advisors informed of what occurs at the intern site. I observed Mike one afternoon in March 2019.

I met with Mike, an experienced and savvy coordinator, as he worked with students and then joined him at an internship worksite. As with any high school program that has many moving parts involving 160 students, a dozen or so teachers, and over a hundred mentors in their workplaces, some things go smoothly, some less so.

One mid-March afternoon, I went to room 136 in MetWest to see Mike and Mayra Acosta (a MetWest graduate and now Resource Program Specialist) work with various students searching for and working in varied internships. Students came in, asked questions about their mentors and sites, and left; others stayed and sat with Mike and Mayra to talk about issues that came up in their classes, Senior Thesis Project, and internships.

I observe Alonzo who had worked as an intern on an Oakland political campaign during the fall semester and is now searching for a new internship. On her laptop screen, Mayra pulls up some possibilities for him to consider. She asks questions about what he learned during the last internship, his current interests, and what he has heard from other students about their internships.

Another student Anthony is talking to Mike about his Senior Thesis Project Defense. On his laptop, Anthony goes through the slides he prepared for his upcoming presentation, based upon his interning at an Oakland Unified school. They go over the STP rubric criteria of rigor, relevance, timeline, and evaluation. The senior gives examples and asks Mike what he thinks. Jose, sitting on a couch, waits his turn to speak with Mayra.

Another student, ninth grader Maria, sits on a couch in the back of the room reading a novel. She comes up to me to say hello; I saw her at a presentation by two students of their Senior Thesis Project Defenses. I ask her where she is interning. She tells me she is working two days a week at the Talent Division (an employee department) of the Oakland Unified District. I ask her what she does, and she explains that she goes over teacher applications to see that each one is completely filled out (e.g., Social Security number, phone number, years of experience in teaching). She also tells me that she wants to intern next in a school to work with children.

In the midst of the one-on-one with Anthony, Mike takes a call from a graduate who asks for help in looking for a job. Mike quickly gives the alum a website to look at and track down a job and the name and phone number of someone Mike knows. He then returns to Anthony and his STP.

Fifteen minutes later, Mike signals me that we are ready to go to an intern site called Hidden Genius where he will meet with Tre, a senior, and his mentor. We go to Mike's car and drive to another part of Oakland. He and I talk about the internship program. He tells me that about one-third of the 160 students in the school thrive in the internships, finding the experience worthwhile enough to use it as a springboard for their Senior Thesis Project and final Exhibition before graduating. Another third, Mike estimates, struggle, but with help from their advisor/teacher, Mike, and the site mentor, they grow intellectually and expand their skills in dealing with nonschool adults and the demands of a workplace. Then there is the final third of students who need intensive, sustained help in getting a placement and then ongoing coaching to stay in the internship. Frequent follow-up by the advisor/teacher and Mike for this bottom third of students is essential for these students to profit from the experience.

On our way to see Tre, we stop at a traffic signal, and Mike calls out to a teenager waiting to cross the street, "Hey, Danielle, how ya doin'?" She acknowledges Mike, and he says to her through the open window, "How come you are not at your internship?" No answer from Danielle. Just a smile. In the car, Mike says that she is interning at a funeral home on the other side of town. He says he will contact her later in the afternoon. He explains that some students have to be fired because of poor attendance, and Danielle, a bright student, has already had to exit a previous placement.

We arrive at the Hidden Genius Project. Tre came to MetWest just last year from an Oakland high school that he was stumbling through. At MetWest, he has caught fire in two different internships, a previous one at Kaiser Permanente (a health organization) and here at Hidden Genius. His mentors at Hidden Genius assigned him projects that required him to learn the game Minecraft and adapt the Python programming language for children (Tre has used the latter for other intern projects). Tre does programming to create software for use by students and adults, some of which will be displayed at a May conference in Cleveland, Ohio.[28]

With Tre, his mentor, and me standing outside the workspace that Tre uses, Mike asks a series of questions of both Tre and the mentor.

Mike takes notes rapidly on his cell phone. A few hours later, the mentor, Tre, and advisor/teacher receive these notes. Mike sends me a copy of what he sent out to the above people (and gives me permission to use it; see Table 6.1).

After the conference with Tre and his mentor, we return to MetWest where Mike has more students to meet and to call Danielle.

The integration of internships with academic subject matter occurs daily in different lessons I observed, but it is spotty, depending a great deal on how involved advisors/teachers are with their students. For those teachers who are not advisors, such as in math and science, the in-class linkages are hit and miss. Overall, however, internships are as central to the school's mission as academic preparation for college attendance. Visible evidence is in the atrium that serves as a communal gathering place for the entire school. Posted on walls for all to see, there are lists of internships that students have and each advisor/teacher with his or her students and the current internships they are working in (see figure 6.3 later).

"SUCCESS" AND "FAILURE" AT METWEST

I can now sum up what I have learned about this small Oakland high school and render a judgment about its institutional and individual "success." As I have stated, "success" is not an either/or verdict. It has as many facets as does the crown of a cut diamond. Depending upon the available light, these facets shine brilliantly. As with SJHA, MetWest's "success" in its two-fold mission is multifaceted, highly political, deserving of adjectives prior to the noun, and yet marked by flaws.

Surely, the media accounts of MetWest have been positive, suggesting institutional "success" in the number of high school graduates entering college and students learning through internships. That the small high school has been around for nearly two decades and now has a waiting list of 150 students eager to attend the school is further evidence that effectiveness in reaching particular goals, longevity, and popularity—mainstream markers of organizational "success"—apply to MetWest.[29]

TABLE 6.1 3/21 Check-In/Internship Visit

Performance	• Harold is Mentor (pseudonym) • Tre has been here, on time, doing excellent work consistently • Missed one day with a doctor's note • Tre has brought in some of his innovations from his Kaiser internship; we may use his code for an attendance / tracking system for our program • Tre is exceeding expectations in his project work and with additional actions/visits/youth engagement events • Tre is developing the skills needed to prepare a high quality presentation for the PYCON

LTI PROJECT
 	
Developing Curriculum for PYTHON CONFERENCE
	Tre will create and facilitate a curriculum for a Python Conference (PYCON) in Cleveland in early May.
	
	KEY ACTIONS AND PROPOSED DUE DATES
	• Due April 5: Tre will research best practices for teaching and facilitating.
	• Due April 5: Tre will analyze core texts (existing curriculum) to find best practices or innovate practices for the best educational impact.
	• Due April 17: Tre will conduct interviews with teachers to learn best practices in facilitating and teaching (Jake Seltzer, Derek Boyd—[Tre's science and math teachers]).
	• Due April 19: Tre will facilitate a demo lesson at MetWest with interested students.
	  – Tre will develop a PRE and POST Diagnostic to measure what students actually learned in the workshop.
	  – Tre will arrange technology and lesson plan.
	  – Mike can help arrange students and classroom space.
	  – Tre will reflect on experience and revise lesson as needed.
	• Due April 23: Tre will present final curriculum to Hidden Genius Mentors for final approval.
	• Due May 2(?): Presentation in Cleveland
	• Due May 16: Final Reflection and Q4 Exhibition
	• What was the key learning?

GOALS FOR GROWTH	I can develop new content knowledge in teaching computer languages: **CORE TEXTS** • Learn to Program with Minecraft • Python for kids – I can make innovations from these core texts I can develop stronger teaching/facilitation skills: • Consult with Jake and Derek . . . about teaching skills I can develop mastery in public speaking skills
NEXT MEETING	Jake or Mike will schedule a meeting to review goals for Mid-April.

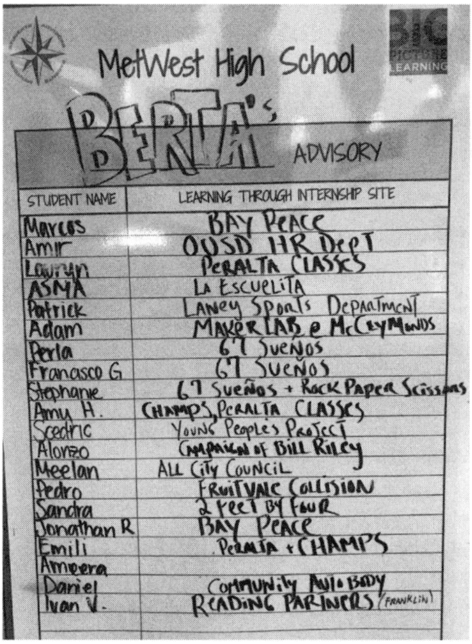

FIGURE 6.3 Berta's Advisory

As with SJHA, I apply the effectiveness criterion of goal achievement and whether the school has achieved those goals with minimum political conflict. On the latter point, the answer is yes. Although there was initial political skirmishing and opposition, the finesse that the teacher founders displayed in getting this small high school adopted by the school board and its continuity for nearly two decades, even with much principal turnover, have generated little pushback from the community.[30] Where there is an emerging conflict, it comes not from the community but from within the district.

There have been internal political battles over expanding the school to 320 students split between two sites. Under pressure to reduce OUSD's budget deficit, district officials have pressed the current principal and staff to establish another MetWest school to double its enrollment in order to reduce the current high per-student cost of maintaining the small high school. Such an expansion may well result in a split MetWest campus but at a political cost in staff disaffection and dilution of the BPL design. As I was writing in the summer of 2019, the principal informed me that MetWest would operate another campus that welcomes forty-two ninth graders in the fall of 2019, growing each subsequent year. Overall, however, there has been very little external opposition to MetWest from parents and mentors at community and business agencies housing school interns.[31]

Beyond this political sign of "success," the other half of the effectiveness judgment depends upon MetWest achieving BPL and OUSD academic goals, including the dominant measures of "success"—that is, test scores, high school graduation, preparation for college yields. In this respect, a mixed record emerges.

Consider OUSD metrics on academic outcomes. MetWest's graduation rate (93 percent) has improved in the past five years and is higher than the district's, and the dropout rate (7 percent) has been going down in past five years and is lower than OUSD's. The number of MetWest seniors prepared for college and university admission over the past five years has gone from 69 percent to 83 percent while the OUSD average was 51 percent (2016).[32]

But reading and math test scores for 2017 show that MetWest students still have a long climb ahead. In reading, 23 percent were above grade level and 29 percent were at grade level—but 47 percent were "multiple years below grade level." In math, high percentages of students did not take the test (35 to 47 percent in 2016 and 2017). Those who did, scored poorly; that is, 51 percent were two or more years below grade level in 2016 and 2017.[33]

In its 2018 report to WASC, the staff's conclusion on reading and math results was: "While MetWest outperformed the district, we still have a long way to go." The staff looked ahead to creating reading and math literacy plans that were vertically and horizontally aligned by grade level and subject, helping struggling students, and collecting data in specific areas that students were having the most difficulty.[34]

With Michelle Deiro named principal in 2018, a number of changes proposed in that WASC report have occurred. As the report said:

[W]e needed to focus on gaining clarity in what we are teaching and why so that we could better assess student outcomes. Our [professional development] goals for the year are: 1) Articulate and document what all students will be expected to learn in each class and internship (create class and LTI learning targets that are aligned with MetWest Vision) and 2) Create and utilize assessments which accurately measure student growth through collaborative work.

Changes did occur. For example, all advisors/teachers now have a common period for preparation to make more collaboration possible. Grade- and department-level teams have been formed to further both intra-staff communication and joint work. All of this is aimed at increasing test scores and other metrics that OUSD, parents, and community activists use to judge school "success."[35]

There is more to judging MetWest's effectiveness, however. Considering the high school's dual vision and BPL's design, documenting what happens to individual graduates after leaving MetWest is crucial to understanding how academics and internships and community activism intersect in helping its graduates negotiate higher education and adulthood.

> MetWest prepares young adults to recognize and take advantage of all resources to further their well-being and the well-being of their communities. Our graduates will have the skills, habits, knowledge, and networks to overcome obstacles to their success, access four-year colleges, engage in fulfilling work, and contribute positively to our world.

Collecting such data to see if these ambitious (and multiple) goals have been met is an enormous job requiring follow-up surveys and interviews to capture over time what occurs to individual students who attended MetWest, graduated, went to college, entered careers, started families, and engaged in their communities. Gathering such longitudinal data is uncommon among US schools in general and rare for particular high schools. Yes, there is strong evidence that MetWest was institutionally "successful" in getting adopted, established, and sustained over time without creating any significant conflict within the community since its founding. This is no small achievement.

It is far harder, however, to ascertain whether MetWest has achieved its mission and goals in furthering individual students' "well-being and the well-being of their communities" during their four years at the high school. Due to lack of data, tidying up amorphous goals into specific terms is tough to do when it comes to educational policies anywhere. At such a complex place as a small urban high school, it is especially difficult. What is missing are data on what occurs in communities and after individual students have graduated, finished college, and entered careers

MetWest Graduates

Apart from media accounts and individual stories told by students, advisors/teachers, administrators, and worksite mentors, I could find no follow-up reports tracking what has occurred to those MetWest graduates who attended college and what they are doing currently. After all, the BPL design and MetWest mission is to have students, most of whom are the first in their families to attend college, go on to complete the college or university they enrolled in. MetWest graduates since the early aughts are now in their twenties and mid-thirties and have launched in careers and families. I could not find such follow-up studies.

Internships

To what degree have the internship experiences been a factor in academic classes, student performance, choosing a college major, and getting a job after completing high school and later earning a degree? It is a reasonable question to ask, given MetWest's mission, the goals of the LTI, and the BPL design.

Internships played a direct role within classes I observed in discussing lessons, listening to students, and interviewing teachers. Among many students, internships became the basis for the Senior Thesis Project and their final public Exhibition. These performance assessments are part of the MetWest experience. Apart from stories I have heard and situations I have observed, there are connections, but, again, I have not seen any reports that document these important linkages.

Community Activism

Displayed continually in the atrium and classrooms are posters, paintings, and printed exhortations to take action in the community. I heard from students (and advisors/teachers) who were active in political protests and campaigns in the fall of 2018. Both MetWest teachers and students, I was told, worked hard in the run-up to the February 2019 teacher strike. The evidence is surely there but uncollected. Scattered among media accounts and anecdotes recounted by students and teachers is much involvement with the community beyond internships. A systematic collection of these data would help in determining in what ways and to what degree the BPL design and MetWest internships account for such community engagement.[36]

With this mixed picture of "success" at MetWest in applying the effectiveness criterion (goal achievement with little political conflict), has this small high school approaching two decades of existence in OUSD expanded the mainstream definition of institutional "success"? Yes, it has. Although I have supplied asterisks to the achievement of some of MetWest's mission and goals, the BPL design is intact. And MetWest's enactment of that design tailored to the demands of OUSD and the community it serves has broadened the meaning of both institutional and individual "success."

But MetWest after nearly two decades is not yet a resilient "success." At best it is a robust "success" on the cusp of resiliency, yet with dark clouds forming in the district office mandate for the school to double in size and have two locations within the next few years. Should that expansion occur, conflicts within the staff, among parents, and community activists could rise to a screech, making any future "success" precarious.

With one eye cocked on the traditional measures of institutional "success" such as test scores, graduation rates, and college attendance and the other eye cocked on individualizing learning and community activism through a blend of academics and work experiences, MetWest has stretched the customary definition of school "success" in US schools to include both personal and community well-being. While all of the data may not be collected yet, it is clear to me that MetWest's definition of "success" has expanded the common (and narrow) definition of the purpose of tax-supported public schooling to include other ways of judging, untidy as it may be, what a "successful" high school should be in a capitalist democratic society.[37]

REFLECTIONS

While I was writing these two chapters on SJHA and MetWest, four points became clear to me. First, both small high schools embody the three core American values I described previously to an extraordinary degree. I can see these values in other US schools, of course. But the mix and blending of individualism, community, and equal opportunity at SJHA and MetWest strike me as uncommon and infrequent since they are embedded deeply in the panoply of the schools' missions, programs, daily schedules, and classroom lessons.

Regardless of whether "self-actualization" or personal well-being or social activism can be agreed upon by staff and students or even measured, the individual student is central to any definition of "success" in both schools. From completing college applications, visiting universities, revealing intimacies in classroom circles, being mentored, or mentoring other students—these schools are geared to individual "success" of students. It is personalized. Being part of a community—"family" is the word used most often by students at both schools—offsets unrestrained individualism and the hard-nosed competition felt in most high schools. Helping one another is a benchmark noted often by both staff and students. Finally, in both schools the core value of equal opportunity shows up repeatedly in community activities, the daily mantra of "everyone goes to college," and the commitment to expand justice to all irrespective of ethnicity, race, religion, gender, or social class.

Second, SJHA and MetWest have expanded traditional definitions of "success" beyond test scores and familiar metrics used in US schools. By merging social activism and academic excellence with individual growth and well-being, both schools have sought a broader, humanistic way of looking at "success" beyond what most US schools embrace. Sure, not everything is neat and tidy at either school when it comes to broadening the definition beyond the narrow and pervasive measures of effectiveness that policy makers use. Furthermore, to get both school sites up and running is testimony to the political moxie that teacher founders and administrators exerted decades ago, along with helpful intermediary groups in the larger community. That SJHA (2011) and MetWest (2002) exist now is proof of what is possible in other regular public schools. But are these two small California high schools "black swans," unpredictable outliers that cannot be replicated anywhere else?[38]

SJHA and MetWest as regular public schools in two large urban districts became "successes" with minimum political pushback over many years. Can this process of expanding and enacting broader definitions of "success" occur in other American public schools?

Here is a spoiler alert for chapter 7: the answer to the first question is "no"; the answer to the second question is "yes."

Third, in writing these two chapters, I realized, slowly to be sure, that SJHA and MetWest mirror many of the principles displayed by early twentieth-century Progressives who pursued John Dewey's ideas. Those pedagogical reformers (as opposed to the larger group of administrative Progressives who pursued efficient school and classroom activities) built schools and classroom programs anchored in the concept of the whole child. They pursued the growth of each child. They used student interests to create projects that were linked to the world outside of classroom walls. Those pedagogical Progressives, however, were then a minority of reformers, and while there were such schools created at the time and have carried on since, the dominant administrative Progressives and their concentration on efficiency held sway until the 1950s. That SJHA and MetWest knowingly (or unknowingly) reached back to these Deweyan Progressives is less important than their creating and sustaining a sharp focus on individual students, expanded teacher roles in advising, mentoring, teaching, student agency, and tightened connections to the community.

Finally, the role that technological devices played in classroom lessons I observed in both high schools was minimal. Tablets, laptops, and desktop computers were easily accessible throughout each school. Chromebooks sat on carts in most classrooms. Students were used to turning to them when teachers directed them to work on assignments or do readings that were already loaded onto the devices.

Except for cell phones. At MetWest, I saw teachers collect all cell phones in baskets or containers at the beginning of a lesson; students retrieved their devices at the end of the period. Student phones were often in use outside of class when they were in the atrium and during brunch and lunch breaks.

At SJHA, district cell phone policy is explicit in banning these devices but gave individual schools latitude in enforcing the ban. SJHA's website laid out those restrictions on classroom use and consequences except when teachers ask students to use them for a specific lesson.[39]

For example, in one English class, according to a newspaper report, teacher Priscilla Farinas told her thirty-one students:

> "This is the one and only time I will have you take out your cellphones," she said, instructing the students to share their definitions of "privilege" via text message as part of a lesson on *The Great Gatsby*.
>
> Students immediately grabbed their mobile devices. Their texts populated a screen in the front of the classroom. Every student appeared focused on their schoolwork. . . . "We're trying to keep you engaged," Farinas said. "This is part of a larger lesson: 'There's a time and a place to use the cellphone.'"[40]

That was in 2015. In February 2019, only one SJHA teacher I observed used a cell phone during a lesson. She used a phone app to generate random student names to call upon for answers to questions about the scene in Hamlet they were studying. Apart from this teacher, no other SJHA teacher I observed asked students to use their cell phones during lessons I watched.

As I reflect on teachers' and students' use of these devices in both schools, they were seldom in the foreground; they were in the background of lessons. Sure, they were present but used when they were integral to a lesson much as paper, pencil, and erasers. Except for cell phones, then, electronic devices were pervasive in both schools but nonessential to the lessons teachers taught.

As a historian and former practitioner, I found writing these two chapters linked my research into early twentieth-century school reform with what I had learned as a teacher, superintendent, and university professor over the past half-century. I consider myself one lucky person to have connected my past, previous school reforms, and the present moment in two small high schools.

In the final chapter, I answer the question posed in the Introduction about whether the Cardozo Project in Urban Teaching was a "success." Then I sum up the main points of this book, and ask: So what? My answers reflect on the past, present, and future of school reform. In thinking about how often school reformers have chased "success" and confronted "failure" by making "fundamental" changes in the age-graded school or as it has come to be known pejoratively by many school reformers as the "factory model" of schooling, I offer another way of thinking about the dominant way of organizing and running schools that David Tyack and I called the "grammar of schooling."

CHAPTER 7

SO WHAT?

In the Introduction to this book, I described the Cardozo Project in Urban Teaching that existed between 1963 and 1970 and my half-century long uncertainty over the worth of what I had spent four years teaching and administering. I asked myself: Was it an institutional "success" or "failure"? I now have an answer that finally scratches the itch that prompted me to write this book.

But first some personal history that inescapably became entangled with societal definitions of both institutional and individual "success" and "failure," including the core American values of individualism, community, and equal opportunity.

Like most Americans, I have been preoccupied with being personally "successful." The youngest of three sons of Russian Jewish immigrant parents and the only one of my brothers to attend college, I mixed family, Judaic, and peer values into a stew of individual ambition, competitiveness, hard work, and love of the friends and community in which I lived. As a young man, I wanted to "succeed," make a name for myself as a teacher, administrator, and professor. I wanted to "succeed" as a husband to Barbara, father to Sondra and Janice, and life-long friend to my Pittsburgh buddies and California pals. Yes, I chased "success" and confronted "failure" as an individual just as others have in this highly competitive culture in which I and other Americans are born, live, and die.

There is a "but." Not only was I a competitive individual, but I also prized being part of a family, a member of a boys club, the neighborhoods we lived in, and my religious community. Being among others and helping one another regardless of background meant a lot to me. In short, I integrated the core values of American culture and juggled them as best I could as a father, husband, teacher, and community member.

That personal history slides easily into discussing the one institution in which I began working in 1955 at the age of twenty: public schools. Then and now public schools, mirroring the larger society, chased institutional "success" and confronted "failure" as they managed the mélange of core American values and responded to societal tremors.

Since their origins in the early nineteenth century, adolescence in the twentieth century, and maturity in the early decades of the twenty-first century, American individualistic values, including competition alongside building community and treating others equitably, have permeated tax-supported public schools.

Sorting out students into winners and losers is (and has been) a primary function of age-graded public schools. Those distinctions have been present for decades in the annual promotion to the next grade, student report cards, suspensions of misbehaving students, and naming of valedictorians and National Merit Scholars. They echo what occurs in the larger society day in and day out.[1]

After all, anyone who has gone to a twentieth reunion of their high school class comes to see that public schools imitate, if not replicate, the larger society. Historically, schools have differentiated those students who will "succeed" from those who will end up mediocre and those who will "fail." Recall Kurt Vonnegut's quoting a friend of his who attended school with him in Indianapolis: "When you get to be our age, you all of a sudden realize that you are being ruled by people you went to high school with. You all of a sudden catch on that life is nothing but high school . . . class officers, cheerleaders, and all." Then Vonnegut commented: "High school is closer to the core of American experience than anything else I can think of. . . . "[2]

Public schools, then, didn't invent core American values; they copied societal ones. Previous chapters pinpointed the sources of these notions of both individual and institutional "success" and "failure" in the meshing of a market-driven economy and democratic governance as early as the seventeenth century. The political and economic structures that branded society as American not only contained and sustained the core values of individualism, community, and equal opportunity but also became the foundation for sorting individual winners from losers, institutional "success" from "failure."

I described and analyzed how sports, business, and schools were key institutions that socialized Americans, both native born and immigrant, into accepting those core values and how those values—particularly competitive individualism (restrained and unrestrained)—are entangled in distinguishing rising stars from down-and-outers.

When it comes to voters and taxpayers, then and now, they expect tax-supported public schools to conserve those values. Americans assume that the next generation will absorb, digest, and display those values after leaving school, allowing those who have acquired credentials and badges of merit to gain individual "success" and duds who sail along unnoticed to accept being losers, often blaming themselves for failing. That, after all, is the American game of life.

With all of this historical and contemporary analysis of institutional and individual "success" and "failure" plus an in-depth look at two schools (chapters 5 and 6) in America, I return to the question I asked earlier: was the Cardozo Project in Urban Teaching a "success" or "failure"?

"SUCCESS" OR "FAILURE"?

To render such a judgment—not scientifically precise by any means but a subjective decision—the degrees of institutional "success" and "failure" that I introduced in earlier chapters and the inevitable contradictions that exist when determining a program's "success" and "failure" have to be elaborated. Especially the inexorable tensions and messiness that appear in drawing conclusions about either organizational "success" or "failure."

I pointed out previously that assessing institutional "success" in a classroom, school, and district is untidy. There are often multiple goals, structural constraints embedded in the age-graded school, limited resources, and unpredictable events intruding. Inevitably, trade-offs have to be made when a policy travels from its origin to adoption to implementation in classrooms, schools, and districts. Top decision-makers, for example, seeking institutional "success" try to build political support for a new district program. They may include, intentionally or not, program particulars such as test scores that ruffle many teachers' feathers, thereby undercutting classroom implementation (e.g., consider the Intensive Partnerships for Effective Teaching in Hillsborough Country, Florida). Thus, one contradiction emerges: a successful political process can lead to an unsuccessful program.[3]

Other tensions can produce untoward outcomes, again over time, of successful programs that wither away because parents and community activists mobilize into political coalitions opposing such programs (e.g., rapid growth of charter schools since the 1990s and political coalitions seeking to cap their growth in 2019). So such institutional judgments, as I have pointed out in analyzing SJHA and MetWest high schools, need adjectives in front of the nouns "success" and "failure." For example, "resilient," "robust," "conflicted," and "precarious" can modify the noun "success." These modifiers introduce essential nuances when making consequential organizational judgments about a spiffy innovation, a broad-reaching school reform, or an individual assessment of a kindergarten teacher's use of ClassDoJo.[4]

Now, I return to my years in the Cardozo Project in Urban Teaching (1963–1967). Earlier, I made clear that the federally funded CPUT had achieved its immediate goals of preparing Peace Corps returnees to become credentialed teachers. Another goal was to get this school-based teacher-education program to be incorporated into the existing budget of the Washington public schools after its federal dollars ran out. Both goals were achieved.

Seventy-five percent of the interns trained in the program over four years were hired as teachers in the District of Columbia and elsewhere. The DC schools adopted the teacher-preparation program in 1967, renaming it the Urban Teacher Corps, and in succeeding years trained a few hundred new teachers. Moreover, CPUT became the model for the National Teacher Corp, a federally funded teacher preparation program that brought teacher-education institutions and urban districts together beginning in 1968. These are sure signs of institutional "success."

Yet the DC Urban Teacher Corps ended in 1970 when a new superintendent closed down the program. The National Teacher Corps died in 1981 after Ronald Reagan was inaugurated president and instituted federal block grants letting each state decide to retain the program or not. Most states spent their federal dollars on other programs. Did "success" disappear?[5]

With the advantage of reflection and further thinking about the slippery notions of organizational "success" and "failure," I can now judge CPUT, the subsequent DC Urban Teacher Corps, and the National Teacher Corps as instances of "conflicted success" while they existed. In retrospect—*when* institutional judgments of "success" and "failure" are made either immediately or a decade or more later are crucial—these programs succumbed to the unrelenting tension of being "successful" programs in a continuous political fight with those who had contrary views of who should prepare teachers and how those teachers should be prepared. Hence, these programs expired due to incessant political battles. Let me elaborate.

I defined institutional "success" as meeting two criteria: achieving program goals with a minimum of political opposition. But these district-driven teacher preparation programs had multiple goals. CPUT's primary goal was to train teachers to enter District of Columbia classrooms and get the district to embrace and fund the program because it was a superior way of attracting a different pool of college graduates and preparing them to teach within a year. While the primary goals were eventually achieved, political opposition from within and outside the district grew. Regular DC staff, central office administrators, and local teacher education institutions contested the Urban Teacher Corps' recruiting, selecting, and training new teachers.

The conflict over who should prepare teachers (the district or universities in the DC area) and how they should be prepared persisted. With a new Washington superintendent, the political coalition to end the Urban Teacher Corps captured the novice superintendent's attention. He ended the program. A similar process unfolded at the national level with the departure of President Jimmy Carter and entry of President Ronald Reagan, whose mantra was that the federal government was the problem, not the solution to the nation's ills. Again, the rollout of block grants rather than categorical ones such as the National Teacher Corps was a political victory for those who championed states deciding use of federal dollars rather than Washington bureaucrats.

And this is why I put CPUT and its progeny into the category of conflicted successes that got chewed up in the political battles over who and how teachers should be prepared. The programs achieved their goals, but persisting political clashes over who should do teacher preparation and how it should be done led to their demise.

So now I understand in ways I did not before that the Cardozo Project in Urban Teaching, the Urban Teacher Corps, and the National Teacher Corps were, indeed, institutionally "successful" programs but failed to survive the political conflicts that eventually consumed them.

That nuanced understanding of institutional "success" and "failure" of an innovation I knew intimately is connected to the larger question about judging school reforms, individual teachers, schools, and districts as winners and losers. Which brings me to the question this chapter addresses: So what?

SO WHAT?

Why should readers care about defining individual and institutional "success" and "failure" in US schools? Why should readers care about the past and present existence of American core values stuffed with notions of "success" and "failure" and how schools transmit these values? Finally, why should readers care about two uncommon public schools that display these shared values and yet expand familiar definitions of organizational "success" to include individual students in ways that most US schools do not?

My answer to these "So what" questions is that definitions of institutional and individual "success" and "failure" applied to US schools show up daily in the taken-for-granted institution called the age-graded school. Within the age-graded school, judgments of "success" and "failure" are inherent in student, teacher, principal, school board, and superintendent actions, memos, and social media. In age-graded schools, numbers and subjective decisions identify winners and losers through student report cards, teacher evaluations, and district accountability ratings.

But even of greater importance is that amid this organization's extraordinary stability in American life, over a century of school reform has tried to overhaul it, even replacing the institution to make it better at what it does and end damaging judgments rendered upon children, teachers, and schools.

For nearly two centuries, this school organization has been both the disseminator of societal definitions of "success" and "failure" and displays of individualism, community, and equal opportunity. The age-graded school with its "grammar of schooling" has had a vise-like grip on how and what teachers teach and students learn. Determining individual winners and losers from kindergarten through twelfth grade and distinguishing between those who are normal from those who deviate from the standard, those who get promoted and those who go to summer school for not passing courses, are inherent to this organizational structure and the rules that govern it. Persistent efforts aimed at substantially altering what happens in schools and classrooms, especially those with mostly children of color, have crashed on the shoals of the age-graded organization and its abiding "grammar of schooling." Intermittent reform efforts to transform this organization through alternative forms of school organization, individualizing instruction through new technologies, and nifty management techniques again and again have lost their way or faded into the background, seldom diminishing popular support for this age-old structure.

So my answer to "So what?" is that *if* (and yes, this is a big "if") one wants to understand individual and organizational "success" and "failure" in American daily life, *if* one wants to alter common patterns of schooling, teaching, and learning that sort student winners from losers, then what has to be done is substantially alter the age-graded school and its "grammar of schooling."

I have briefly described and analyzed the age-graded school and repeated reform attempts to rework that organization and its underlying "grammar of schooling." Yet the fact remains that the age-graded school's capacity to school hundreds of millions of children and youth for nearly two centuries, its longevity, and its global ubiquity—I would be stingy to avoid the word—have been a clear institutional "success." If it ain't broke, the cliché runs, why fix it?

This school organization has stayed the course for decades because of its universal access and strong popular support generation after generation. It is anchored in the American imagination and culture as a "real school" where young children attend at age five (now ages three and four in many districts) and leave at ages seventeen or eighteen. It is the place where American values are displayed and taught.[6]

Nearly all Americans have gone through public or private age-graded schools. Strangers on airplanes and buses can connect when they talk about their schools. They remember how a school smells and looks. They still complain about school lunches. They can recount their best and worst teachers. Report cards, honor rolls, tests, and homework are as common as eating scrambled eggs and toast for breakfast. Yet the age-graded school is neither an iconic nor admired organization such as Ford and IBM were and Apple, Amazon, and Google have become.

No song or poem has immortalized the age-graded school. Still, it remains the most influential institutional mechanism that shapes for good or ill children's knowledge, skills, attitudes, and behavior over a dozen or more years. Ditto for those adults who work within these organizations.

As pointed out earlier, reforms aimed at improving how it works have poured over the age-graded school, and it has changed over time. Adding kindergarten and prekindergarten to the elementary school and increasingly community colleges to the secondary level has led to near-universal access into this institution. Accommodating children with disabilities, giftedness, and educational disadvantages who deviated from the norm, the age-graded school has demonstrated flexibility by responding to political coalitions of parents and activists who fought for the above changes.

But abandoning the organization and moving to nongraded schools are fundamental changes, not incremental ones, and have been rare over the past century. Thus, the stunning continuity and popular acceptance of the age-graded school mean that the "grammar of schooling" has re-mained in intact.

GRAMMAR OF SCHOOLING

David Tyack and I defined the phrase in this way:

> By the "grammar" of schooling we mean the regular structures and rules that organize the work of instruction. Here we have in mind, for exam-ple, standardized organizational practices in dividing time and space, classifying students and allocating them to classrooms, and splinter-ing knowledge into "subjects." Continuity in the grammar of instruc-tion has frustrated generations of reformers who have sought to change these standardized organizational forms.[7]

What is the connection between a "grammar of schooling" and lin-guistic grammar? Both have structures and rules that are seldom made explicit. Both operate in regular patterns. Neither has to be consciously specified to run smoothly.

Regularities, the essence of a "grammar of schooling," govern age-graded schools. Students are divided by ages from prekindergarten through senior high school. In elementary schools, a single teacher in a classroom teaches the content and skills in five or more subjects pre-scribed for that grade. Students stay with that teacher most of the school day. The teacher judges the performance and behavior of each student, deciding which will be promoted or retained for the next grade.[8]

The comprehensive high school is also age-graded: ninth graders are mostly fourteen years old and seniors are eighteen or so. Organized into departments, subject-matter teachers take attendance, assign home-work, enter grades in report cards, and determine whether a student passes or fails.

Then there is the Carnegie Unit, a defining feature of the high school. The Carnegie Unit is a single credit awarded for each academic subject based upon time spent sitting in classrooms for a school year. Beginning in the ninth grade, the number of academic credits a student collects is counted toward graduation.[9]

WHAT HAS KEPT THE "GRAMMAR OF SCHOOLING" IN PLACE FOR SO LONG?

The answer to the question is straightforward: popular social beliefs that the age-graded school, free to all, is a "real school." It rewards merit and provides a ladder to achieve personal "success" for generation after generation of children and youth.

This trust in the school as a meritocracy where the smartest and hardest working students will garner kudos is pervasive. Of equal importance is the current widespread belief among parents that every high school graduate should go to college. Schools and colleges are escalators to financial and social "success." Social mobility is an aspiration of both native-born and immigrant parents for their sons and daughters. Getting diplomas and degrees from public schools and colleges is the way for each individual to "succeed" in society as studies of lifetime earnings linked to credentials confirm. Taxpayers and voters expect schools to instill and display these values. This web of social beliefs has sustained the age-graded school even when concerted reform efforts sought to alter the "grammar of schooling."[10]

A second reason for the durability of the "grammar of schooling" is that state and district curriculum standards, tests, and accountability mechanisms are fastened to the age-graded school. State standards are grade and subject specific, spelling out what content and skills should be learned in first grade and tenth grade, for example. No Child Left Behind (2002–2015) tested students in math and reading in grades three through eight and at least once in high school. These policies continue in the Every Student Succeeds Act (2016–present) but leave decisions to state, not federal, officials. These state and federal policies act as an iron cage reinforcing popular beliefs that the age-graded school and its pervasive "grammar" are a "real school" and the one best way to educate the next generation and rise in material wealth.

Efforts to Change the "Grammar of Schooling"

These powerful social beliefs have persisted before, during, and after major challenges to the age-graded school occurred. In the early twentieth century, for example, reformers attempted to break the tight grip of the elementary age-graded school and the "grammar of schooling." As described in chapter 1, the Dalton Plan in a small Massachusetts town and the Winnetka Plan in an affluent Chicago suburb sought to individualize instruction to fit the strengths and limitations of each student. In individual contracts between teachers and students (the Dalton Plan) and in the Winnetka Plan that dispensed with age-grading, teachers taught differently. And in doing so, the plan tried to reduce the untoward classroom effects of the "grammar of schooling." Each of these reforms did gain a foothold in US schools, spread, but ultimately disappeared.[11]

For high schools, a similar pattern occurred. Initially, selective public high schools appeared in the seventeenth century in New England (the Boston Latin Grammar School was founded in 1635). By the early nineteenth century, the handful of these elite schools attended by students from affluent families grew larger as tax-supported public high schools opened on the eastern seaboard. The innovation spread through New England and the Midwest before and after the Civil War. Few families sent their sons and daughters to these schools since the workplace and farm provided jobs for those leaving school at ages twelve and up. In the 1890s, for example, only one out of ten seventeen-year-olds was enrolled in a tax-supported public high school.[12]

But with child labor laws being enforced and the onset of the Great Depression in the 1930s, youth stayed in school. Administrative and pedagogical Progressives created the comprehensive high school with multiple curricula and services for all students, not just those academically inclined (about thirty of one hundred seventeen-year-olds graduated in 1930). This innovative organization—still age-graded—made it possible for most American teenagers to enter the ninth grade and get a diploma by the end of the twelfth grade. By 1950, nearly sixty of one hundred seventeen-year-olds graduated.[13]

With the spike in enrollments and rising graduation rates in districts with comprehensive high schools, concerns over too much catering to students' varied interests and sinking academic performance surfaced in the 1950s, leading critics to question the thoroughness of the high school curriculum and softening of standards. Few students, for example, took advanced math courses, physics, and Latin compared to selective high schools in the early decades of the twentieth century. Criticism of US high schools mounted particularly after the 1954 *Brown v. Board of Education* decision triggered protests over segregated schools across the country. The Soviet Union's launch of the Sputnik satellite in 1957 also sparked a US curricular reaction in the New Math and an array of innovative science courses. Top policy makers and power elites began asking whether US high schools could be both excellent and equal—a question that is still being asked in 2019.

That question fueled the next half-century of reform. During the 1960s and 1970s, educational policy makers responding to political and social tremors in the culture shuttled back and forth trying to equally conserve values and alter society while accommodating both excellence and equity. Civic and business leaders pressed policy makers to increase equal opportunity through busing to desegregate schools, opening up advanced classes to all students, and relaxing graduation requirements. But a slow-growing economy and rising discontent over Germany and Japan outselling US companies in the 1970s led a later generation of business, civic, and educational reformers to press schools to turn out skilled graduates who could enter the workplace able to compete with workers in other nations.

A Nation at Risk, in scorching language, pointed to low graduation requirements, soft academic subjects, and US students' poor scores on international tests.[14]

That report and subsequent policy actions in the 1980s and 1990s ended up with nearly all states increasing their graduation requirements and tightening academics in the comprehensive high school. This pattern of seeking academic excellence for everyone without limiting opportunity for heretofore neglected groups has remained a tenet of school reformers for the past half-century. But when policies advancing both values were put into place, instead of loosening the "grammar of schooling," they added steel bars.[15]

There were also school reformers in these years who offered other high school models that departed from the traditional age-graded high school. The small school movement to downsize large comprehensive high schools (1500-plus students) and tailor them to be both demanding academically and cultivators of deep learning in students spread across the nation, powered by federal laws and philanthropic dollars. Many of these efforts sought to reshape the "grammar of schooling." Here are two examples.[16]

SMALL HIGH SCHOOLS: THE COALITION OF ESSENTIAL SCHOOLS (CES)

A former headmaster at Phillips Academy, ex-dean of the Harvard Graduate School of Education, and professor at Brown University, Ted Sizer believed deeply in John Dewey's concept of "democratic pluralism" and the importance of learning both knowledge and skills through face-to-face interactions with students in smaller settings than existing high schools.

Begun in 1984 with an initial cohort of eight high schools, no one model of a secondary school was pushed. Instead, Sizer and his staff formulated ten principles upon which educators should build schools that fit their setting. Among those principles were

LEARNING TO USE ONE'S MIND WELL: The school should focus on helping young people learn to use their minds well. Schools should not be "comprehensive" if such a claim is made at the expense of the school's central intellectual purpose.

LESS IS MORE: DEPTH OVER COVERAGE: The school's goals should be simple: that each student master a limited number of essential skills and areas of knowledge. While these skills and areas will, to varying degrees, reflect the traditional academic disciplines, the program's design should be shaped by the intellectual and imaginative powers and competencies that the students need, rather than by "subjects" as conventionally defined. The aphorism "less is more" should dominate: curricular decisions should be guided by the aim of thorough student mastery and achievement rather than by an effort to merely cover content. . . .

PERSONALIZATION: Teaching and learning should be personalized to the maximum feasible extent. Efforts should be directed toward a goal that no teacher have direct responsibility for more than 80 students in the high school and middle school and no more than 20 in the elementary school. To capitalize on this personalization, decisions about the details of the course of study, the use of students' and teachers' time and the choice of teaching materials and specific pedagogies must be unreservedly placed in the hands of the principal and staff.

STUDENT-AS-WORKER, TEACHER-AS-COACH: The governing practical metaphor of the school should be "student-as-worker," rather than the more familiar metaphor of "teacher as deliverer of instructional services." Accordingly, a prominent pedagogy will be coaching students to learn how to learn and thus to teach themselves. . . .

DEMONSTRATION OF MASTERY: Teaching and learning should be documented and assessed with tools based on student performance of real tasks. Students not yet at appropriate levels of competence should be provided intensive support and resources to assist them quickly to meet standards. Multiple forms of evidence, ranging from ongoing observation of the learner to completion of specific projects, should be used to better understand the learner's strengths and needs, and to plan for further assistance. Students should have opportunities to exhibit their expertise before family and community. The diploma should be awarded upon a successful final demonstration of mastery for graduation: an "Exhibition." As the diploma is awarded when earned, the school's program proceeds with no strict age grading and with no system of "credits earned" by "time spent" in class. . . .

DEMOCRACY AND EQUITY: The school should demonstrate non-discriminatory and inclusive policies, practices, and pedagogies. It should model democratic practices that involve all who are directly affected by the school. The school should honor diversity and build on the strength of its communities, deliberately and explicitly challenging all forms of inequity.[17]

These principles produced structures displaying Deweyan ideas of teaching and learning (e.g., block scheduling, integrated subjects, cooperative learning, and senior year projects). CES schools were smaller than comprehensive high schools and less susceptible to the traditional "grammar of schooling" prevalent in nearly all US high schools.

Receiving a large grant from the Bill and Melinda Gates Foundation in 2003, CES advanced the small high school movement.[18]

As a result of flexibility in applying these tenets, CES schools differed from one another. Central Park East Secondary School in New York City under Deborah Meier clearly differed from Thayer High School in New Hampshire under Dennis Littky, yet both tailored the principles to their setting.[19]

What began as Ted Sizer's groundbreaking effort to reform the United States' twenty-four thousand secondary schools over three decades ago reached one thousand plus schools by 1997, the year Sizer retired. Although the national organization closed its doors in 2018, many small US high schools retain CES components, including SJHA and MetWest.[20]

OUTCOME-BASED EDUCATION

Often squeezed together with "competency-based learning" and "mastery learning," "outcome-based education," beginning in the late 1970s, is an umbrella term that has covered the other concepts but is now seldom used by educators. All three ideas sparkled as reforms, enjoying fleeting flashes in the 1990s and into the early decades of the twenty-first century. Today, one hardly hears the phrase "outcome-based education" while "competency-based learning" gets a second act in the spotlight, one it had decades earlier. Regardless of the phrase, all three are connected in a fundamental way. [21]

They organize content around activities that lead to student proficiency in demonstrating specific knowledge, skills, and behavior without regard to how long it takes. Some students can learn the concept of thermodynamics in an hour; others, a few days. Some students can master quadratic equations in days; for others, mastery may take weeks.

A high school that organizes students around the time spent to fully grasp a concept or skills (with accompanying performance tasks to prove student understanding) is a school that rejects the basic premise of the "grammar of schooling," where the Carnegie Unit commands counting the time students sit in an algebra or physics classroom. The assumption driving the Carnegie Unit is that spending thirty-six weeks in a class translates into students mastering math and science concepts and practicing the relevant skills on tests. Most high school students would snicker were the assumption spoken aloud.

So devotees of outcome-based education, mastery learning, or competency-based programs at different times since the 1970s have tried to organize schools and districts to demonstrate how individual students can learn at their own pace and avoid marching to the Carnegie Unit drummer.

Some outcome-based programs and secondary schools are self-paced, meaning that individual students in each grade and subject move at different rates through, say, English or biology courses using online lessons and worksheets, and participating in discussions with teachers. Other programs dispense with age-graded structures completely in a brick-and-mortar building or through wholesale use of online courses (or both). Today the common phrase to describe schools and programs organized in this way is that they are competency-based.[22]

COMPETENCY-BASED EDUCATION

Many states have competency-based programs through waivers, incentive grants, and mandates. A few states such as New Hampshire have embraced competency-based education fully. Beginning in 2005, the state eliminated the Carnegie Unit and mandated competency-based practices in all of its schools. Implementation varies, but it remains the state policy in 2019.[23]

Elsewhere, some districts have moved in this direction, such as Lindsay Unified School District near Fresno, California. Beginning in 2006, top officials of the four-thousand-student K–12 district began the process of defining what they wanted students to know and do. Stating the performance they expected of their students, district officials dropped the Carnegie Unit, grade levels, and As and Ds, and created a performance-based system fitted to where students actually are and what they had to know and do to achieve their goal of graduating high school.[24]

Or consider Northern Cass School District in North Dakota. Receiving a state waiver to move toward abolishing all grade levels and adopting a competency-based program for all students, the district set up a pilot in the middle grades to have teachers and students work through such a program. As one journalist described:

> About a dozen Northern Cass students working on laptops made themselves comfortable in a large classroom with mobile furniture, beanbag pillows and a plush blue couch. The kids were rounding out eighth or ninth grade, but that had little to do with their choices of self-paced lessons in several subjects. Some had finished all the material pegged to their grade level months ago and had moved on, while others were taking more time.
>
> Two teachers, known as "academic advisors," were on call to field questions and ensure everybody stayed on task (the teachers also lead weekly seminars or labs to bolster the computer work).
>
> These students, and a couple dozen others circulating through the classroom for three periods each day, make up Jaguar Academy (named for the district's feline mascot). As a first-year pilot, Jaguar Academy is just part of the larger overhaul. But it's one of the district's first steps toward a grade-free future.[25]

Short of districts or schools abandoning grade levels, some programs such as Teach To One work within existing age-graded schools but offer math to, say, sixth through eighth graders in skill-driven lessons tailored specifically to each student's grasp of the skill and performance, allowing that student to move to the next level at his or her pace. Teacher/advisors work closely with students, helping some to decipher algebraic equations and others who wrestle with decimals and fractions.[26]

States, districts, and schools adopting competency-based education are committed to using online and offline lessons anchored in discrete skills and knowledge and tailored to the abilities and performance of individual students. The knowledge and skills are packaged by software designers and teachers and delivered to individual students daily and weekly. Students use software applications that permit them to self-assess their mastery of the specific knowledge and skills embedded in discrete lessons. Some students perform well ahead of their peers, others maintain steady progress, and some need individual help from teachers. Such competency-based programs are concrete instances of what has been the Holy Grail of those opposed to age-graded schools: personalized learning.

In effect, these instances of a few states, districts, and schools abandoning age-graded schools with a single teacher for twenty-five students, homework, teachers meting out grades, and promotion or retention in grade alter the traditional "grammar of schooling" by creating another kind of "grammar of schooling."

Thus, multiple ways of organizing schools, structuring teaching, and learning have occurred often in the history of tax-supported public schools. There are, indeed, different "grammars of schooling."

Note, however, even with the instances I cite, the vast majority of US schools remain firmly age-graded and practicing the familiar "grammar of schooling" in defining what constitutes an institutionally "successful" school and individually "successful" teacher and student.

Yet that "vast majority" of districts still tinker with age-graded structures. Incremental changes occur. Districts, for example, create alternative schools, innovative magnets, and teacher-run charters. They also set up new continuation schools—students who dropped out of high school enter these settings to earn their diplomas often through competency-based online programs. Nearly all of these kinds of schools, however, have been organized as age-graded schools following the traditional "grammar of schooling."

And that most difficult political and organizational process of creating different "grammars" of schooling, especially in the high school, continues in 2019. There is, for example, XQ: The Super School Project.

TRANSFORMING THE TRADITIONAL COMPREHENSIVE HIGH SCHOOL

Neither for the first nor the last time has the American high school been the target of wholesale reform. There have been multiple attempts to alter completely—or in the words of one philanthropist, "reimagine"—the century-old institution.

The original comprehensive high school in the 1920s, with its multiple curriculum tracks, catered to a broad range of student interests and aptitudes. It was an innovation that "transformed" the previous elite high school of the 1890s where all students took the same academic courses. Since then, repeated efforts to reform the reform have occurred.

In the 1950s, for example, former Harvard University president James Bryce Conant called for an overhaul of the high school; a decade later, attacks on the sterile comprehensive high school produced a flurry of alternative and "free" high schools, including the innovation by Principal Frank Brown at Melbourne High School (Brevard County, Florida).

Brown reorganized this comprehensive high school into five phases or levels. Students were grouped by achievement on standardized tests rather than age and independent study was made an option for many students. After Brown left the principalship a few years later, the concept lingered on elsewhere in the county and in scattered high schools across the nation. It was and is an anomaly.[27]

In the 1970s and 1980s, critiques of the comprehensive high school stirred reformers anew. Ted Sizer launched the Coalition of Essential Schools (see above) in the mid-1980s with its "common principles," and hundreds of those high schools flowered across the nation.

And in the 1990s, a serious effort to alter the comprehensive high school began with small high schools in big cities like Deborah Meier's Central Park East Secondary school, the Urban Academy, and others. Then the Bill and Melinda Gates Foundation poured over $2 billion into creating small high schools.[28]

Yet "small high schools" such as MetWest and Social Justice Humanitas Academy persist even after donor money has dried up. While school size may not be associated with improved academic performance, small schools (five hundred or fewer students) have personalized the experiences of many students heretofore ignored in large high schools. My point is that decade after decade reformers have sought to "reimagine" the comprehensive high school. It has never been frozen in amber.[29]

Every attempt to "transform" the comprehensive high school since the 1920s came up with solutions only to see that a subsequent generation of reformers supplied different answers to the same questions.

Knowing that history and the particulars of past efforts to "transform" the high school is essential to the current generation of reformers. And this is where XQ: The Super School Project enters the century-long cascade of high school reforms.

Established by Laureen Powell Jobs (widow of Steve Jobs, the cofounder of Apple), the Super School Project launched a multimillion dollar competition in 2015. Powell said:

> The system was created for the work force we needed 100 years ago. Things are not working the way we want it to be working. We've seen a lot of incremental changes over the last several years, but we're saying, 'Start from scratch.'"[30]

Seven hundred teams of educators from all states submitted proposals to "reimagine" the comprehensive high school and receive cash for their innovations. A year later, the XQ Institute announced that ten teams had won $10 million each over five years to create their "reimagined" high school. Subsequent grants have been made since 2016, and there are now nineteen teams promised $136 million. The high schools range from ones that offer four years of computer science to ones working with the homeless and others that are wholly project-based learning. Three of the winners had track records in that they had already operated schools such as Summit School charters based in California and the Leadership Academy in Washington, DC. By 2019, three of these winning schools—none of the above—had died and gone to reform heaven. Whether the Super School Project will spill over to regular high schools and alter their structures and view of "success" and "failure" is too early to say. If the past were any guide to the future, Las Vegas oddsmakers would bet against XQ reinventing the American high school.[31]

Most high school reformers in the twentieth and twenty-first centuries envisioned that pilot projects, innovative programs, and lighthouse schools would get adopted and gradually reshape conventional high schools across the nation. Other reformers imagined a grand change—a transformation—within a short time (e.g., one to three years), overturning the existing organization. That rarely happened, since major curricular and organizational changes in comprehensive high schools, when they do occur, having stable staff and resources often take five to ten years. Incremental changes to existing structures, veteran reformers knew, were the norm.

In most instances, civic, business, and donor leaders saw these models slowly changing the existing twenty-four thousand traditional high schools much like incoming waves eroding a rocky shoreline. The structures of the age-graded high school and its companion "grammar of schooling" would dwindle away and be replaced by hybrids of the old and new versions of teaching and learning, containing expanded notions of organizational "success." Such changes have indeed occurred but rarely.[32]

The question, then, of whether innovative charter schools, magnets, and alternative high schools (including those richly funded by XQ) can move from the periphery to the center of schooling, from inhabiting a niche in a system to becoming an entirely new system, remains open. Surely changes have occurred in the nation's high schools over the past century. And just as surely, age-graded structures, the "grammar of schooling," and a constricted view of institutional "success" remain in place in nearly all the nation's schools. Based upon the historical record of age-graded schools with their "grammar of schooling" continuing to being typical, holding one's breath for major or rapid changes in high schools to go viral would be unwise.

Which brings me to the final "So what?" of this book. Are the two schools I described extreme outliers that cannot be duplicated? Or are they possible models for many regular high schools to copy? I asked these questions previously and answered the first with a "no" and the second with a "yes." Here I elaborate on those answers.

ALTERING THE AGE-GRADED SCHOOL AND ITS "GRAMMAR OF SCHOOLING": THE DREAM AND REALITY

Reformers dream of ridding schools of the asphyxiating "grammar of schooling," replacing it with "ambitious teaching" and "deep learning." They dream of applying technological devices to personalize learning. They dream of students going deeply into content, grasping tough concepts, and applying problem-solving skills to answer complex questions. They dream of making schools both excellent and equitable.

Some of those dreams have been realized in scattered rural, suburban, and urban elementary and secondary schools across the country. I say "scattered" because they are few and spread out, a tiny sliver of the entire decentralized system of US schooling.

Any reformer eager to tackle the age-graded school and its "grammar of schooling" must keep in mind that there are nearly one hundred thousand schools located in thirteen thousand-plus school districts in fifty states. States govern districts. They allow local school boards within the state to make policy for students, teachers, and administrators within their boundaries. There is no federal superintendent of schools, just as there is no national ministry of education.

Certainly, as I have noted previously, the age-graded school and its "grammar of schooling" have incrementally changed over time. Where once there were bolted-down desks, movable classroom furniture is the norm. Large group instruction occurs in elementary school classrooms, but the dominant pattern today is a mix of small groups, partner activities, individual work, and whole group instruction. Where there were once fifty-plus students in classrooms in many classrooms, there are now twenty-five-plus. Instead of daily forty-minute periods in high school schedules, many schools have blocks of time when teachers meet with students for sixty to ninety minutes a few days a week. In earlier decades, high school graduation requirements were minimal, but for nearly four decades, they have been ratcheted upward. Districts, schools, and teachers are directly held responsible for student outcomes, contrary to the laissez-faire attitude of state and local school boards toward accountability a half-century ago. While still the authority figure, the teacher today is better trained in content and skills, much less formal in attire, far more knowledgeable of children's behavior, and increasingly avid in working individually with students than her great-grandmother who taught in the 1930s.

Often such adopted changes preserve stability. Social scientists label such organizational adaptations "dynamic conservatism." Like many other organizations, public schools bob and weave in order to retain their "real" school structures. They "fight to remain the same." Hardly any of these incremental changes would please critics of the age-graded school who want grander, deeper, and wholesale changes, but they are nonetheless alterations that have occurred.[33]

Many times reformers have attempted to go beyond such incremental changes. These well-meaning efforts at far-reaching designs have a sad history of being shooting stars that fall to earth after a glorious display of light. Note the short life span of nongraded schools and open-space schools in the 1960s and 1970s, well-funded Annenberg reforms in the 1990s, and federally funded Comprehensive School Reform models in the 1990s and early 2000s. Then there is the current fever over "deep learning" as a way of teaching and learning that will transform what occurs in both elementary and secondary classrooms across the nation.

Deep Learning

Funded by the William and Flora Hewlett Foundation, one grantee described the instructional reform known as "deep learning":

> To counter-act the "shallow learning" that too many students experience—a focus on rote memorization, multiple choice tests, textbooks and curriculum that is a mile wide and inch deep—the foundation has been working to help schools adopt deeper learning. For students, it means they can develop content knowledge alongside the skills of critical thinking, communication, collaboration, learning how to learn and growth mindsets.[34]

Hallelujahs for "deeper learning" appear from the current US Secretary of Education and show up in state-adopted goals for K–12 systems. Donors have grasped the concept as a strategy to inspire and direct the passion of many reformers eager to alter how and what teachers teach and how students learn. One analysis of donor grants made between 2010 and 2016 said:

> Our analysis identified 107 grantees, 312 grants and more than 700 deliverables. The 10 grantees who produced the greatest number of these more than 700 deliverables include researchers (Stanford University),

public policy organizations (NASBE, CCSSO and the Alliance for Excellent Education), practitioners (EL Education, Envision Education and Big Picture Company) and media outlets (American Public Media).[35]

Whether this well-intentioned effort to reform instruction and learning in the nation's schools will produce cherries or lemons, I cannot say. But as I was writing during the summer of 2019, books, articles, and claims about "deeper learning" occurring in the nation's classrooms abound. Such acclaim is neither the first nor last time that enthusiasm fueled by donor grants created euphoric policy talk, occasional state and district policy adoption, but only limited policy implementation in schools and classrooms.[36]

In the past, these good-hearted schemes came to naught for many financial, political, and programmatic reasons. But one reason in particular often goes unnoted in analyses of institutional "failure" of these attempts at transforming the traditional public school and how students learn: dumping the age-graded school and its "grammar of schooling" is a politically complex and difficult task.

I have already pointed out that a sticky web of strongly held social beliefs encircles the age-graded schools, making the organization and its "grammar of schooling" publicly accepted as night follows day. Students listening to teachers, doing homework, taking tests, trying to get As or Bs are expected in school. Equally powerful is the abiding belief that such a "real" school holds the key to each child's future as an adult. Getting credentials from these age-graded schools supplies tickets to higher education and a comfortable income, family, and familiar American signs of individual "success"—nice clothes, car, home, cable television, and vacations. These durable social beliefs buttressed by curricular standards, tests, and accountability regulations keep the traditional school organization in place, letting most Americans take for granted this "grammar of schooling" as being the best (or perhaps the only) way to educate the next generation.

For well over a century, reform-driven policy makers, donors, and entrepreneurs have sought to rid the nation of its traditional age-graded schools and have hit a wall that few have the political savvy and will to either penetrate or climb over.

Consider Max Ventilla, an ex-Google entrepreneur who in 2013 started a chain of small private, nongraded, Progressive schools called AltSchool in New York City and the San Francisco Bay area. These ungraded "micro-schools" used project-based learning complete with individually designed "playlists," small classes, and experienced teachers. Were John and Evelyn Dewey alive, they would have enrolled their six children in AltSchool.

But running these micro-schools was expensive. The business plan (Ventilla raised venture capital of $176 million) depended upon tuition and licensed software bought by public schools. This plan didn't work out as Ventilla had dreamed, however. Spending $40 million a year and taking in $7 million in revenue is a recipe for financial disaster. Ventilla closed some of the micro-schools in 2017, brought in experienced educators from public schools, and two years later turned over AltSchool to another company.[37]

On a post to his blog six months before AltSchool closed, Ventilla said: "People often ask what I wish I'd known before starting AltSchool and I say: However difficult you think working in education is . . . multiply that by 10 [original bold-face]. Life at a startup is hard, but education is exponentially harder." To be sure, many other school reformers in the past have said such words privately. If veteran educators were in hearing range of these words, many would quietly say to themselves, "no kidding." To Ventilla's credit, few school reformers are as frank about altering schools.[38]

And that sheer complexity of schooling is why some reformers with initially grand schemes to transform the age-graded school have figured out that making incremental changes that chip away at the age-graded school and replacing the chips with slices of another kind of "grammar of schooling" is a fruitful direction to take, albeit one that may take at least a decade.

There are schools scattered across the United States, mostly in urban districts enrolling children of color, that clearly deviate from the norm of age-graded schools. These districts and schools have incrementally enlarged traditional definitions of "success" to include individual well-being while incorporating core American values of individualism, community, and equal opportunity. In doing so, they have created different "grammars of schooling."

I have described two such schools. Many more plow the same ground, albeit with different plowshares, as they slowly and purposely make incremental changes moving toward a broader vision that incorporates both institutional and individual definitions of "success."

Consider existing networks of schools such as Big Picture Learning schools (65 schools), Expeditionary Learning (152), Democracy Prep (19), High Tech High (16), Summit Public Schools (11), International Network of Public Schools (28), and Schools of Opportunity awardees (52). I am sure I have overlooked other networks and individual schools—there are a number of open classroom schools that popped up during the 1960s and 1970s that exist today as well as similar ventures begun decades earlier. But the ones I have identified have attracted media attention and researcher studies. They have also been around a decade or longer.[39]

None of these networks began with a design to swiftly replace the existing age-graded school and its "grammar of schooling." Some are charter networks that had an initial design that underwent alterations as years went by. Other networks have partnered with districts and schools that sought a different way to school their students. These schools extended the traditional measures of "success" to include individual students' well-being and their contribution to both the school and community. In such districts, these schools found protected niches where they could slowly grow, using existing resources, and enact their two-fold vision piece by piece, year by year. Did they have issues over whether their institutional and individual definitions of "success" had sufficient data to convince students, parents, and the larger public? Yes, they did.

As in the two schools I visited, institutional measures of "success" were attended to and made available to the district, state, and community. But when it came to individual measures of "success" in student well-being, completing a college degree, and post-college careers, little data were at hand. Whether these networks had collected individual measures to show goal achievement, I do not know. Overall, then, these networks remain anchored within the age-graded format but have incrementally created different "grammars of schooling." When it comes to showing publicly that individual students have achieved confidence, developed higher self-esteem, contributed to the community, and become the best they can be, they have fallen short.

These networks and individual schools sprinkled across thousands of districts, however, are still a tiny fraction of the nearly one hundred thousand schools across the nation.

My rough estimate is that far less than 1 percent are schools that depart from the age-graded model of schooling. But there is a larger fraction, perhaps 3 percent, that uses the age-graded school as a shelter for different structures of teaching and learning while maintaining a façade of a "grammar of schooling." The shelter and façade give these schools the appearance of traditional age-graded structures, but behind the façade is another "grammar of schooling" that stretches measures of "success" for both the school and individual student.

I believe that having enlarged definitions of "success" and multiple "grammars of schooling" are worthwhile goals for US schooling. Why?

Having institutional and individual definitions of "success" is both historically fitting and difficult to achieve. "Fitting" in two senses. Americans juggle multiple definitions of "success" as they grow up, enter the workplace, have families, and enter middle age. Competing to get noticed and approved, becoming financially comfortable, and being a winner still dominate American culture, but competing views of individual "success" drawn from religious teachings and growing self-awareness (e.g., being a "good" person, helping others) become personal goals beyond acquiring wealth. In short, within the larger culture, there are (and have been) rival conceptions of individual "success." Since public schools have mirrored the larger society's ideas and movements, having more than one way to define "success" is fitting.

Moreover, schools have historically contained more than one version of individual "success." Recall that the Progressive reforms bridging the late nineteenth and early twentieth centuries stressed the importance of the "whole child," student decision-making, and individual well-being. Those ideas were embedded in curricular and instructional reforms across decades (i.e., open classrooms, individualized instruction, social-emotional skills, and personalized learning)—even when dominant school reforms in the 1950s focused on more math and science to compete with the Soviet Union during the Cold War and since the mid-1980s, thus binding schools to the economy. "Learning by doing," student agency, and the "whole child" persisted over time in protected niches within public schools. But these views of individual "success" embedded in pedagogical Progressivism occupied the periphery, not the center of public schooling.

The powerful web of popular beliefs in "real" schools as age-graded has shoved Progressive pedagogy with its concern for the psychological, emotional, physical, and social totality of a child and belief in student decision-making to the outer circle of district programs. Moreover, because of class size and teaching load, the demands of Progressive pedagogy upon teachers creating instructional materials and working individually with students far exceed the normal school day. There is only so much teachers can do if they want a life outside of the 8 a.m. to 3 p.m. school day.

While that emphasis on Progressive teaching and learning has slipped in and out of public view as other reform movements swept over American schools, SJHA and MetWest High School, along with the networks I mentioned above, have resurfaced that Progressive impulse for individual children and student agency. That impulse has moved the current reform center of gravity a few inches away from nearly four decades of total focus on what schools can do for society, i.e., strengthen the economy. These schools have joined institutional and individual definitions of "success" within the structures of the age-graded school while, at the same time, altering the familiar "grammar of schooling" into something quite different. Such instances reaffirm anew that there is not just one way to school children and youth.

Today's ubiquitous age-graded school arose from a choice that policy makers made nearly two centuries ago. It was (and is) the "one best system" that has characterized US schools since the late nineteenth century. There are—and have been—other ways to organize schools.

In ungraded schools groups of mixed-age students learn at different paces the prescribed content or a curriculum jointly constructed by teachers and students. Schools that require students to work in community internships for part of the school day structure their classes and daily schedule differently. Cyber schools where students learn at home or at different sites are other ways of organizing a school. And there are combinations of all of these.

Each of these ways of operating schools contains a "grammar of schooling," that is, a theory of learning and teaching, implicit and explicit rules to follow, and an organizational framework that shapes the social and individual behavior of both children and teachers in schools and classrooms. Each way of organizing schools transmits core American values. Each of these schools has individual and institutional definitions of "success" and "failure" that both mirror existing definitions and, in some instances, enlarge traditional ones.

Historically, then, many ways of organizing schools have existed. Thus, multiple "grammars of schooling" have been around. Yet age-graded structures continue to dominate school organization.

But my critique of age-graded schools is not a preface for a call to eliminate all such organizations. I do not wish to see age-graded schools replaced wholesale either by fiat or by retail choice. The history of school reform has taught me that trying to transform public schools by mandate or "reimagination" is a fool's errand.

Seekers of transformed schools ignore that charters and regular schools are just fine for many students and their parents. High-achieving age-graded schools in cities, suburbs, exurbs, and rural communities where both children and parents are satisfied should continue—especially when tax-supported public schools are expected in a democracy to serve all children.

In many urban districts where children of color are the majority, there are schools such as the Knowledge Is Power Program (KIPP), Success Academies, Core Knowledge, and International Baccalaureate schools. These schools attract parents who want the familiar "grammar of schooling" to continue since they believe in them as "real" schools, or such places have already worked for them and now want that experience for their daughters and sons. Until these parents become dissatisfied with the schooling their children receive, these age-graded organizations will remain the places that the majority of US students attend.

What I seek is more variation in organizing schools, more choices for alternative arrangements, more "grammars of schooling." MetWest, SJHA, and the numerous networks of schools mentioned above build different "grammars of schooling" behind the façade and under the umbrella of the traditional age-graded school. Donors willing to invest in different, incremental ways of putting a school together and local districts that seek different ways for children to learn do exist. Parents and teachers have joined hands to create schools that depart from the familiar model. Private schools that have public versions like Waldorf and Montessori add to the mix of different ways to run schools. More such slow cooking of a school with a different kind of "grammar" is necessary in a diverse nation. It is essential that core American values are transmitted to the next generation and that definitions of "success" compete with one another, acknowledging openly that there is no certainty on how to best achieve desired results for a highly diverse population in an institution with multiple goals. Remember the overall purpose of tax-supported public schools is to both conserve and change. Contradictory as it sounds, that is precisely what these schools have done for nearly two centuries.

So I support far more alternatives to traditional age-graded organizations than exist now knowing full well that the age-graded school and its distinctive "grammar of schooling" will not fade away.[40]

For those readers who have reached this final page, you have my answer to the "So what" question.

NOTES

INTRODUCTION

1. The schools were Grimke Elementary School, Banneker and Garnet-Patterson Junior High Schools, and Cardozo High School in Washington, DC. Grimke Elementary School closed in the 1980s; Banneker Junior High School was converted into a magnet high school called Banneker Academic High School in 1980. Cardozo High School, the original site for the project, is now a grade seven through twelve secondary school.
2. *Cardozo Project in Urban Teaching, 1965–1966* (Washington, DC: Model School Division, Public Schools of the District of Columbia, 1965); Larry Cuban, *To Make a Difference: Teaching in the Inner City* (New York: Free Press, 1970).
3. Office of Staff Development, *The Urban Teacher Corps: Description and Philosophy, 1963–1968* (Washington, DC Public Schools, 1968).
4. Bethany Rogers, "'Better' People, Better Teaching: The Vision of the National Teacher Corps, 1965–1968," *History of Education Quarterly* 49, no. 3 (2009): 347–72; Wikipedia, "Teacher Corps," https://en.wikipedia.org/wiki/Teacher_Corps.

   Between 1963 and 1967, Cardozo High School faculty had a handful of white teachers—less than 10 percent of the faculty. Since then, percentages of nonminority teachers ebbed and flowed, seldom rising to over 15–20 percent of the faculty. Those figures changed slowly as Hispanic students entered Cardozo. Not until the Chancellor of the DC schools determined that the entire administration and faculty of a school would be replaced did more white and Hispanic teachers join the faculty. Reconstitution occurred twice at Cardozo, in 2008 and 2013.

   Emma Brown, "With 'Reconstitution,' School Officials Hope for School Turnaround," *Washington Post*, June 10, 2013, https://bitlylink.com/yxxVg; Greg Toppo and Mark Nichols, "Decades After Civil Rights Gains, Black Teachers a Rarity in Public Schools," *USA Today*, February 1, 2017, https://www.usatoday.com/story/news/nation-now/2017/02/01/decades-after-civil-rights-gains-black-teachers-rarity-public-schools/96721684/; "DCPS Fast Facts, 2017–2018," https://dcps.dc.gov/sites/default/files/dc/sites/dcps/publication/attachments/DCPS%20Fast%20Facts%202017-18.pdf.

5. In visiting Cardozo High School May, 19–21, 2014, I examined the *Purple Wave* (annual high school yearbook) for 2008 and 2009—many yearbooks were missing—and found that in the academic subjects, about one-third of the teachers were white.

6. The Cline Report is unpublished and in the author's possession.

7. Larry Cuban, "The 'Failure' of New Technologies to Transform Traditional Teaching in the Past Century," in *Failure Up Close*, ed. Jay Greene and Michael McShane (Lanham, MD: Rowan and Littlefield, 2018), 17–34.

8. Carl Kaestle, *Pillars of the Republic: Common Schools and American Society, 1780–1860* (New York: Hill and Wang, 1983); Frederick McClusky, "The Introduction of Grading in the Schools of New England," *Elementary School Journal* 21, no. 1 (1920): 34–46.

9. I elaborate on the "grammar of schooling" and its historic role in school reform in chapter 7.

   Frederick McClusky, "Introduction of Grading into the Public Schools of New England, Part II," *Elementary School Journal* 21, no. 2 (1920): 132–45.

10. According to National Public Radio producer, Neenah Ellis, there were 190,000 one-room schoolhouses in the United States, and there are now [2005] less than 400, mostly in the Western states. "One-Room Schools Holding on in Rural America," December 22, 2005, https://www.npr.org/templates/story/story .php?storyId=5064420.

    Ran Abramitzky and Leah Boustan, "Immigrants and Cultural Assimilation: Learning from the Past," VOX, July 4, 2016, http://voxeu.org/article/immigrants -and-cultural-assimilation.

11. Graduation rate figure comes from "Fact Sheet: President Obama Announces High School Graduation Rate Has Reached New High," The White House Office of the Press Secretary, October 17, 2016, https://obamawhitehouse.archives .gov/the-press-office/2016/10/17/fact-sheet-president-obama-announces -high-school-graduation-rate-has.

12. David Tyack, *One Best System* (Cambridge, MA: Harvard University Press, 1974), 44–45; Robert Levin, "Age-Grading," in *Historical Dictionary of American Education*, ed. Richard Altenbaugh (Westport, CT: Greenwood Publishing Group), 11–13. For global presence of age-graded schools, see "Primary Education," https://en.wikipedia.org/wiki/Primary_education, and "Secondary Education," https://en.wikipedia.org/wiki/List_of_secondary_education_systems_by _country.

13. The text that advocated nongraded elementary schools is John Goodlad and Robert Anderson, *The Non-graded Elementary School* (New York: Harcourt, Brace, and Company, 1959).

14. For "real school" reference, see Mary Metz, "Real School: A Universal Drama amid Disparate Experience," in *Education Politics for the New Century*, ed. D. Mitchell and M. Goertz (New York: Falmer Press, 1990), 75–91; also see John Meyer and Brian Rowan, "Institutionalized Organizations: Formal Structures as Myth and Ceremony," *American Journal of Sociology* 83 (1977): 340–63. For an example of the rationale and operation of nongraded schools, see Goodlad and Anderson, *The Non-graded Elementary School*.

15. Elena Silva et al., *The Carnegie Unit: A Changing Education Landscape* (Stanford, CA: Carnegie Foundation for the Advancement of Teaching, 2015).

CHAPTER 1

1. Patrick Welsh, "Four Decades of Failed School Reform," *Washington Post*, September 27, 2013.

2. Ron Haskins, "Social Programs That Work," *New York Times*, December 31, 2014.

3. I say "supposedly" because Stan Pogrow has written about Success For All and its statistical analyses of data raising serious questions about the principal investigator's conclusions. See "Success For All Does Not Produce Success for Students," *Phi Delta Kappan* (September 2000): 67–80; "Rejoinder: Consistent Large Gains and High Levels of Achievement Are the Best Measures of Program Quality: Pogrow Responds to Slavin," *Educational Researcher* (November 1999): 24–26, 31.

Historically, three links bind institutional and individual definitions of "success" and "failure" since educational Progressives dominated school reform between 1890 and 1940.

First, there are the multiple goals of tax-supported public schools over the past century and a half. "Success" is attained when graduates are literate, prepared for the workplace, and are civically engaged. Schools serve social, economic, and political purposes, and when they do it well, they are institutionally a "success."

But schools are also judged a "success" when they boost individual students to become personally "successful." Parents want their sons and daughters to be financially comfortable and rise in social status. Public schools, then, offer a private good to parents called social mobility. So tax-supported schools offer both institutional and individual benefits.

Second, the age-graded school with its "grammar of schooling" (see Introduction and chapter 7) not only allows both individual and institutional definitions of "success" and "failure" but also maintains both definitions simultaneously. There are rules, for example, for when each student gets promoted or retained, receives test scores, takes home individual report cards, and graduates high school. Individuals get named to honor rolls and as valedictorians. Individual high performers receive awards from perfect attendance to college scholarships. For those individuals who deviate from norms of the age-graded school, they are identified for special treatment, suspended, or leave school. Schools, then, prize individual merit and well-being.

Gathering all of the above individual data generated by the "grammar of schooling" into categories also permits educators, policy makers, researchers, and parents to judge institutional "success" and "failure.

The final link between institutional and individual definitions of "success" and "failure" is numbers. Numerical measures are crucial. Historically, how much property one owned, money earned, and other signs of financial "success" were noted in a community as markers of personal "success." Calculating institutional "success" in contemporary schools looks at test scores, high school dropout and graduation rates, and percentage of seniors admitted to college.

4. Multiple goals, the "grammar of schooling," and the American love affair with numbers are the links I see historically between institutional and individual definitions of "success" and "failure."

5. David Tyack and Elisabeth Hansot, *Managers of Virtue* (New York: Basic Books, 1986); David Labaree, "Progressivism, Schools, and Schools of Education: An

American Romance," *Pedagogica Historica* 41, no. 1–2 (2005): 275–88; Tracy Steffes, *School, Society, and State* (Chicago: University of Chicago Press, 2012).

6. Raymond Callahan, *Education and the Cult of Efficiency* (Chicago: University of Chicago Press, 1962), 50.

7. Joseph Rice, *Public School System of the United States* (New York: The Century Company, 1893).

8. Rice, *Public School System*, 139–40.

9. Leonard Ayres, *Laggards in Our Schools* (New York: Charities Publication Committee, 1909).

10. Callahan, *Education and the Cult of Efficiency*, 51.

11. I use "technocratic" to mean experts making nonpolitical, scientifically based decisions. For the agendas of these "administrative Progressives," see Ellwood Cubberley, *Public School Administration* (New York: Houghton Mifflin, 1929); Callahan, *Education and the Cult of Efficiency*; Jal Mehta, "The Penetration of Technocratic Logic into the Educational Field: Rationalizing Schooling from the Progressives to the Present," *Teachers College Record* 113, no. 5 (2013): 1–40; Donald Schon, *The Reflective Practitioner* (New York: Basic Books, 1983).

12. Robert Kanigel, *The One Best Way* (Boston: Viking, 1997); Steffes, *School, Society, and the State*, 36–44.

13. Callahan, *Education and the Cult of Efficiency*, 68–69.

14. Tyack and Hansot, *Managers of Virtue*; Lawrence Cremin, *The Transformation of the School* (New York: Vintage Press, 1961); David Labaree, "Progressivism, Schools and Schools of Education," 275–88.

15. John Dewey, *Experience and Education* (New York: Macmillan, 1938), 29.

16. Cremin, *The Transformation of the School*, 295–99; Susan Whitcomb, "How Progressive Education Came to Winnetka," *The Gazette* (Winnetka, IL: Winnetka Historical Society, 2009), http://www.winnetkahistory.org/gazette/how-progressive-education-came-to-winnetka/.

17. Evelyn Dewey, *The Dalton Laboratory Plan* (New York: E. P. Dutton and Company, 1922).

18. Diane Ravitch, *Left Back: A Century of Failed School Reforms* (New York: Simon & Schuster, 2000), 285.

19. Adam Laats, *The Other School Reformers: Conservative Activism in American Education* (Cambridge, MA: Harvard University Press, 2015).

20. David Labaree, "Public Goods, Private Goods: The American Struggle over Educational Goals," *American Educational Research Journal* 34, no. 1 (1997): 39–81.

21. Eric Foner, *The Story of American Freedom* (New York: W.W. Norton, 1998); James Patterson, *Grand Expectations: The United States, 1945–1974* (New York: Oxford University Press, 1997); Jill Lepore, *These Truths* (New York: W.W. Norton, 2018).

22. David Tyack, *The One Best System* (Cambridge, MA: Harvard University Press, 1974); Diane Ravitch, *The Troubled Crusade, 1945–1980* (New York: Basic Books, 1985); David Tyack, Elisabeth Hansot, and Robert Lowe, *Public Schools in Hard Times* (Cambridge, MA: Harvard University Press, 1984).

The binary judgment of either "success" or "failure" of US schools has been central to reformers historically defining a "crisis" in public schools. The either/or dichotomy is familiar to anyone over the age of thirty-five in the United States who follows the ups and downs of school reform. What developed early in the twentieth century is another word that is located on the downward path toward failure: mediocrity. Negatively charged, the word is equated with "average," a label that few Americans would adopt for themselves. Used to describe a middle place of so-so quality, just adequate performance is a short hop, skip, and jump from failure. Like receiving a "C–" on a report card. Here is the President of Columbia University saying in 1907 that democracy should not bring Americans "down to the level of the average." Nor should Americans in a democracy accept a "doctrine of mediocrity." [Cited in David Gamson, *The Importance of Being Urban* (Chicago: University of Chicago Press, 2019)].

A Nation at Risk: The Imperative for Educational Reform was neither the first mention of "mediocrity" nor the last but left a distinct impression that it is an unhealthy place for US schools to be in a highly competitive world where the quality of education shapes how well national economies compete for global customers.

> We report to the American people that while we can take justifiable pride in what our schools and colleges have historically accomplished and contributed to the United States and the well-being of its people, the educational foundations of our society are presently being eroded by a rising tide of *mediocrity* that threatens our very future as a Nation and a people. . . . If an unfriendly foreign power had attempted to impose on America the *mediocre* educational performance that exists today, we might well have viewed it as an act of war [italics added].

23. National Commission on Excellence in Education, *A Nation at Risk: The Imperative for Educational Reform* (Washington, DC: Department of Education, 1983), 5, https://files.eric.ed.gov/fulltext/ED226006.pdf.
24. Hugh Graham, *The Uncertain Triumph: Federal Education Policy in the Kennedy and Johnson Years* (Chapel Hill, NC: University of North Carolina Press, 1984); Harvey Kantor and Robert Lowe, "Educationalizing the Welfare State and Privatizing Education," in *Closing the Opportunity Gap*, ed. Prudence Carter (New York: Oxford University Press, 2013), 25–39.
25. David Halberstam, *The Best and the Brightest* (New York: Ballantine Books, 1993); Mehta, "The Penetration of Technocratic Logic into the Educational Field," 1–40.
26. Milbrey McLaughlin, *Evaluation and Reform: The Elementary and Secondary Education Act of 1965, Title I* (Santa Monica, CA: RAND Corporation, 1974), 2–4.
27. National Commission on Excellence in Education, *A Nation at Risk*, 5.

Mediocrity, as used in describing US schooling, means inferior quality of a product and performance. It is a slur slung at those who are "average" or in the middle of a distribution—the C student or the student who finishes fifteenth out of forty in the 100-meter dash. Both tried hard but came up short in earning that "average" grade or finishing in the middle of the pack in the race.

Striving for success is as American as, well, apple pie. Some individuals will rise to the top, be successful, by dint of hard work and talent; others, equally as hard working, settling in to the middle of the distribution, will not taste the sweet tang of success. It is a meritocratic system, many say. Sure, Americans want equal opportunity to succeed, but it is stellar performance that wins the gold medal, gets the Fulbright scholarship, and receives the most valuable player award.

Every individual can't be excellent in a culture where intellectual, artistic, athletic, and creative talents are distributed unequally across the population. Especially when economic inequality, social discrimination, and who one knows continue to play a large part in divvying up success and failure in the United States. Yet calls for pursuing academic excellence in schools while maintaining equitable opportunity across the board in order for individuals to succeed rather than fail have spurred reformers time and again. And it is that constant tension between the pursuit of excellence in individual performance and valuing equal opportunity that has given being in the middle—where most of us are—a bad name. Many call it mediocrity.

28. I do not find being in the middle shameful in a seemingly meritocratic society of winners and losers. Being "average" is not an epithet. Nor is it a compliment to anyone in American culture. "Mediocre" and "mediocrity" have become particularly useful words in the rhetoric school reformers use since *A Nation at Risk*. See Todd Rose, *The End of Average* (New York: HarperOne, 2017).

29. Norton Grubb and Marvin Lazerson, *The Education Gospel* (Cambridge, MA: Harvard University Press, 2007); Larry Cuban, *The Blackboard and the Bottom Line* (Cambridge, MA: Harvard University Press, 2007).

Charles Lindblom, *Politics and Markets* (New York: Basic Books, 1980). For the story of how financier J. P. Morgan helped rescue the United States in 1895 from a depleted gold reserve by sponsoring the selling of bonds (after the US Congress authorized the international sale), see Rob Wile, "The True Story of the Time J. P. Morgan Saved America from Default," *Business Insider*, January 13, 2013, https://www.businessinsider.com/morgan-1895-crisis-and-1862-gold-loophole-2013-1.

30. Also see the New American Development Corporation in the 1990s that the federal government and corporate leaders established to design new models of schooling called "New America Schools." Jeffrey Mirel, "Unrequited Promise, *EducationNext*, 2, no. 2 (2002), https://www.educationnext.org/unrequited-promise/.

31. Stephen Holmes, "School Reform Alliance for Business Moves In," *New York Times,* February 1, 1990; Lewis Gerstner, CEO of IBM, brought together business, government, and educational leaders in a series of national "summits" during the 1990s. See the overview of the 1999 "National Education Summit" at https://issuu.com/achieveinc/docs/post-summit.

32. Ron Edmonds, "Effective Schools for the Urban Poor," *Educational Leadership* 37, no. 1 (1979): 15–18, 20–24; Pamela Bullard and Barbara Taylor, *Keepers of the Dream: The Triumph of Effective Schools* (Chicago: Excelsior Foundation, 1999).

33. Laura Desimone, "How Can Comprehensive School Reform Models Be Successfully Implemented?," *Review of Educational Research* 72, no. 3 (2002): 433–79.

34. David Hoff, "Big Business Going to Bat for NCLB," *Education Week*, October 16, 2006.

35. Sam Dillon, "Failure Rate of Schools Overstated, Study Says," *New York Times*, December 15, 2011; Thomas Dee and Brian Jacob, "Impact of No Child Left Behind on Student Achievement," National Bureau of Economic Research, Working Paper 15531, November 2009; Jazelle Hunt, "President Obama Signs the Every Student Succeeds Act," *NBC News,* December 10, 2015, https://

www.nbcnews.com/news/nbcblk/no-child-left-behind-replacement-focuses
-marginalized-groups-n477791.

In *Organizing Schools for Improvement: Lessons from Chicago* (Chicago: University of Chicago Press, 2009), Anthony Bryk and colleagues provide a detailed study of why students in one hundred public elementary schools in Chicago improved substantially in reading and math over a seven-year period where students in another one hundred schools did not do so. Using longitudinal evidence, the study yields a set of school practices and community conditions that promoted improvement, noting that the absence of these features spells nonimprovement.

The five features are school leadership, professional capacity, parent–community ties, student-centered learning climate, and instructional guidance. In contrast to many current reform efforts that seek improvement via one or two of these features, this study shows that substantial school improvement requires building the social organization and orchestrating initiatives across the entire topography of a school.

36. Beyond the school, Bryk et al. analyzed community contexts to find ways internal practices of improving schools are inexorably entwined with local neighborhoods. They raised serious questions about the US's capacity to improve schooling in its most neglected communities. For schools in these communities, the task of improvement is much tougher than most donors, policy makers, and practitioners had expected.

37. Frederick Hess, "School Reform at a Crossroads," *National Review*, October 19, 2015, https://www.nationalreview.com/magazine/2015/10/19/school-reform -crossroads/.

38. Kevin Parker and Bill Davey, "Computers in Schools in the USA: A Social History," in *Reflections on the History of Computers in Education*. IFIP Advances in Information and Communication Technology, vol. 424, ed. A. Tatnall and B. Davey (Berlin: Springer, 2014), 203–11; "Technology Is Transforming What Happens When a Child Goes to School," *Economist*, July 22, 2017, https://www .economist.com/briefing/2017/07/22/technology-is-transforming-what-happens -when-a-child-goes-to-school; Natasha Singer, "How Google Took Over the Classroom," *New York Times*, May 13, 2017.

39. Robert Kanigel, *The One Best Way* (Cambridge, MA: MIT Press, 2005).

40. Callahan, *Education and the Cult of Efficiency*, 69.

41. Callahan, 67–79.

42. Tyack and Hansot, *Managers of Virtue*, 121–39.

43. "Sidney Pressey," A Hypertext History of Instructional Design, http://faculty .coe.uh.edu/smcneil/cuin6373/idhistory/pressey.html; Audrey Watters, "The First Teaching Machines," February 3, 2015, http://hackeducation.com/2015 /02/03/the-first-teaching-machines.

44. Cited in Martha Casas, "The Use of Skinnerian Teaching Machines and Programmed Instruction in the United States, 1960–1970," (2002): 9, ERIC document 469942, https://files.eric.ed.gov/fulltext/ED469942.pdf.

45. Tina Trujillo, "The Modern Cult of Efficiency," *Educational Policy* 28, no. 2 (2014): 207–32.

46. Amazon's net worth in 2018 comes from Flora Carr, "Amazon Is Now More Valuable Than Microsoft and Only Two Other Companies Are Worth More,"

Fortune, February 15, 2018, http://fortune.com/2018/02/15/amazon-microsoft -third-most-valuable-company/.

47. Will Knight, "Inside Amazon," *MIT Technology Review*, July 23, 2015, https:// www.technologyreview.com/s/539511/inside-amazon/.

48. Kanigel, *The One Best Way*, 501.

49. Wayne Au, "Teaching Under the New Taylorism," *Curriculum Studies* 43, no. 1 (2011): 25–45; Joan Berman and Shari Golan, "The Effects of Standardized Testing on Teaching and Learning," CRESST, UCLA, 1991, https://cresst.org /wp-content/uploads/TECH334.pdf; Paul Decker et al., "Education and the Economy: An Indicators Report," (Washington, DC: US Department of Education, National Center for Education Statistics, 1997); National Council of Teachers of English, "How Standardized Tests Shape—and Limit—Student Learning," 2014, http://www.ncte.org/library/NCTEFiles/Resources/Journals /CC/0242-nov2014/CC0242PolicyStandardized.pdf.

50. Daarel Burnette II, "A–F School Rankings Draw Local Pushback," *Education Week*, March 7, 2017; Education Commission of States, *Rating States, Grading Schools* (Denver, CO: Education Commission of States, 2014).

51. Jennifer Steele et al., *Using Student Performance to Evaluate Teachers* (Santa Monica, CA: RAND Corporation, 2011); Linda Darling Hammond et al., *Getting Teacher Evaluation Right: A Background Paper for Policy Makers* (Washington, DC: National Academy of Education, 2011); Eduardo Porter, "Grading Teachers by the Test," *New York Times*, March 24, 2015.

52. Frank Grittner, "Individualized Instruction: An Historical Perspective," *Modern Language Journal* 59, no. 7 (1975): 323–31.

53. Arne Duncan, "The New Normal: Doing More with Less" (remarks of US Secretary of Education at the American Enterprise Institute Panel, "Bang for the Buck in Schooling," Washington, DC, November 17, 2010).

54. US Department of Education, "Increasing Educational Productivity," 2011, https://www.ed.gov/oii-news/increasing-educational-productivity.

55. Cited in David Gamson, *The Importance of Being Urban: Designing the Progressive School District, 1890–1940* (Chicago: University of Chicago Press, 2019), 10.

56. K. Brooke Stafford-Brizard, "The Case for Expanding the Definition of 'Personalization' to Meet the Needs of the Whole Child," *EdSurge*, September 23, 2018; Barbara Pape and Tom Vander Ark, "Policies and Practices That Meet Learners Where They Are," *Global Digital Promise*, http://digitalpromise.org/wp-content /uploads/2018/01/lps-policies_practices-r3.pdf.

57. Nina Lopez et al., "Competency-Based Education and Personalized Learning Go Hand in Hand," *Competency Works*, November 30, 2017, https://www .competencyworks.org/equity/competency-based-education-and-personalized -learning-go-hand-in-hand/; Susan Patrick, "A National and Global Perspective on Personalized Learning and Competency-Based Education Systems," iNACOL, Personalized Learning Summit, 2017, https://bitlylink.com/wkF2C.

58. Nichole Dobo, "Automated Learning," *Slate*, February 9, 2015. I wrote about a similar class in Ascend Charter School (Oakland Unified School District, CA), which had an updated program aimed at sixth through eighth graders who worked in different modules within a converted school library; see Larry Cuban, *The Flight of the Butterfly and the Path of the Bullet: Using Technology to Transform Teaching and Learning* (Cambridge, MA: Harvard Education Press, 2018), 107–14.

59. Rebecca Mead, "Learn Different: Silicon Valley Disrupts Education," *New Yorker*, March 7, 2016; Chris Weller, "The Founder of Khan Academy Built the Ultimate School for Kids to Work and Play Together—Take a Look Inside," *Business Insider*, October 6, 2017; David Osborne, "Schools of the Future: California's Summit Public Schools," Progressive Policy Institute, January 2016.

60. Jim Rickabaugh et al., "A School Where Learning Is Personal," *Educational Leadership* (March 2017): 22–27.

61. Larry Cuban, "Second Draft: A Continuum of Personalized Learning," September 28, 2018, https://larrycuban.wordpress.com/2018/09/27/second-draft-a-continuum-of-personalized-learning/.

CHAPTER 2

1. Monica Torres, "Americans' Ideas of Success Go Beyond Income," *Ladders*, January 25, 2108, https://www.theladders.com/career-advice/survey-americans-ideas-of-success-go-beyond-income.

An original account of the survey can be found at https://www.thermosoft.com/en-US/blog/making-it-in-america.

No data are given in the survey about who the respondents were or the methodology of the instrument. Since people reported their annual wages topped $57,000, I infer that they were already middle class. In 2017, the average annual wage was just under $38,000. See Eduardo Porter, "Catching the Wave," *New York Times*, May 3, 2019.

2. Jeff Desjardins, "How Do Americans Quantify Success?," *World Economic Forum*, February 1, 2018, https://www.weforum.org/agenda/2018/02/heres-how-americans-quantify-success.

3. Beliefs come from experiences and are assumed to be true; values derive from these beliefs. Both beliefs and values guide behavior. Quote is in Carl Degler, *Out of Our Past* (New York: Harper & Row, 1959), 1.

4. James Truslow Adams, *Epic of America* (Boston: Little, Brown & Co., 1931), 404–405.

5. Gunnar Myrdal, *An American Dilemma: The Negro Problem and Modern Democracy* (New York: Harper & Brother, 1944), xliv.

6. Robert Bellah et al., *Habits of the Heart* (Berkeley, CA: University of California Press, 1995), viii.

7. Cotton Mather, "A Christian at His Calling, 1701," in *The American Gospel of Success*, ed. Moses Rischin (Chicago: Quadrangle Books, 1965), 23–30.

8. Benjamin Franklin, "The Way to Wealth," in *The American Gospel of Success*, ed. Moses Rischin, (Chicago: Quadrangle Books, 1965), 33–38.

9. Alex de Tocqueville, *Democracy in America*, Volume 2, section 2, http://xroads.virginia.edu/~hyper/detoc/ch2_02.htm.

10. Cited in Scott Sandage, *Born Losers: A History of Failure in America* (Cambridge, MA: Harvard University Press, 2005), 46.

11. Andrew Grove, *Only the Paranoid Survive* (New York: Crown Business, 1999), 6.

12. Claire Miller, "Sky's the Limit for Girls, but Boys Feel Limited," *New York Times*, September 18, 2018.

13. Jill Lepore, *These Truths* (New York: W. W. Norton, 2018), 156.

14. Patricia Cohen, *A Calculating People: The Spread of Numeracy in Early America* (Chicago: University of Chicago Press, 1982).

15. Sandage, *Born Losers*, 5–6, 17–18; this idea that individuals are responsible for their lack of "success" in society, that is, the rich are rich because they work hard and the poor are poor because they don't work hard enough or choose not to work, has been an abiding belief—often as strong among the unemployed and poor themselves—that has led to political action in the twentieth and twenty-first centuries. State and federal subsidies—often called "welfare"—for those unemployed or below a government-set poverty line since the 1930s were constantly challenged and gradually reduced, into the mid-1990s. To be eligible for government funds, one had to work or show that one had tried to find a job. These rules were linked to the seventeenth-century social belief that if you work hard, you will succeed and those who have not worked hard will fail. See Ofer Sharone, "Why Do Unemployed Americans Blame Themselves While Israelis Blame the System," *Social Forces* 91, no. 4 (2013): 1429–50; Matthew Desmond, "Why Work Doesn't Work Anymore," *New York Times Magazine*, September 16, 2016.

16. "The McGuffey Reader," *The American Gospel of Success*, ed. Moses Rischin (Chicago: Quadrangle Books, 1965), 45.

17. Herbert Hoover, "'Rugged Individualism' Campaign Speech, 1928," *Digital History*, http://www.digitalhistory.uh.edu/disp_textbook.cfm?smtid=3&psid=1334.

18. Sandage, *Born Losers*, 265.

19. According to *Wiktionary*, there are 319 pages of words with the prefix "self-." See https://en.wiktionary.org/wiki/Category:English_words_prefixed_with_self-. Also see Christopher Lasch, *The Culture of Narcissism* (New York: W. W. Norton, 1991); Tom Wolfe, "The Me Decade and the Third Great Awakening," *New York Magazine*, August 23, 1976; Rosemary Sword and Philip Zimbardo, "The Elephant in the Room," *Psychology Today*, February 28, 2017, about President Donald Trump.

20. Cited in Bellah et al., *Habits of the Heart*, 167.

21. Cited in E. J. Dionne, *Our Divided Political Heart: The Battle for the American Idea in an Age of Discontent* (New York: Bloomsbury USA, 2013), 70–71.

22. Gavin Francis, "Resistance to Immunity," *New York Review of Books*, May 23, 2019.

23. Dionne, *Our Divided Political Heart*, 97.

24. Cited in Daniel Bell, *The Cultural Contradictions of Capitalism* (New York: Basic Books, 1976), 261.

25. Sandage, *Born Losers*, 221.

26. Taylor Branch, *Parting the Waters: America in the King Years, 1954–1963* (New York: Simon & Schuster, 1988); Lepore, *These Truths*, chapters 14 and 15.

27. Thurgood Marshall quote is cited in Lepore, *These Truths*, 577.

28. Bell, *The Cultural Contradictions of Capitalism*, 260.

29. Alan Brinkley, *Liberalism and Its Discontents* (Cambridge, MA: Harvard University Press, 2000); Irving Kristol, "The Neoconservative Persuasion," *Weekly Standard*, August 25, 2003.

30. Michael Tomasky, "America's Coming Oligarchy," *New York Times*, April 15, 2019; Joseph Stiglitz, "Progressive Capitalism Is Not an Oxymoron," *New York Times*, April 21, 2019; Jane Mayer, *Dark Money* (New York: Anchor Press, 2017).

31. Thomas McCraw, ed., *Creating Modern Capitalism* (Cambridge, MA: Harvard University Press, 1997), 1–8.

32. Thomas Jefferson in drafting the Declaration changed the "pursuit of property" to the "pursuit of happiness." Carol Hamilton, "Why Did Jefferson Change 'Property' to the 'Pursuit of Happiness'?," *History News Network*, January 27, 2008, https://historynewsnetwork.org/article/46460.

33. Andrew Sorkin, "Buffet Still Champions Capitalism," *New York Times*, May 6, 2019.

34. Satya Padala, "Recessions Since the Great Depression," *International Business Times*, February 11, 2011, https://www.ibtimes.com/recessions-great-depression-265903.

35. Hugh Willis, "Capitalism, the United States Constitution and the Supreme Court," 1934, https://www.repository.law.indiana.edu/cgi/viewcontent.cgi?article=2254&context=facpub.

36. Congressional Budget Office, "Trends in Family Wealth, 1989–2013," August 2016, https://www.cbo.gov/sites/default/files/114th-congress-2015-2016/reports/51846-familywealth.pdf.

37. Trump quote comes from C-Span video, "Donald Trump Campaign Rally in Worcester, Massachusetts," November 18, 2015; User-created clip, December 5, 2018, Video, 0:15, https://www.c-span.org/video/?c4764764/american-dream-dead.

38. By 1821, twenty-one out of twenty-four states had dropped property qualifications for voting. Lepore, *These Truths*, p. 183.

39. Yoni Appelbaum, "Losing the Democratic Habit," *Atlantic* (October 2018): 74–77.

40. Appelbaum, "Losing the Democratic Habit," 76.

41. Frederick Douglass, "What to the Slave Is the Fourth of July?," July 5, 1852, http://teachingamericanhistory.org/library/document/what-to-the-slave-is-the-fourth-of-july/.

42. Lepore, *These Truths*; James Patterson, *Grand Expectations: The United States, 1945–1974* (New York: Oxford University Press, 1997); David Kennedy, *Freedom from Fear* (New York: Oxford University Press, 2001); Robert Wiebe, *The Search for Order, 1877–1920* (New York: Macmillan, 1967); Mayer, *Dark Money*. Presidents George W. Bush and Donald Trump received fewer popular votes than Albert Gore in 2000 and Hillary Clinton in 2016.

43. John Halpin and Marta Cook, *Social Movements and Progressivism* (Washington, DC: Center for American Progress, 2010); Estelle Freedman and John D'Emilio, *Intimate Matters: History of Sexuality in America*, 3rd edition (Chicago: University of Chicago Press, 2012); Thomas McCraw, ed., *Creating Modern Capitalism* (Cambridge, MA: Harvard University Press, 1997), 348. For recessions in the nineteenth century, see Charles Calomiris and Gary Gorton, "The Origins of Banking Panics: Models, Facts, and Bank Regulations," in *Financial Markets and Financial Crises*, ed. Glenn Hubbard (Chicago: University of Chicago Press, 1991), 109–74. For recessions since the Great Depression, see Padala, "Recessions Since the Great Depression."

44. Stanford Encyclopedia of Philosophy, "Enlightenment," August 20, 2010, https://plato.stanford.edu/entries/enlightenment/.

45. Cohen, *Calculating People*.

46. Paul DiMaggio and Walter Powell, "The Iron Cage Revisited: Institutional Isomorphism and Collective Rationality in Organizational Fields," *American*

Sociological Review 48 (1983): 147–60; Stephen Kalberg, "Max Weber's Types of Rationality," *American Journal of Sociology* 85, no. 5 (1980): 1145–79; Arthur Elstein et al., "Medical Problem Solving: A Ten-Year Retrospective," *Evaluation and the Health Professions* 13, no. 1 (1990): 5–36.

47. Herbert Simon, "Bounded Rationality and Organizational Learning," *Organization Science* 2, no. 1 (1991): 125–34; James March and Herbert Simon, *Organizations* (New York: John Wiley and Sons, 1958); Daniel Kahneman, *Thinking, Fast and Slow* (New York: Farrar, Straus & Giroux, 2011).

CHAPTER 3

1. Michael Sandel, "What Isn't for Sale?," *Atlantic*, April 2012.
2. Michelle Mark, "Meet America's Top 10 Land Barons," *Business Insider*, August 18, 2017, https://www.businessinsider.com/who-are-the-top-10-land-owners -in-the-us-2017-8.
3. Michael Lind, *Land of Promise* (New York: Harper, 2012), 26–47.
4. David Kennedy, *Freedom from Fear: The American People in Depression and War, 1929–1945* (New York: Oxford University Press, 2001).
5. Thomas McCraw, "American Capitalism," in *Creating Modern Capitalism*, ed. Thomas McCraw (Cambridge, MA: Harvard University Press, 1997), 303–50; Charles Lindblom, *The Market System* (New Haven, CT: Yale University Press, 2001).
6. Committee for Economic Development, "Regulation and the Economy: The Relationship and How to Improve It," September 27, 2017, https://www.ced .org/reports/regulation-and-the-economy; Kennedy, *Freedom from Fear*; Margaret O'Mara, *The Code: Silicon Valley and the Remaking of America* (New York: Penguin Press, 2019).
7. Harold Hyman, *American Singularity: The 1787 Northwest Ordinance, the 1862 Homestead and Morrill Acts, and the 1944 G.I. Bill* (Athens, GA: University of Georgia Press, 1986); David Potter, *People of Plenty* (Chicago: University of Chicago Press, 1954).
8. Alfred Chandler, *The Visible Hand: The Managerial Revolution in American Business* (Cambridge, MA: Harvard Belknap, 1977).
9. Jeff Nilsson, "Why Did Henry Ford Double His Minimum Wage," *Saturday Evening Post*, January 3, 2014, https://www.saturdayeveningpost.com/2014/01 /ford-doubles-minimum-wage/.
10. Robert Gordon, *The Rise and Fall of American Growth* (Princeton, NJ: Princeton University Press, 2016); Joseph Stiglitz, *The Price of Inequality* (New York: W. W. Norton, 2012).
11. Gordon, *The Rise and Fall of American Growth*; Stephan Thernstrom, *Poverty and Progress: Social Mobility in a Nineteenth Century City* (Cambridge, MA: Harvard University Press, 1964).
12. Kimberly Amadeo, "Consumer Spending Trends and Current Statistics," *Balance*, October 5, 2018; Martin Crutsinger, "U.S. Consumer Spending Surges 1% in September," *USA Today*, October 30, 2017.
13. Potter, *People of Plenty*, 167.
14. Natalie Zmuda, "Ad Campaigns Are Finally Reflecting Diversity of U.S.," *Ad Age*, March 10, 2014; Lenika Cruz, "'Dinnertimin' and 'No Tipping': How Advertisers Targeted Black Consumers in the 1970s," *Atlantic*, June 7, 2015,

https://www.theatlantic.com/entertainment/archive/2015/06/casual-racism
-and-greater-diversity-in-70s-advertising/394958/.

15. Bradley Johnson, "Big Game Punting: Super Bowl Scores $5.4 Billion in Ad
Spending over 52 years," *Ad Age*, January 11, 2018, https://adage.com/article
/special-report-super-bowl/super-bowl-ad-spending-history-charts-52-years
/311881/; William Arruda, "Super Bowl Ads Spark Controversy—Diversity,
Inclusion, and Unity Common Themes," *Forbes*, February 6, 2017, https://www
.forbes.com/sites/williamarruda/2017/02/06/super-bowl-ads-spark-controversy
-diversity-inclusion-and-unity-are-common-themes/; see YouTube ad, "Coca
Cola—It's Beautiful," video originally published on dagbladet.no/dbtv.no on February 4, 2014, https://www.youtube.com/watch?reload=9&v=VQsSET3ce54.

16. Elizabeth Weiss, "American Ads, American Values," *New Yorker*, March 14, 2014.

17. Henry Gates, Jr., "Why Are There So Many Black Athletes?," *Root,* September 1,
2014, https://www.theroot.com/why-are-there-so-many-black-athletes
-1790876918.

18. Jay Coakley, "Sport in Society: Inspiration or Opiate," in *Sport in Contemporary
Society*, ed. Stanley Eitzen (New York: Worth Publishers, 2001), 20–38.

19. US Anti-Doping Agency, "Lance Armstrong Receives Lifetime Ban," August
24, 2012, https://bitlylink.com/kGPSO; US Anti-Doping Agency, "What Sport
Means in America: A Study of Sport's Role in Society," 2011, http://www
.truesport.org/library/documents/about/what_sport_means_in_america
/what_sport_means_in_america.pdf.

20. George Kirsch, "Is Baseball Still the National Pastime?," Letter to the Editor,
New York Times, October 3, 2013, https://www.nytimes.com/2013/10/04
/opinion/is-baseball-still-the-national-pastime.html.

21. Twain quote found at http://www.twainquotes.com/Baseball.html.

22. Robert Lipsythe, *Sportsworld* (New York: Quadrangle Books, 1975), 12.

23. Scott Allen, "Richard Nixon, Vince Lombardi and Their Intertwined Year in
Washington in 1969," *Washington Post*, December 12, 2016.

24. Hannah Hutyra, "115 Vince Lombardi Quotes to Use in the Game of Life,"
https://www.keepinspiring.me/vince-lombardi-quotes/.

25. Philip Jackson, *Life in Classrooms* (New York: Holt, Rinehart & Winston, 1968),
34–35.

26. Margaret LeCompte, "Learning to Work: The Hidden Curriculum of the
Classroom," *Anthropology and Education Quarterly* 9, no. 1 (1978): 22–37.
Robert Merton, *Social Theory and Structure* (New York: Free Press, 1957).
Sociologist Peter Berger distinguished the two functions with these examples:

> Thus the "manifest" function of antigambling legislation may be to suppress
> gambling, its "latent" function to create an illegal empire for the gambling
> syndicates. Or Christian missions in parts of Africa "manifestly" tried to con-
> vert Africans to Christianity, "latently" helped to destroy the indigenous tribal
> cultures and this provided an important impetus towards rapid social trans-
> formation. Or the control of the Communist Party over all sectors of social
> life in Russian "manifestly" was to assure the continued dominance of the
> revolutionary ethos, "latently" created a new class of comfortable bureaucrats
> uncannily bourgeois in its aspirations and increasingly disinclined toward
> the self-denial of Bolshevik dedication. Or the "manifest" function of many

voluntary associations in America is sociability and public service, the "latent" function to attach status indices to those permitted to belong to such associations."

27. Peter Berger, *Invitation to Sociology* (New York: Anchor Books, 1963), 40–41.

28. Robert Merton, "The Unanticipated Consequences of Purposive Social Action," *American Sociological Review* 1, no. 6 (1936): 894–904.

29. Establishing public schools to instill these values in the young is a political decision. For centuries, newly formed nations concerned about replicating themselves have decided again and again to build citizens proud of and willing to protect the country against internal and external enemies (e.g., France and the United States in the nineteenth century; Soviet Union, China, and Cuba in the twentieth century). See Yinghong Cheng and Patrick Manning, "Revolution in Education: China and Cuba in Global Context, 1957–76," *Journal of World History* 14, no. 3 (September 2003): 359–91, http://www.manning.pitt.edu/pdf /2003.RevolutionInEducation.pdf; Jonathan Tudge, "Education of Young Children in the Soviet Union: Current Practice in Historical Perspective," *Elementary School Journal* 92, no. 1 (1991), http://www.journals.uchicago.edu/doi /abs/10.1086/461683; J. David Markham, "The Revolution, Napoleon and Education," *Research Subjects: 19th Century Society*, https://www.napoleon-series.org /research/society/c_education.html.

30. David Tyack and Larry Cuban, *Tinkering Toward Utopia* (Cambridge, MA: Harvard University Press, 1995), 85–109.

31. Timon Covert, *Rural School Consolidation*, No. 6 (Washington, DC: US Office of Education, Department of the Interior, 1930); Joseph Kett, *Merit: The History of a Founding Ideal from the American Revolution to the Twenty-First Century* (Ithaca, NY: Cornell University Press, 2013), 108.

32. Margaret Nelson, "From the One-Room Schoolhouse to the Graded School: Teaching in Vermont, 1910–1950," *Frontiers* 7, no. 1 (1983): 14–20; Carol Weinstein, "Classroom Design as an External Condition for Learning," *Educational Technology* 21, no. 8 (1981): Part Two, 12–19; Kara Turner, "'Getting It Straight': Southern Black School Patrons in the Struggle for Equal Education in the Pre- and Post-Civil Rights Eras," *Journal of Negro Education* 72, no. 2 (2003): 217–29.

33. Kett, *Merit*, 118, 120.

34. Robert Dreeben, *On What Is Learned in School* (Reading, MA: Addison-Wesley, 1968); Stephen Brint et al., "Socialization Messages in Primary Schools: An Organizational Analysis," *Sociology of Education* 74, no. 3 (2001): 157–80.

35. N. L. Englehardt, Jr., "Trends in School Architecture and Design," *Review of Educational Research* 12 (1942): Part 2, 171–77; Weinstein, "Classroom Design as an External Condition for Learning," 12–19.

36. Kett, *Merit*, 107–108, 118.

37. John Goodlad and Robert Anderson, *The Non-graded Elementary School* (New York: Harcourt, Brace, and Company, 1959); Charles Silberman, *Crisis in the Classroom* (New York: Random House, 1971); John Goodlad, *A Place Called School* (New York: McGraw-Hill, 1984).

38. David Armstrong, "Team Teaching and Academic Achievement," *Review of Educational Research* 47, no. 1 (1977): 65–86; Faith Boninger et al., *Personalized*

Learning and the Digital Privatization of Curriculum and Instruction (Boulder, CO: National Education Policy Center, 2019).

39. For a "real school" reference, see Mary Metz, "Real School: A Universal Drama Amid Disparate Experiences," *Journal of Education Policy* 4, no. 5 (1989): 75–91. For nongraded private schools, see Rebecca Mead, "Learn Different: Silicon Valley Disrupts Education," *New Yorker*, March 7, 2016; Malaina Kapoor, "A Day at the Khan Lab School," *EducationNext*, Fall 2015.

40. Lawrence Cremin, *Popular Education and Its Discontents* (New York: Harper Collins, 1991); David Labaree, "The Winning Ways of a Losing Strategy: Educationalizing Social Problems in the United States," *Educational Theory* 58, no. 4 (2008): 447–60.

41. Jal Mehta, *The Allure of Order: High Hopes, Dashed Expectations, and the Troubled Quest to Remake American Schooling* (New York: Oxford University Press, 2015); Labaree, "The Winning Ways of a Losing Strategy," 447–60.

42. Peter Robison, "Welcome to Capitalism Camp," *Bloomberg Businessweek*, November 29, 2016, https://www.bloomberg.com/news/features/2016-11-29/welcome -to-capitalism-camp-for-kindergartners; Brendan O'Connor, "Capitalism Camp for Kids," *New York Times*, May 25, 2019.

CHAPTER 4

1. Former US Secretary of Education Arne Duncan, quoted in Gabrielle Levy, "Rethinking Education in America," *U.S. News & World Report*, July 27, 2018, https://www.usnews.com/news/the-report/articles/2018-07-27/america s-schools-arent-working-for-americas-kids.

2. John Kingdon, "How Do Issues Get on Public Policy Agendas," in *Sociology and the Public Agenda*, ed. William Wilson (New York: Sage Publications, 1993), 40–50.

3. "The American Recovery and Reinvestment Act of 2009: Education Jobs and Reform," US Department of Education, February 18, 2009, https://www2 .ed.gov/policy/gen/leg/recovery/factsheet/overview.html.

4. For other descriptions of policy elites doing school reform, see David Callahan, *The Givers* (New York: Vintage, 2018). Dorothy Shipps elaborates further on policy elites steering school reform agendas in "The New Politics of Education Reform," in *Shaping Education Policy*, 2nd ed., ed. Douglas Mitchell et al., (New York: Routledge, 2018), 238–68. For a history of this phrase and similar ones (e.g., "power elites"), see William Domhoff, "Power Structure Research and the Hope for Democracy," WhoRulesAmerica.net, April 2005, http://observatory-elites.org /wp-content/uploads/2012/06/Power-Structure-Research-.pdf.

5. Callahan, *The Givers*, 89.

6. Sarah Reckhow, *Follow the Money: How Foundation Dollars Change Public School Politics* (New York: Oxford University Press, 2013); Frederick Hess and Jeff Henig, eds., *The New Education Philanthropy: Politics, Policy, and Reform* (Cambridge, MA: Harvard Education Press, 2015).

7. Diane Ravitch, *Reign of Error* (New York: Vintage, 2014); Julie Mead and Suzanne Eckes, *How School Privatization Opens the Door for Discrimination* (Denver, CO: National Education Policy Center, 2018); Daniel Rodgers, "The Uses and Abuses of 'Neoliberalism,'" *Dissent*, Winter 2018, https://www.dissentmagazine .org/article/uses-and-abuses-neoliberalism-debate.

8. Stan Karp (speech, Northwest Teachers for Justice, Seattle, Washington, October 1, 2011, http://rethinkingschools.org/news/NWTSJKarpOct11.shtml).

9. Diane Ravitch, "A Moment of National Insanity," *Washington Post*, March 1, 2012.

10. William Eggers and Paul Macmillan, "Government Alone Can't Solve Society's Biggest Problems," *Harvard Business Review*, September 19, 2013, https://hbr.org/2013/09/government-alone-cant-solve-societys-biggest-problems.

11. Leadership Public Schools now have three high schools in the network. I have in my possession minutes from board of directors meetings I attended and notes I have taken. For information on LPS, see http://www.leadps.org/; and Tom Vander Ark, "Blended Case Study: Leadership Public Schools," *Getting Smart*, July 25, 2012, https://www.gettingsmart.com/2012/07/blended-case-study-leadership-public-schools/.

12. Linda Darling Hammond, "Instructional Policy into Practice: The Power of the Bottom over the Top," *Educational Evaluation and Policy Analysis* 12, no. 3 (1990): 339–47; Charles Payne, *So Much Reform, So Little Change* (Cambridge, MA: Harvard Education Press, 2008); Joyce Epstein, "Perspectives and Previews on Research and Policy for School, Family, and Community Partnerships," in *International Handbook of Educational Change*, eds. Andy Hargreaves et al. (New York: Routledge, 1996), 209–46.

13. David Tyack and Elisabeth Hansot, *Managers of Virtue* (New York: Basic Books, 1986); Joseph Cronin, *The Control of Urban Public Schools* (New York: Free Press, 1972); Tracy Steffes, *School, Society, and the State* (Chicago: University of Chicago Press, 2012).

14. Tyack and Hansot, *Managers of Virtue*; Cronin, *The Control of Urban Public Schools.*

15. For districts hiring cadres of efficiency engineers, see Raymond Callahan, *Education and the Cult of Efficiency* (Chicago: University of Chicago Press, 1962).

16. Steffes, *School, Society, and the State*, 38–39; Edward Buchner, *Educational Surveys,* (Washington, DC: Department of the Interior, Government Printing Office, 1923).

17. David Gamson, *The Importance of Being Urban: Designing the Progressive School District, 1890–1940* (Chicago: University of Chicago Press, 2019), 40–43; Steffes, *School, Society, and the State*, 38–39.

18. David Savage, "The Long Decline in SAT Scores," *Educational Leadership* (January 1978): 290–93; Diane Ravitch, "Education in the 1980s: A Concern for 'Quality,'" *Education Week*, January 10, 1990.

19. Patrick McGuinn, *No Child Left Behind and the Transformation of Federal Education Policy, 1965–2005* (Lawrence, KS: University Press of Kansas, 2006).

20. Harvey Kantor, "Education, Reform, and the State: ESEA and Federal Education Policy in the 1960s," *American Journal of Education* 100, no. 1 (1991): 47–83; Lorraine McDonnell, "No Child Left Behind and the Federal Role in Education: Evolution or Revolution?," *Peabody Journal of Education* 80, no. 2 (2005): 19–38.

21. Lauren Camera, "Federal Education Funding: Where Does the Money Go?," *U.S. News & World Report*, January 14, 2016.

22. Michael Kirst and Gail Meister, "Turbulence in American Secondary Schools: What Reforms Last," *Curriculum Inquiry* 15, no. 2 (1985): 169–86; Larry Cuban, "Reforming Again, Again, and Again," *Educational Researcher* 19, no. 1 (1991): 3–13.

23. Charles Teddlie and Sam Stringfield, "A History of School Effectiveness and Improvement Research in the USA Focusing on the Past Quarter Century,

Part 1," in *International Handbook of School Effectiveness and Improvement*, ed. Tony Townsend (Dordrecht, The Netherlands: Springer, 2007), 131–66.

24. Janet Quinn et al., *Scaling Up the Success For All Model of School Reform* (Santa Monica, CA: RAND Corporation, 2015). Stan Pogrow has criticized Success For All for its statistical analysis over the years, questioning the claims made about the program's success. See "Success For All Does Not Produce Success for Students," *Phi Delta Kappan* 82, no. 1 (2000): 67–80. Also see Retraction Watch, "After Lawsuit Threat, Journal Forces Author to Heavily Revise Education Paper," March 15, 2017, https://retractionwatch.com/2017/03/15/lawsuit-threat -journal-forces-author-heavily-revise-education-paper/.

25. Margaret Moustafa and Robert Land, "The Research Base of Open Court and Its Translation into Instructional Policy in California," January 2001, http:// www.csun.edu/~krowlands/Content/SED610/The%20Research%20Base%20of %20Open%20Court.pdf; What Works Clearinghouse, "Open Court Reading," August 2012, https://ies.ed.gov/ncee/wwc/Docs/InterventionReports/wwc _opencourt_081412.pdf.

26. W. Richard Scott and Gerald Davis, *Organizations and Organizing* (New York: Routledge, 2006).

27. Donald Schon, "From Technical Rationality to Reflection in Action," in *Supporting Lifelong Learning: Perspectives on Learning*, vol. 1, ed. Julia Clarke et al. (New York: Routledge/Open University, 2002), 40–61.

28. David Labaree, "Public Goods, Private Goods: The American Struggle over Educational Goals," *American Educational Research Journal* 34, no. 1 (1997): 39–81; Amanda Datnow, "Power and Politics in the Adoption of School Reform Models," *Educational Evaluation and Policy Analysis* 22, no. 4 (2000): 357–74.

29. John Meyer and Brian Rowan, "Institutionalized Organizations: Formal Structure as Myth and Ceremony," *American Journal of Sociology* 83 (1978): 340–63; W. Richard Scott, *Organizations: Rational, Natural, and Open Systems*, 5th ed. (New York: Prentice Hall, 2002).

30. Madeline Will, "How Teacher Strikes Are Changing," *Education Week*, March 5, 2019.

31. Larry Cuban, *How Teachers Taught* (New York: Teachers College Press, 1993); Sam Dillon, "Teachers' Union Shuns Obama Aides at Convention," *New York Times*, July 4, 2010.

32. Jonathan Zimmerman, "Education in the Age of Obama: The Paradox of Consensus," in *The Presidency of Barack Obama: A First Historical Assessment*, ed. J. E. Zelizer (Princeton, NJ: Princeton University Press), 111–26.

33. Kate Taylor and Mokoto Rich, "Teacher Unions Fight Standardized Testing, and Find Diverse Allies," *New York Times*, April 20, 2015; Louis Freedberg, "California Leads Drive to Reverse Focus on Standardized Tests," *EdSource*, November 30, 2015, https://edsource.org/2015/california-leads-drive-to-reverse-focus -on-standardized-tests/91114.

34. Rachel Shurman, "Micro(soft) Managing a 'Green Revolution' for Africa: The New Donor Culture and International Agricultural Development," *World Development* 112 (2018): 180–92; Callahan, *The Givers*, 158–62.

35. Brian Stecher et al., *Intensive Partnerships for Effective Teaching Enhanced How Teachers Are Evaluated but Had Little Effect on Student Outcomes* (Santa Monica, CA: RAND Corporation, 2018).

36. Jason Song and Jason Felch, "Times Updates and Expands Value-added Ratings for Los Angeles Elementary School Teachers," May 7, 2011, http://www.latimes.com/local/la-me-value-added-20110508-story.html.

37. Thomas Kane, "Capturing the Dimensions of Effective Teaching," *Education-Next*, Fall 2012, https://www.educationnext.org/capturing-the-dimensions-of-effective-teaching/.

38. Marlene Sokol, "Sticker Shock: How Hillsborough County's Gates Grant Became a Budget Buster," *Tampa Bay Times*, October 23, 2015.

39. Brian Stecher et al., *Improving Teacher Effectiveness, Final Report* (Santa Monica, CA: RAND Corporation, 2018), 488.

40. Milbrey McLaughlin, "Learning from Experience: Lessons from Policy Implementation," *Educational Evaluation and Policy Analysis* 9, no. 2 (1987): 171–78; Brian Rowan et al., "School Improvement by Design: Lessons from a Study of Comprehensive School Reform Programs," Consortium for Policy Research in Education, 2009, https://www.researchgate.net/publication/234594682_School_Improvement_by_Design_Lessons_From_a_Study_of_Comprehensive_School_Reform_Programs.

41. Stecher et al., *Improving Teacher Effectiveness, Final Report*, 488.

42. For example, three states had stopped depending upon teacher evaluation policies that used student test scores (Florida, New Jersey, and Wyoming). See "This Teacher Evaluation Trend Was the Reform Du Jour. Now States Are Backing Away," *NEPC Newsletter*, July 11, 2019; Eduardo Porter, "Grading Teachers by the Test," *New York Times*, March 24, 2015; Rachel Cohen, "Teachers Tests Test Teachers," *American Prospect*, July 18, 2017; Kaitlin Pennington and Sara Mead, "For Good Measure? Teacher Evaluation Policy in the ESSA Era," Bellwether Education Partners, December 2016; Edward Haertel, "Reliability and Validity of Inferences About Teachers Based on Student Test Scores" (lecture, William Angoff Memorial Lecture, Washington, DC, March 22, 2013); Matthew Di Carlo, "Why Teacher Evaluation Reform Is Not a Failure," August 23, 2018, http://www.shankerinstitute.org/blog/why-teacher-evaluation-reform-not-failure.

43. Haertel, "Reliability and Validity of Inferences About Teachers Based on Student Test Scores."

44. Allan McConnell, "Policy Success, Policy Failure, and Grey Areas In-Between," *Journal of Public Policy* 30, no. 3 (2010): 357–59.

45. Di Carlo, "Why Teacher Evaluation Reform Is Not a Failure."

46. Daniel Koretz, *The Testing Charade* (Chicago: University of Chicago Press, 2017), 137–59.

47. McConnell, "Policy Success, Policy Failure, and Grey Areas In-Between," 354, 357–359.

CHAPTER 5

1. UCLA Center X, "Leading with Social Justice and Humanity: Jose Luis Navarro," Just Talk: Voices of Education and Justice, April 27, 2017, https://centerx.gseis.ucla.edu/leading-with-social-justice-and-humanity-jose-luis-navarro/.

2. Simone Sebastian, " Small, Unorthodox School Has Big Results," *SFGate*, June 15, 2006, https://www.sfgate.com/education/article/OAKLAND-Small-unorthodox-school-has-big-2533238.php.

3. I interviewed staff and observed lessons at MetWest on five different occasions totaling about fifteen hours. I collected print and nonprint documents about the school on site and through official publications. At Social Justice Humanitas Academy (SJHA), I spent two days and evenings interviewing staff and observing classrooms. I also collected print and nonprint media articles, accreditation reports, and videos of students and classroom lessons. The SJHA website included much information about the school, promotional videos, and student comments that I collected and used. MetWest has yet to create a working website.

4. This statement is taken from the SJHA website at http://www.sjhumanitas.org /about-us/our-vision-and-mission/.

5. See the SJHA website.

6. See the SJHA website.

7. Luis Valdez and Domingo Paredes, "In Lak'Ech: You Are My Other Me," Voices in Urban Education, http://vue.annenberginstitute.org/perspectives/lak%E2% 80%99ech-you-are-my-other.

8. Demographics come from the Institute for Educational Leadership, "2015 Award for Excellence," http://www.communityschools.org/assets/1/Asset Manager/Humanitas2015Awardee.pdf.

   See the Institute for Educational Leadership, "2015 Award for Excellence"; see also Great! Schools.org, "Cesar Chavez Learning Academies: Social Justice Humanitas Academy," https://bitlylink.com/VKAz6.

9. Principal Jeff Austin informed me in an email on June 19, 2019, that US History has been added to Advanced Placement offerings (in author's possession).

10. See Great! Schools.org.

11. UCLA Center X, "Leading with Social Justice and Humanity: Jose Luis Navarro"; Jeff Austin, "When Teachers Share a Vision, They Do Great Things," http://www .sjhumanitas.org/when-teachers-share-a-vision-they-do-great-things/; Jeff Austin (principal, Social Justice Humanitas Academy), interview with the author, February 26, 2019.

12. Social Justice Humanitas Academy, "Western Association of Schools and Colleges/California Department of Education, Focus on Learning Accreditation Manual," (2014): 56 (in author's possession).

13. Marisa Saunders et al., *Getting to Teacher Ownership: How Schools Are Creating Meaningful Change* (Providence, RI: Annenberg Institute for School Reform, 2017), 25.

14. Tina Barseghian, "What a Teacher-Powered School Looks Like," KQED News, *Mind/Shift*, May 20, 2014, https://www.kqed.org/mindshift/35819/what-a -teacher-powered-school-looks-like; Barnett Berry and Kim Farris-Berg, "How Teacher-Powered Schools Work and Why They Matter," *American Educator* (Summer 2016): 11–17, 44; Kathy Boccella, "At These Schools, Teachers Get a Say in How Things Are Run," *Philadelphia Inquirer*, July 20, 2018, https://www .philly.com/philly/education/souderton-charter-building-21-workshop-school -teacher-powered-schools-20180720.html.

   While many schools will tout one or more of these programs as their enacting of "social justice," SJHA has all of these programs in place. Although some readers may question that a school moving nearly all students through courses that state colleges and universities require as an example of "social justice," founding teacher and later principal, Jose Navarro, saw it as a prime example:

> I think it gives people choices. I teach economics and I believe, economically speaking, wealth is a quantity of quality choices. I think my students deserve to have as many choices as possible, instead of choices being made for them, either because of the color of their skin or where they're from. I also think that the more people [they] are exposed to, they tend to be more understanding. I want my kids to continue to learn and the way I see it, college is the easiest answer. And, to get to college, students need to be educated with high expectations.

15. See UCLA Center X, "Leading with Social Justice and Humanity: Jose Navarro."
16. John Rawls, "Justice as Fairness: Political not Metaphysical," *Philosophy and Public Affairs* 14, no. 3 (1985): 223–51.
17. "SJHA Dream," video, 10:03, featuring SJHA students and teachers, http://www.sjhumanitas.org/about-us/.
18. "SJHA Dream," video.
19. Social Justice Humanitas Academy, "Focus on Learning Accreditation Manual," 196.
20. Bill Raden, "A California Public School That Betsy DeVos Wouldn't Recognize," *Beyond Chron*, April 10, 2018, http://beyondchron.org/california-public-school-betsy-devos-wouldnt-recognize/.
21. "SJHA Dream," video.
22. Social Justice Humanitas Academy, "Focus on Learning Accreditation Manual," 196.
23. "SJHA Dream," video.
24. Leveraging Equity and Access in Democratic Education (LEADE), "Social Justice Humanitas Academy," a report from LEADE project at UCLA Center X, Summer 2018 (in author's possession). John Rogers and colleagues collected over 2,100 responses from students in six pilot schools in LAUSD. All six schools enroll majority Latino students.
25. Jean Merl, "A Bore No More: Humanities Classes Designed for 'Community' of Teachers, Students Draw Rave Reviews," *Los Angeles Times*, February 21, 1991.
26. Merl, "A Bore No More."
27. "The New School," video, 12:17, February 12, 2014, published by the Los Angeles Education Partnership, details how these Sylmar teachers teach in their Humanitas program and then decided to propose a separate school in a newly built high school nearby, https://www.youtube.com/watch?v=LHXHTm XPCVg&feature=youtu.e.
28. Austin, "When Teachers Share a Vision."
29. Los Angeles Unified School District, "Public School Choice, 2.0," https://achieve.lausd.net/Page/4356.
30. Kim Farris-Berg and Kristoffer Kohl, "Teachers Design and Run L.A. Unified 'Pilot' Schools," *Education Week*, November 10, 2014.
31. Los Angeles Unified School District, Office of School Choice, "Los Angeles Pilot Schools Manual, 2016–2017, 11–23, https://achieve.lausd.net/cms/lib /CA01000043/Centricity/Domain/262/Pilot%20Manual%2016-17_v3_02.03.17.pdf.

32. Sara Maldonaldo, "A Decade of Innovation: Report Shows LAUSD Pilot Schools Closing the Opportunity Gap," Center for Powerful Schools, March 20, 2018, http://powerfuled.org/a-decade-of-innovation-report-shows-lausd-pilot-schools-closing-opportunity-gap/.

33. Matt Barnum, "Do Community Schools and Wraparound Services Boost Academics? Here's What We Know," *Chalkbeat*, February 20, 2018, https://www.chalkbeat.org/posts/us/2018/02/20/do-community-schools-and-wraparound-services-boost-academics-heres-what-we-know/.

34. Raden, "A California Public School That Betsy Devos Wouldn't Recognize."

35. Institute for Educational Leadership, "2015 Award for Excellence."

36. Bill Raden, "Community School District Launches in LA," Capital & Main, January 3, 2017, https://capitalandmain.com/community-school-district-movement-launches-in-los-angeles-0103.

37. Of SJHA's fifteen academic subject teachers, I observed nine. Either my schedule or their unavailability (or both) prevented me from entering all of these classrooms. I have selected a few that represent a cross section of the lessons I observed.

   The mission of Facing History and Ourselves is "[T]o engage students of diverse backgrounds in an examination of racism, prejudice, and antisemitism in order to promote the development of a more humane and informed citizenry." See the website at https://www.facinghistory.org/.

   The poster "Protect DACA" (Deferred Action for Childhood Arrivals) refers to the US immigration policy launched under President Barack Obama in 2012 that allows undocumented children under sixteen brought to the country to receive a two-year deferral from deportation and eligibility for a work permit (the estimated number of DACA children and adults ranges between seven hundred thousand to eight hundred thousand). Plans to phase out DACA were announced in September 2017 and ended in March 2018, but court actions have delayed the end of the program as of mid-2019. See Richard Gonzales, "5 Questions about DACA Answered," NPR, September 5, 2017, https://www.npr.org/2017/09/05/548754723/5-things-you-should-know-about-daca; and Wikipedia, "Deferred Action for Childhood Arrivals," https://en.wikipedia.org/wiki/Deferred_Action_for_Childhood_Arrivals.

38. Note also that Jesus Barraza and Melanie Cervantes created the print "Viva La Mujer" ("Long Live the Woman"). See https://shop.dignidadrebelde.com/product/viva-la-mujer-print-small-2016.

39. Social Justice Humanitas Academy, "Focus on Learning Accreditation Manual," 8:

   The Social Justice Humanitas Academy's Habits of Mind are ten values that are critical for each student's personal and academic success. These are the values that all adults on our campus will uphold as well as they model the benefits of lifelong learning, academic optimism, self-efficacy, and self-actualization.

40. Social Justice Humanitas Academy, "Focus on Learning Accreditation Manual," 192:

   The math department [in 2014] has initiated the use of College Preparatory Mathematics (CPM) curriculum, which is aligned with the Common Core

Standards and Standards of Mathematical Practices. CPM emphasizes small cooperative learning groups, where students rely on their team members to make sense of math concepts. Teachers serve as facilitators in students' learning process. During lessons, students use inquiry and investigative skills to think critically about solutions for problems. This curriculum encourages students to critically think everyday they have integrated math.

41. On the previous day, all students attended a Black History assembly marking the month devoted to the history of African Americans. Marcella DeBoer had scheduled her advisory group of students to discuss the assembly and had prepared a lesson.

42. Nora Fleming, "'The Anger Pushed Me Through': On Founding a School," *Edutopia*, January 23, 2017, https://www.edutopia.org/article/anger-pushed-me -through-founding-school-nora-fleming.

43. Quote comes from Principal Jeff Austin in SJHA's application to become a 2019 School of Opportunity in February 2019. Austin's words are in response to "Criterion 4: Use a Variety of Assessments Designed to Respond to Student Needs." (In author's possession.)

44. Allan McConnell, "Policy Success, Policy Failure, and Grey Areas In-Between," *Journal of Public Policy* 30, no. 3 (2010): 345–62.

45. McConnell, "Policy Success, Policy Failure, and Grey Areas In-Between," 354.

46. McConnell, 351. My definition is a variation of McConnell's on p. 351 of above article.

47. Adjectives are located in McConnell, 352–58.

48. McConnell, 352.

49. Jeff Austin (principal, Social Justice Humanitas Academy), interview with the author, February 26, 2019; quote comes from Jeff Austin's comment on draft of this chapter, June 19, 2019.

50. Mission and vision come from the Social Justice Humanitas Academy website at http://www.sjhumanitas.org/about-us/our-vision-and-mission/.

51. Emily Cataldi et al., "First Generation Students," *Stats in Brief,* US Department of Education, February 2018, NCES 2018-421; Richard Whitmire, "Alarming Statistics Tell the Story Behind America's College Completion Crisis: Nearly a Third of All College Students Still Don't Have a Degree Six Years Later," *The 74,* April 8, 2019, at https://bitlylink.com/J2OVw.

52. See the SJHA website.

53. The phrase comes up repeatedly in SJHA videos of students and teachers, the words of founding principal, Jose Navarro, and in an interview with Jeff Austin, February 25, 2019.

Scott Kaufman, "Self-Actualization People in the 21st Century: Integration with Contemporary Theory and Research on Personality and Well-Being," *Journal of Humanistic Psychology*, 2018, https://scottbarrykaufman.com/wp-content /uploads/2018/11/Kaufman-self-actualization-2018.pdf.

54. Scholars also have investigated the invention of the commonly pictured Maslow pyramid, locating it in management studies. In fact, according to Kaufman, Maslow never used the graphic of a pyramid. Douglas McGregor, a management professor, applied Maslow's ideas to business leaders through

his Theory X and Theory Y but did not use the graphic. Todd Bridgman et al. trace the representation of a pyramid to a psychologist writing in a 1960 article in *Business Horizons*. See Scott Kaufman, "Who Created Maslow's Iconic Pyramid?," *Scientific American*, April 23, 2019, https://www.scottbarrykaufman.com /who-created-maslows-iconic-pyramid/; and Todd Bridgman et al., Who Built Maslow's Pyramid?," *Academy of Management Learning and Education* 18, no. 1 (2019), https://journals.aom.org/doi/10.5465/amle.2017.0351.

55. Itai Ivtzan et al., "Wellbeing Through Self-Fulfillment: Examining Developmental Aspects of Self-Actualization," *Humanistic Psychologist* 41, no. 2 (2013): 119–32.

CHAPTER 6

1. Tina Trujillo et al., "Enduring Dilemmas in Democratic Urban District Reform: The Oakland Case," in *The Shifting Landscape of the American School District: Race, Class, Geography, and Perpetual Reform of Local Schools*, eds. David Gamson and Emily Hodge (New York: Peter Lang, 2018), 187–222; EdData, Alameda County, Oakland Unified School District, https://www.ed-data.org/district /Alameda/Oakland-Unified; Dean Murphy, "Dream Ends for Oakland School Chief as State Takes Over," *New York Times*, June 8, 2003; Katy Murphy, "Oakland's Small School Movement, 10 Years Later," Scope Center for Opportunity Policy in Education, May 6, 2009, https://edpolicy.stanford.edu/news/articles /899; Michele Maitre, "School Leaders Say Oakland's Community School Movement Will Continue, Even Without Tony Smith," *EdSource*, May 27, 2013, https://edsource.org/2013/school-leaders-say-oaklands-community-school-movement-will-continue-even-without-tony-smith/32558.

2. Ali Tadayon, "Grand Jury Report: Oakland Unified Operating Too Many Schools," *East Bay Times*, June 28, 2018; Ali Tadayon, "Oakland Unified Scrambles to Identify as Many as 24 Schools That Could Be Closed in Five Years," *East Bay Times*, January 8, 2019.

3. Theresa Harrington, "Oakland School Board Cuts $20.2 Million from Budget, Including 100 Jobs," *EdSource*, March 4, 2019.

4. Gary Yee and Larry Cuban, "When Is Tenure Long Enough," *Educational Administration Quarterly* 32, no. 1 (1996): 615–41; Michael Fullan, *Whole School Reform: Problems and Promises* (Ontario: Ontario Institute for Studies in Education, University of Toronto, June 2001). Fullan estimates eight years for a district "turnaround," meaning improved student achievement. In my experience as a superintendent and research I have done on sitting superintendents, it takes five-plus years at the minimum and up to a decade to show positive results. See Larry Cuban, *As Good As It Gets: What School Reform Brought to Austin* (Cambridge, MA: Harvard University Press, 2010); Larry Cuban, "The Turnstile Superintendency?," *Education Week*, August 22, 2008.

5. Joel Shannon, "'When We Strike, We Win;' Tentative Agreement Reached in Oakland Teacher Strike," *USA Today*, March 1, 2019; Thomas Ultican, "Oakland Is California's Destroy Public Education Petri Dish," *San Diego Free Press*, April 4, 2018. In addition, I have tracked the arrival and departure of Oakland superintendents since the 1960s.

6. EdData, Alameda County, Oakland Unified School District, https://www
.ed-data.org/district/Alameda/Oakland-Unified.

7. Information on founders comes from documents and an interview with Michelle Deiro, current principal, February 1, 2019, and Young Whan Choi, April 4, 2019. Because the first Big Picture Learning high school, located in Providence, Rhode Island, was called the "Met," the Oakland high school was named MetWest. A brief history of the network is at the Big Picture Learning website at https://www.bigpicture.org/apps/pages/index.jsp?uREC_ID=389353&type =d&pREC_ID=882353.

8. Joseph McDonald, "Scaling Up the Big Picture," 2005, "Unpublished study funded by an anonymous foundation, 2002–2005" (in author's possession).

9. Oakland Unified School District, "MetWest High School Progress Report," for April 17, 2018, visit from Accrediting Commission for Schools, Western Association of Schools and Colleges, 2.

10. Oakland Unified School District, "MetWest High School Progress Report," 2–3.

11. The names of MetWest principals come from interviews with Michelle Deiro and Young Whan Choi, Internet searches, and videos. See, for example, Charlie Plant, "Welcome from Charlie Plant," video, 2:44, May 9, 2018, https://www
.harborfreightfellows.org/apps/video/watch.jsp?v=207148.

12. Michelle Deiro (principal, MetWest), in an interview with the author, April 4, 2019.

13. The mission statement comes from the Big Picture Learning website at https://
www.bigpicture.org/.

14. "How It Works," Big Picture Learning, https://www.bigpicture.org/apps/pages
/index.jsp?uREC_ID=389353&type=d&pREC_ID=882356.

15. See the Lafayette School District website at http://www.lafayetteschools.org
/bigpicture.

16. Principal Michelle Deiro pointed out to me that MetWest has no formal policy on teacher looping with students for four years. At MetWest, it can be two to four years depending upon the teacher. Email message to author, July 3, 2019.

17. Michelle Deiro, email message to author, July 3, 2019. See also "10 Distinguishers," Big Picture Learning, https://www.bigpicture.org/apps/pages/index
.jsp?uREC_ID=389353&type=d&pREC_ID=902235.

18. Of the ten BPL design features described above, for MetWest I will focus on the advisor/teacher role as enacted within classroom lessons, the internship experience, school leadership and organization, and assessment of work in classroom and school.

19. Michelle Deiro, interviews with the author, February 1, 2019, and April 4, 2019.

20. Great! Schools.org, "MetWest High School," https://www.greatschools.org
/california/oakland/12550-Metwest-High-School/.

21. Michelle Deiro, interviews with the author, February 1, 2019, and April 4, 2019; Young Whan Choi, interview with the author, April 4, 2019.

22. For a description of Alternative Education in OUSD and where MetWest fits, see http://www.ousdcharters.net/uploads/4/1/6/1/41611/feb_2009_brochure
_428_pm_.pdf.

23. Teachers' managing additional roles beyond subject matter expertise is a feature of many small high schools since the mid-1990s. Higher and expanded expectations of student-teacher relationships are embedded in the Social Justice Humanitas Academy and MetWest, as my observations and interviews

document. Also see Kate Phillippo, *Advisory in Urban High Schools: A Study of Expanded Teacher Role*s (New York: Palgrave, 2013).

24. In 2005, Oakland Unified School District required a capstone project for all seniors. Some schools implemented it; others did not. Not until 2014, according to Young Whan Choi, did a teacher-designed rubric to assess quality of senior projects become generally used across the district. See Young Whan Choi, "Oakland's Graduate Capstone Project: It's About Equity," *Learning Policy Institute Blog*, October 26, 2017, https://learningpolicyinstitute.org/blog/oaklands -graduate-capstone-project-its-about-equity.

25. Former Civil Rights worker Robert Moses, who was also a math teacher, founded The Young People's Project initially in Mississippi. The project aims at increasing math literacy for educationally disadvantaged children and youth. See http://nsfstemforum.edc.org/wp-content/uploads/2015/11/Milner.pdf.

26. Rachel Gross, "A California High School That Values College and the Real World," *New York Times*, June 23, 2010.

27. Katrina Schwartz, "Interests-to-Internships: When Students Take the Lead in Learning," *Mind-Shift*, June 16, 2016, https://www.kqed.org/mindshift/45453 /interests-to-internships-when-students-take-the-lead-in-learning.

28. The website describing The Hidden Genius Project is at http://www.hidden geniusproject.org/.

29. Michelle Deiro, interview with the author, April 4, 2019; see above citations of media accounts on MetWest.

30. Allan McConnell, "Policy Success, Policy Failure, and Grey Areas In-Between," *Journal of Public Policy* 30, no. 3 (2010): 345–62.

31. Michelle Deiro, interview with the author, April 4, 2019; Michelle Deiro, email message to the author, July 3, 2019.

32. Oakland Unified School District, "MetWest High School Progress Report," 5–6.

33. Oakland Unified School District, 7–9.

34. Oakland Unified School District, 10.

35. Oakland Unified School District, 13

36. Rebecca Klein, "These Teachers Have a Plan to Fight Back Against Donald Trump," *Huffington Post*, January 16, 2017.

37. I sent a penultimate draft of this chapter to principal Michelle Deiro. She read it and corrected errors I had made in describing the school and its program.

38. Wikipedia, "Black Swan Theory," https://en.wikipedia.org/wiki/Black_swan _theory.

District policy for SJHA banned the use of cell phones but gave schools latitude in enforcing the ban. At SJHA (see http://www.sjhumanitas.org/about-us /policy-forms/), the policy was

> We understand that cell phones are important for personal communication and, at times, aid in student organization and learning. However, they can also be a major distraction to your education. Should you choose to bring your devices to school, you are to use them responsibly and appropriately according to the following guidelines.
>
> - Electronic devices can be used before school, after school & during lunch/passing periods
> - Electronic devices must be silenced and out of sight during class

- Devices may be used in class for instructional purposes when **explicitly permitted by the teacher** (original boldface)
- Students leaving the classroom for any reason, must leave their device with the teacher while they are gone

Students are subject to the following consequences when they violate the Electronics/Cell Phone Policy:

- **1st Violation:** Device taken away for the remainder of the day. Student may pick up in the Main Office after school
- **2nd Violation:** Device taken away for remainder of the day. Parent/guardian notified and required to pick up device between 7:30am–3:00pm
- **3rd Violation:** Device taken away for remainder of the day & will receive 3 BEHAVIOR stamps. Parent/guardian notified and required to pick up device between 7:30am–3:00pm

39. **Additional Violations:** The device will be taken away. Student & parent/guardian must attend meeting with counselor and administrator to receive the device.
40. Daniela Gerson, "Cellphones Make a Comeback in the Classroom, with Teachers' Support," *Los Angeles Times*, November 15, 2015.

CHAPTER 7

1. Sarah Deschenes, Larry Cuban, and David Tyack, "Mismatch: Historical Perspectives on Schools and Students Who Don't Fit Them," *Teachers College Record* 103, no. 4 (2001): 525–47.
2. Sara Davidson, "The High School Revolutionaries," *New York Times*, April 26, 1970.
3. Allan McConnell, "Policy Success, Policy Failure, and Grey Areas In-Between," *Journal of Public Policy* 30, no. 3 (2010): 357–59.
4. I have added "robust" to adjectives that Allan McConnell uses to indicate that there are decided strengths to "success" in face of continuing conflicts that are important to note; "resilience" in this context means that problems have been solved, changes still occur, adaptations are made, and "success" is maintained. See Louis Freedberg, "Drive to Cap Charter School Growth Stalls," *EdSource*, June 3, 2019, https://edsource.org/2019/drive-to-cap-california-charter-school-growth-stalls/613242; Natasha Singer, "Class DoJo: A Tale of Two Classrooms," *New York Times*, November 17, 2014.
5. Bethany Rogers, "'Better People, Better Teaching': The Vision of the National Teacher Corps," *History of Education Quarterly* 49, no. 3 (2009): 347–72.
6. The phrase "real school" comes from Mary Metz, "Real School: A Universal Drama amid Disparate Experiences," *Journal of Education Policy* 4, no. 5 (1989): 75–91.
7. David Tyack and Larry Cuban, *Tinkering Toward Utopia* (Cambridge, MA: Harvard University Press, 1995), 85.
8. Decades ago, Seymour Sarason called my attention to the taken-for-granted "regularities" that dominate public schools in *The Culture of the School and the Problem of Change* (Boston: Allyn and Bacon, 1971).
9. The Carnegie Foundation for the Advancement of Teaching, "What Is the Carnegie Unit?," August 4, 2014, https://www.carnegiefoundation.org/faqs/carnegie-unit/.

10. Megan Brennan, "Seven in 10 Parents Satisfied with Their Child's Education," *Gallup News Alerts*, August 27, 2018, https://news.gallup.com/poll/241652/seven -parents-satisfied-child-education.aspx; David Cohen and Barbara Neufeld, "The Failure of High Schools and the Progress of Education," *Daedalus* 110, no. 3 (1981): 69–89; Paul Tough, *The Years That Matter the Most: How College Makes or Breaks Us* (New York: Houghton Mifflin Harcourt, 2019).

11. Frank Grittner, "Individualized Instruction: An Historical Perspective," *Modern Language Journal* 59, no. 7 (1975): 323–33; Wikipedia, "Dalton Plan," https:// en.wikipedia.org/wiki/Dalton_Plan.

12. William Reese, *The Origins of the American High School* (New Haven, CT: Yale University Press, 1999).

13. Cohen and Neufeld, "The Failure of High Schools and the Progress of Education," 75.

14. National Commission on Excellence in Education, *A Nation at Risk: The Imperative for Educational Reform* (Washington, DC: Department of Education, 1983), https://www2.ed.gov/pubs/NatAtRisk/risk.html.

15. Jack Schneider, *Excellence for All* (Nashville, TN: Vanderbilt University Press, 2011). Historians of education David Tyack and Diane Ravitch, from contrasting perspectives, have documented reforms of the late twentieth century in their books. See Tyack and Cuban, *Tinkering Toward Utopia*; and Diane Ravitch, *Left Back: A Century of Failed School Reform* (New York: Simon & Schuster, 2000).

 Deep learning has been defined in many ways. The Hewlett Foundation, an advocate for this approach to reforming schools, defines it by six competencies that students must have to "achieve at high levels."

 • Master core academic content.
 • Think critically and solve complex problems.
 • Work collaboratively.
 • Communicate effectively.
 • Learn how to learn.
 • Develop academic mindsets.

16. See "Deeper Learning Competencies," Hewlett Foundation, April 2013, https:// hewlett.org/wp-content/uploads/2016/08/Deeper_Learning_Defined__April _2013.pdf.

17. These principles are listed at the Coalition of Essential Schools' website at http://essentialschools.org/common-principles/.

18. For the description of the $18.7 million grant from the Bill and Melinda Gates Foundation in 2003, see "Coalition of Essential Schools Receives $18.7 million from Bill & Melinda Gates Foundation," https://www.gatesfoundation.org /Media-Center/Press-Releases/2003/09/Coalition-of-Essential-Schools -Receives-Grant.

19. See, for example, Kathleen Cushman, "Behavior in a Thoughtful School: The Principle of Decency," *Horace*, October 12, 1991, http://essentialschools.org /horace-issues/behavior-in-a-thoughtful-school-the-principle-of-decency/.

20. Dirk Zuschlag, "R.I.P. Coalition of Essential Schools," *Green and Write*, February 16, 2017, Michigan State University College of Education, https://edwp.educ .msu.edu/green-and-write/2017/r-i-p-coalition-of-essential-schools/.

21. For the conservative and progressive politics surrounding outcome-based education, see Peter Shrag, "The New School Wars: How Outcome-Based Education Blew Up," *American Prospect*, Winter 1995. For a roundup of outcome-based education and examples from districts, see Ron Brandt, "An Overview of Outcome-Based Education," ASCD, *Curriculum Handbook*, 1998. Competency-based programs and tests enjoyed a brief moment in the gleaming spotlight of reform in the 1970s. See also William Spady, "Competency Based Education: A Bandwagon in Search of a Definition," *Educational Researcher* 6, no. 1 (1977): 9–14.

22. Christopher Sessums, "What Is OBE: Unboxing Outcomes-Based Education," *DL2*, September 26, 2016, https://www.d2l.com/blog/what-is-obe/; Kyle Spencer, "A New Kind of Classroom: No Grades, No Failing, No Hurry," *New York Times*, August 11, 2017.

23. National Conference of State Legislatures, "What Is Competency-Based Education," September 8, 2017, http://www.ncsl.org/research/education/competency.aspx; Julia Freeland, "New Hampshire's Journey Toward Competency-Based Education," *EducationNext*, February 1, 2015, https://www.educationnext.org/new-hampshires-journey-toward-competency-based-education/.

24. Christina Quattrocchi, "How Lindsay Unified Redesigned Itself from the Ground Up," *EdSurge*, June 17, 2014, https://www.edsurge.com/news/2014-06-17-how-lindsay-unified-redesigned-itself-from-the-ground-up; for a promotional video of the district, see "Competency-Based Education: Engaging Students and Personalizing Learning," *ExcelinEd*, Video, 2:30, https://www.youtube.com/watch?time_continue=1&v=MRtd4lrXn_A.

25. Chris Berdik, "What's School Without Grade Levels?," *The Hechinger Report*, July 30, 2018.

26. Tim Newcomb, "Teach to One: Inside the Personalized Learning Program That Bill Gates Calls 'The Future of Math,'" *The 74*, June 16, 2016, https://www.the74million.org/article/teach-to-one-inside-the-personalized-learning-program-that-bill-gates-calls-the-future-of-math/.

27. James Conant, *The American High School Today* (New York: McGraw-Hill, 1959); Allan Graubard, "The Free School Movement," *Harvard Educational Review* 42, no. 3 (1972): 351–73; Richard Doremus, "Whatever Happened to . . . Melbourne High School?," *Phi Delta Kappan* 63, no. 7 (1982): 480–82.

28. Peter Meyer, "New York City's Small-Schools Revolution," *EducationNext*, May 12, 2015; Jack Schneider, "Small Schools: The Edu-Reform Failure That Wasn't," *Education Week*, February 9, 2016; Los Angeles Times Editorial Board, "Gates Foundation Failures Show Philanthropists Shouldn't Be Setting America's Public School Agenda," *Los Angeles Times*, June 1, 2016.

29. Tyack and Cuban, *Tinkering Toward Utopia*; Ravitch, *Left Back*.

30. Jennifer Medina, "Laurene Powell Jobs Commits $50 Million to Create New High Schools," *New York Times*, September 14, 2015.

31. Alexander Russo, "Will the XQ 'Super Schools' Live Up to Their Name? *EducationNext*, 2017; Matt Barnum, "Laurene Powell Jobs Has Given Millions to Reinvent the American High School. Is It Working?," *Chalkbeat*, June 27, 2019.

32. National Center for Education Statistics, "Fast Facts," 2016, https://nces.ed.gov/fastfacts/display.asp?id=84.

33. Donald Schon, *Beyond the Stable State* (New York: Norton, 1973), 32.

34. Phil Gonring and Brinnie Ramsay, "Building the Deeper Learning Field, Grant by Grant," Hewlett Foundation, November 12, 2016, https://hewlett.org /building-deeper-learning-field-grant-grant/.

35. NASBE is National Association of State School Boards; CCSSO is Council of Chief State School Officers.

36. See Jal Mehta and Sarah Fine, *In Search of Deeper Learning: The Quest to Remake the American High School* (Cambridge, MA: Harvard University Press, 2019). For a deep analysis of Hewlett's role in pushing "deeper learning," see "Hewlett-Packard and the Pitfalls of 'Deeper Learning' in an Internet of Things World," *Wrench in the Gears*, July 7, 2019, https://wrenchinthegears.com/.

37. Tony Wan, "AltSchool Gets an Alt-Name and New Leadership," *EdSurge*, June 28, 2019, https://bitlylink.com/YMlwt.

38. Max Ventilla, "AltSchool in 2019: Progress and Lessons Learned," January 25, 2019, *Altitude Learning*, https://www.altschool.com/post/altschool-in-2019 -progress-and-lessons-learned.

39. See Big Picture Learning, https://www.bigpicture.org/; Expeditionary Learning is now called EL—see https://eleducation.org/impact/school-design/by-the -numbers; Democracy Prep, http://democracyprep.org/; High Tech High, https://www.hightechhigh.org/; Internationals Network, http://international snps.org/; Schools of Opportunity, http://schoolsofopportunity.org/; Summit Public Schools, https://summitps.org/.

40. For mission and schools, see Alliance for Public Waldorf Education, http:// www.allianceforpublicwaldorfeducation.org/our-mission/; Montessori Public is a website that includes its mission, the number of public Montessori schools, and a description of the approach—see https://www.montessoripublic.org /public-montessori/.

ACKNOWLEDGMENTS

Every book has its creation story. For this one, there is nothing exotic or path breaking. In my career as a teacher, administrator, and professor since 1955 (I retired in 2001 but continued to teach and write), I have spent my professional time in researching and writing on questions about educational policy and practice that tugged at me for answers. For that I am most grateful. But now as the sun is setting on my career, I wanted to pull disparate threads together from my earlier writings that touched larger issues in the journey that educational policy takes toward the classroom.

In *Chasing Success and Confronting Failure in American Public Schools*, I wanted to answer a question that has bothered me for a long time. Given my knowledge of the history of efforts to alter what occurs in schools and classrooms, why has the constant refrain of school reform failing again and again and schools never changing sounded off kilter? A few years ago, I had a chance to explore the question of the supposed failure of school reform and lack of change in US schools when Jay Greene and Michael McShane asked me to do a chapter in their edited collection called *Failure Up Close: What Happens, Why It Happens, and What We Can Learn from It.*

Writing that chapter got me thinking about the dominance of current policy definitions of "success" and "failure" in public schools. So I began asking myself a bunch of questions: Had those policy definitions been around for just the past few years? Decades? Centuries? Had these notions of "success" and "failure" changed over time? Where did they come from? How and why did tax-supported public schools adopt these definitions of "success" and "failure"? What do these definitions look like when applied to actual schools and classrooms? And, finally, can contemporary definitions of "success" be stretched to encompass other goals for teachers and students in public schools?

Like much of my previous writings, these questions started on the busy four-lane highway of reform-driven policy making and then hopped on two-way roads and eventually one-way streets of educational practice to see what happened to those adopted policies when they finally appeared in schools and classrooms. Some reforms stuck; some morphed in familiar ways of running schools and teaching. And some disappeared. The above questions bugged me enough to travel anew this familiar path of policy-to-practice.

Those questions spurred me to send Harvard Education Press yet another proposal to write the book you have in hand. I have answered these and related questions in this book, partially scratching the itch that got me this far. I say "partially" because I am uncertain whether what I have written here misses questions about stability and change in US schools that I should have asked or errs in what I have concluded. As I said above, the creation story for this book is neither exotic nor path breaking. It is what it is.

And for getting this book written and then published, I have many people to thank. The anonymous reviewers who recommended publishing this book gave me valuable suggestions of further readings about success and failure in American culture beginning in the colonial era and continuing to the present. A special tip of the hat to colleague David Labaree, who suggested I read articles and books I had not known. Those readings plus the literature suggested by the reviewers opened my eyes to both expand and deepen the argument and provide richer evidentiary support. I thank them all.

Jeff Austin, principal of Social Justice Humanitas Academy in San Fernando, I thank for inviting me to visit the school, interview, and observe teachers; and providing both time and documents for me to use in getting a clearer sense of the school's ethos.

Michelle Deiro, principal of MetWest High School in Oakland, I thank for the time she gave me in answering my many questions and granting access to teachers who welcomed me into their classrooms and to sessions where students presented their senior projects.

At both schools, I thank the teachers and other staff who let me observe their work, responded to drafts of my descriptions of lessons, and gave me permission to write about them in my blog.

Social Justice Humanitas Academy:

- Sasha Guzman
- Lourdes Lizarraga
- Brenda Arias
- Marcella DeBoer
- Robert Martinez
- Jennie Rosenbaum

MetWest High School:

- Nick Palmquist
- Shannon Carey
- Lawrence Teng
- Mike Cellemme

Finally, I want to thank Harvard Education Press's Director, Doug Clayton, for the confidence he has demonstrated in publishing my work over the years, Editor Jayne Fagnoli, and Editorial and Production Director Sumita Mukherji for their unstinting work in bringing this book to readers.

I cannot escape the expected acknowledgment that for all of the thanks I give to those who helped me on this journey, I alone am responsible for the content and conclusions I reached. While I hope that this book is error-free, I have written enough to know that is a fantasy. Any errors readers find, they are mine alone.

—Larry Cuban, October 2019

ABOUT THE AUTHOR

LARRY CUBAN is Professor Emeritus of Education at Stanford University. His background in the field of education prior to becoming a professor included fourteen years of teaching high school social studies in big city schools, directing a teacher education program that prepared returning Peace Corps volunteers to teach in inner-city schools, and serving seven years as a district superintendent.

His major research interests focus on the history of curriculum and instruction, educational leadership, school reform, and the uses of technology in classrooms. In addition to his HEP books, he is also the author of *As Good As It Gets: What School Reform Brought to Austin* (Harvard University Press, 2010) and *Hugging the Middle: How Teachers Teach in an Era of Testing and Accountability* (Teachers College Press, 2009).

INDEX

abolitionists, 57–58
academic credits, 8, 193, 199–200
academic performance, 22, 32, 76,
 112–113
 See also student outcomes
accountability
 for academic performance, 22
 attitudes toward, 206
 control over, 26
 mechanisms, 25, 104, 194
 policy elites and, 83, 101
 regulations, 24, 32, 34, 78, 91
 standards-based, 135
 teacher, 106
achievement gaps, 91
Acosta, Mayra, 172
adaptability, 93–97, 104–105, 138
Adequate Yearly Progress, 26
administrative Progressives, 12–15, 28,
 32–34, 88, 195
advertising, 65–66
advisory structure, 153–154
African American teachers, 4
age-graded schools, 190–194, 202
 alternatives to, 213–214
 critiques of, 29
 curriculum in, 77
 definitions of success and, 77
 factory model of schooling and, 78,
 184
 history of, 6–8
 progress in, 76

reform of, 205–214
society and, 79–80
spread of, 92
standardization of, 72–73
student sorting in, 186
AltSchool, 78, 209
Amazon, 30
American Creed, 42, 51
American Dream, 41, 42, 51, 55–56,
 80, 214
American Recovery and Reinvestment
 Act, 81
American Revolution, 58
American values. *See* core values
Annenberg reforms, 207
The Apprentice, 67
Arias, Brenda, 126–128
Articles of Confederation, 56
assessment, 154, 165–169
assimilation, 79
athletes, 68
Austin, Jeff, 113–114, 119–120, 135,
 140, 142
authentic assessment, 154, 165–169
automation, 79
autonomy
 individual, 55
 of local districts, 103
 school, 121, 140, 155, 156
 of teachers, 95, 96, 97
Avach, Sally, 45, 47
Ayres, Leonard, 89

Bagley, William, 18
Barnard, Henry, 6
baseball, 69
belonging, 48
Berlin, Isaiah, 50
biases, 59–60
Big Picture Learning schools, 148–150,
     152–157, 169, 171
Bill and Melinda Gates Foundation,
     82, 99–108, 199, 203
black athletes, 68
Black Tuesday, 63
bonuses, for teachers, 100
Boston Latin Grammar School, 195
bottom-line thinking, 104–105
Broad Foundation, 82
Bromley, David, 149
Brown, Frank, 203
Brown v. Board of Education, 196
Brown v. Board of Education, 20
Bryk, Anthony, 26
Buffet, Warren, 54
Bush, George W., 98
business, 61–67, 84, 98, 105, 187
business practices, 30–31, 33–34
Business Roundtable, 82

Callahan, David, 83
Cantu, Perla, 109
capitalism, 42, 46, 52–55, 57, 61–67, 85
Cardozo High School, 3
Cardozo Project in Urban Teaching
     (CPUT), 1–5, 9, 185, 187–190
Carey, Shannon, 157–161, 169,
     170–171
Carnegie Unit, 8, 193, 199–200
Carter, Jimmy, 189
Cellemme, Mike, 170, 171–174
cell phones, 183
Central Park East Secondary School,
     199, 203
CES. *See* Coalition of Essential Schools
charter schools, 7, 26, 84, 92, 98, 101,
     188
child labor laws, 195
Civil Rights Act, 20
Civil Rights movement, 20, 52, 58, 90

civil society, 48–50
Civil War, 51
ClassDoJo, 188
classrooms
     at MetWest High School, 145–147,
          157–165
     at Social Justice Humanitas Acad-
          emy, 124–131
     standardization of, 74–75
     technology use in, 182–183
Clinton, Bill, 25, 48–49, 98
Coalition of Essential Schools (CES),
     197–199, 203
Cold War, 19, 212
Coleman Report, 4
college attendance, 194
college outcomes, 141
Common Core standards, 34, 84, 98,
     100
Common Schools, 6, 98
community, 48–50, 60, 66, 68, 80, 107,
     181
community activism, 179–181
community schools, 122–123, 139, 148
competency-based education, 34,
     199–202
competition, 47
comprehensive high schools, 8, 193,
     195–196, 202–205
Comprehensive School Reform Act,
     25, 207
computers, 27, 29, 31
Conant, Jams Bryce, 203
conflicted success, 189–190
Congressional Budget Office, 55
conservatives, 17–20
Constitutional Convention, 58
consumerism, 65–66
continuation schools, 202
Core Knowledge schools, 213
core values
     community, 48–50, 60, 66, 68, 80,
          107, 108, 181
     equal opportunity, 50–53, 60, 66, 68,
          80, 84, 107, 181, 196
     ideas of success and failure and,
          42–60

individualism, 40, 42–48, 52, 60, 63, 66, 68, 80, 107, 181, 185–186
market economy and, 61–67
public schools and, 70–72, 181, 186–187
sports and, 67–71
transmittal of, 61–80, 214
corporate America, public schools and, 24–25
corporate school reform, 83–84, 86–87
corruption, 87–88
CPUT. *See* Cardozo Project in Urban Teaching
crime, 104
Cubberley, Ellwood, 28, 33
curriculum
hidden, 72, 75–76
standards, 7, 25, 34, 90, 100, 194–196
cyber schools, 213

Dalton Plan, 17, 195
data-driven algorithms, 27
David A. Boody Intermediate School, 34–35
DeBoer, Marcella, 130–131
Declaration of Independence, 54, 56, 57, 58
deep learning, 207–208
Degler, Carl, 42
Deiro, Michelle, 151, 177–178
democracy, 53, 63, 81, 84, 98, 115, 154, 198
democratic governance, 42, 43, 58, 64, 186
democratic pluralism, 197
Desjardins, Jeff, 41
de Tocqueville, Alexis, 44, 47, 48
Dewey, John, 16, 33, 182, 197
Dionne, E. J., 50
Direct Instruction, 25
discrimination, 51, 104
donors, 21, 23, 29, 83, 86–88, 90, 93, 98, 100, 104, 135, 207, 214
See also policy elites
Douglass, Frederick, 57

dropouts, 21, 74, 76
Duncan, Arne, 32, 81
Dwight School, 73
dynamic conservatism, 206–207

economic inequality, 51–53, 55–56, 58, 65, 104
economic panics, 54–55
Edmonds, Ron, 26
Educate America Act, 98
education
See also learning; schools
competency-based, 34, 199–202
outcome-based, 199–200
educational conservatives, 17–20
educational engineers, 15, 23, 88–89
educational software, 32
effectiveness
metrics, 90
of schools, 21–27, 32, 90
of SJHA, 140–144
standard of, 94, 99, 104–105, 107–108, 137–138
of teachers, 99–108
technology-driven, 30–32
efficiency
cult of, 32
measures of, 89, 90
of schools, 15–16, 19, 21, 22, 27–28, 32, 88–89
technology-driven, 30–32
Elementary and Secondary Education Act, 4, 20, 90, 91
Emancipation Proclamation, 51
Emerson, Ralph Waldo, 45, 47
emotional intelligence, 150
Enlightenment, 58–59
equal opportunity, 50–53, 60, 66, 68, 80, 84, 107, 181, 196
equity, 114–115, 198
Every Student Succeeds Act, 7, 26, 78, 91, 92, 194
Expected Schoolwide Learning Results (ESLRs), 150, 156

factory model of schooling, 78, 184
faculty demographics, 3, 4

failing schools, 20–22
  agenda for turning around, 104
  contemporary views of, 20–22
  criteria for judging, 81–108
  judgments on, 76–77
  NCLB criteria for, 26
  past views of, 12–20
failure
  contemporary examples of, 109–184
  definitions of, 186–187, 190–191, 213
  determining, 5–10
  differences in defining, 11–12, 22,
    136
  judging overall, 136–140, 187–190
  at MetWest High School, 174–181
  origins of views on, 41–60
  as personal, 46, 187
  at Social Justice Humanitas Acad-
    emy, 134–135
fairness, 115
family engagement, 154
Farinas, Priscilla, 183
federal funding, 21, 22, 79, 91–92
federal policy, 21, 24–26, 98, 100–101
  See also specific policies
Federal Reserve, 55
fidelity standard, 93, 94, 99, 138
Fifteenth Amendment, 51
football, 69–70
Ford, Henry, 64
Fourteenth Amendment, 51
Franklin, Benjamin, 44, 47, 57, 58

Garrison, William Lloyd, 57
gerrymandering, 60
Goals 2000, 98
Gordon, Eve, 151
grading system, 76
graduation rates, 21, 26, 31, 39, 41, 77,
  81, 100, 195
graduation requirements, 79, 90, 206
"grammar of schooling," 97, 184, 191,
  193–197, 202
  belief in, 208
  definition of, 6–7, 193, 213
  reform of, 205–214
  standardization and, 72–80

Great Depression, 19, 52, 55, 63, 65, 195
Great Recession, 55, 81
Great Society, 20, 21
groupthink, 21
Grove, Andy, 45, 47
Guzman, Sasha, 124

Hamilton, Alexander, 62
Haskins, Ron, 11
Hayes, Cathy, 34
hidden curriculum, 72, 75–76
high schools
  comprehensive, 8, 193, 195–196,
    202–205
  reform of, 196–197, 202–205
  small, 196–199, 203
Hillsborough County school district,
  101–103, 188
Homestead Act, 64
Hoover, Herbert, 47
human capital, 31, 82
humanism, 16–17
Humanitas program, 118–120, 122

immigrants, 64–65, 79, 109
incremental change, 8, 83, 202, 204,
  205–207, 209–211, 214
Independent Study schools, 156
individualism
  as core value, 42–48, 50, 52, 60, 63,
    66, 80, 107
  sports and, 68
  success and, 181, 185–186
individualized learning, 17
industrialization, 64
inequality, 51–53, 55–56, 58, 65, 104, 115
information economy, 98
Intensive Partnerships for Effective
  Teaching (IPET), 99–108, 188
International Baccalaureate schools,
  213
internships, 154–157, 166, 169–174,
  175, 179
Invisible Hand, 53–54

Jackson, Philip, 71
Jefferson, Thomas, 62

job losses, 81
job preparation, 98, 99
Jobs, Laureen Powell, 204
Jobs, Steve, 204
Johnson, Lyndon, 20, 91
Judd, Charles, 28
junior high school, 8

Karp, Stanley, 84
Kaufman, Scott, 142
Kelly, Aseem, 115
Kennedy, John F., 20
Kennedy, Robert, 22
Khan Lab Schools, 78
Kirkpatrick, William, 18
Knowledge Is Power Program (KIPP), 213

Laats, Adam, 18
labor unions, 58
Ladies' Home Journal, 14
LAEP. *See* Los Angeles Education Partnership
laggards, 74, 76
Laird, Mel, 70
LAUSD. *See* Los Angeles Unified School District
leadership, 154
learning
    competency-based, 34, 199–202
    deep, 207–208
    individualized, 17
    mastery, 34, 198, 199–200
    personalized, 32, 33–39, 78, 153, 197–198
    proficiency-based, 34
    rote, 13
Learning Through Internship (LTI), 154–157, 166, 169–174
Lecompte, Margaret, 71
Lepore, Jill, 45
Lincoln, Abraham, 50–51
Lindsay Unified School District, 200
Littkey, Dennis, 199
Lizzarraga, Lourdes, 139
Locke, John, 54
Lombardi, Vince, 70

longevity, 92, 95, 99
Los Angeles Education Partnership (LAEP), 118
Los Angeles Unified School District (LAUSD), 118–124
low-income students, 82, 91, 100

Mann, Horace, 6, 98
market-driven economy, 42, 53–55, 61–67, 80, 85, 186
    See also capitalism
Marshall, Thurgood, 51
Martinez, Robert, 128–129
Maslow's hierarchy of needs, 141–142
mastery learning, 34, 198, 199–200
Mather, Cotton, 44, 47
McClung, Sean, 151
McConnell, Allan, 107
McCoy, Kris, 170–171
McGuffey's Second Eclectic Reader, 46–47
media, 67, 84
Meier, Deborah, 199, 203
Melbourne High School, 203
meritocracy, 194
Merton, Robert, 72
MetWest High School, 109–110, 145–184, 203
    assessment at, 165–169
    background on, 147–149
    as Big Picture Learning school, 149–150, 152–157
    classroom lessons at, 145–147, 157–165
    community activism and, 179–181
    core values and, 181–182
    demographics of, 149
    graduates of, 179
    internships at, 169–174, 175, 179
    mission of, 150–151, 152
    school leadership, 151–152
    student outcomes, 150–151
    success and failure at, 174–181
    teachers at, 145–147, 161
    technology use at, 182–183
    test scores at, 177
micro-schools, 209
middle class, 55–56, 58, 65, 81

minority students, 82
  access to better schools by, 25–26
  achievement gaps and, 91
  effective teachers and, 100
  inequalities for, 26
  segregated schools and, 74
money, 41, 46, 194
Montessori schools, 214
multi-age teams, 78

National Education Association, 28
National Teacher Corps, 2, 4, 5,
  188–190
A Nation at Risk report, 23, 30, 81, 82,
  90, 98, 196
Navarro, Jose, 109, 113–114, 119, 134,
  142
neoliberalism, 86
New American schools, 25
New Education, 15
New Hampshire, 200
New Math, 196
Nineteenth Amendment, 51
Nixon, Richard, 69–70
No Child Left Behind, 25, 26, 78, 91,
  92, 98, 194
nongraded schools, 78, 192, 207, 213
Northern Cass School District, 201

Oakland Unified School District
  (OUSD), 147–149, 176
Obama, Barack, 81, 91, 98, 100
open-space schools, 207
organizational policy, 8–9
outcome-based education, 199–200

Palmquist, Nick, 145–147, 169
parental choice, 26
parent engagement, 154
Parkhurst, Helen, 17
patronage systems, 87–88
pedagogical Progressives, 16–17, 32,
  33, 182, 195
personalized learning, 32, 33–39, 78,
  153, 197–198
pilot schools, 120–122, 140
Plant, Charlie, 151

*Pocket Manual of Rules of Order for Delib-
  erative Assemblies*, 56
policy elites
  criteria used by, 91–99
  criticism of, 83–84
  differences among, 83–85
  judgments in success and failure by,
    82–91
  of last century, 87–89
  purposes of, 98–99
  school reform and, 81–82, 100–101
policy making, 91–99, 136–137
political action, 5
politics, 8, 87–88, 98, 105, 136, 139–140
poor, 46
poor students, 26
popularity, of reforms, 92, 95, 99, 138
postindustrial society, 79
post-secondary planning, 155
Potter, David, 65–66
poverty, 65, 104
Pressey, Sidney, 28–29
process, of policy adoption, 8, 99, 105,
  136, 137, 139
productivity, 32
professional development, 155
professionalism, 89
proficiency-based learning, 34
programs, 8, 105, 136
Progressives, 12–20, 28, 32, 33, 58, 82,
  87, 98–99, 182, 195, 211–212
project-based instruction, 36–38
property, 46, 53, 54
Public School Choice program, 120,
  122
public schools
  See also schools
  core values and, 70–72, 181,
    186–187
  corporate America and, 24–25
  critiques of, 77–80
  functions of, 186, 214
  funding of, 21, 22, 49, 79, 89, 91–92
  governance of, 206
  hidden curriculum of, 72, 75–76
  political purposes of, 79
  responsibilities of, 18–19

selective, 195
societal issues and, 24
standardization of, 72–80

Quincy Grammar School, 6–7

Race to the Top, 81, 98, 101, 105
rags-to-riches stories, 46
rationality, 58–60
Ravitch, Diane, 18, 84
Rawls, John, 115
Reagan, Ronald, 2, 189–190
reality shows, 67
recessions, 54–55
restorative justice, 115
Rice, Joseph, 13
Robert's Rules of Order, 56
Roosevelt, Theodore, 63
Rosenbaum, Jennie, 122–123
rote learning, 13
Rugg, Harold, 18
rugged individualism, 47, 52, 63
Russell, James, 14

salaries
    education levels and, 194
    teacher, 100
Sandage, Scott, 47
Sandel, Michael, 61
Sayers, Gale, 69
Schlesinger, Arthur, Jr., 57
scholastic aptitude test (SAT), 90
Schon, Donald, 94–95
school boards, 14, 87–89, 206
school choice, 26, 120, 122
school culture, 154
school reform
    adaptability of, 93–97, 104–105, 138
    competency-based education and,
        200–202
    corporate, 83–84, 86–87
    deep learning and, 207–208
    determining success and failure in,
        5–10
    educational conservatives and, 17–20
    efficiency-based, 38–39
    federal policy and, 24–26

    grammar of schooling and, 194–197
    of high schools, 202–205
    history of, 6, 87–89, 191, 194–197,
        213
    history of, in Los Angeles,
        118–124
    incremental, 7, 83, 202, 204,
        205–207, 209–211, 214
    Intensive Partnerships for Effective
        Teaching initiative, 99–108
    judgments on, 94–99
    longevity of, 92
    market-based ideas for, 85
    outcome-based education and,
        199–200
    policy elites and, 81–82, 96–99
    popularity of, 92
    in Progressive era, 12–20, 98–99,
        182, 211–212
    radical changes and, 8
    reality of, 205–214
    small school movement, 155,
        196–199, 203
    teachers and, 96–97
    technology and, 27–32
    top-down, 88, 90, 99, 101
schools
    See also public schools
    age-graded. *see* age-graded schools
    Big Picture Learning, 149–150,
        152–157, 169, 171
    charter, 7, 26, 84, 92, 98, 101, 188
    Common Schools, 6, 98
    community, 122–123, 139, 148
    continuation, 202
    Core Knowledge, 213
    effectiveness of, 21–27, 32, 90
    efficiency of, 15–16, 19, 21, 22,
        27–28, 32, 88–89
    evaluation of, 31
    "failing," 12–22, 76–77, 104
    funding of, 21, 22, 49, 79, 89,
        91–92
    as meritocracies, 194
    micro-schools, 209
    nongraded, 78, 192, 207, 213
    open-space, 207

schools, *continued*
  pilot, 120–122, 140
  segregated, 196
  standardization of, 72–80
  technologies in, 27–32, 182–183
school surveys, 89
scientific management, 15–16, 21, 24,
    27–28, 30, 88
Scopes Trial, 18
Scott, Hugh, 2
segregated schools, 196
selective public high schools, 195
self-actualization, 110, 117, 140,
    141–144, 181
self-government, 56–57
self-interest, 53–54
self-made man, 46, 47
Senior Thesis Project (STP), 165–169
Sizer, Ted, 197, 199, 203
Skinner, B. F., 29
slavery, 51, 57–58
small school movement, 155, 196–199,
    203
Smith, Adam, 53
Smith, Tony, 148
social efficiency, 23, 25–26
social inequality, 104
social intelligence, 150
social justice, 114–115
Social Justice Humanitas Academy
    (SJHA), 109–144, 203
  academic results at, 112–113
  classroom lessons at, 124–131
  core values and, 181–182
  demographics of, 112
  effectiveness criterion applied to,
    140–144
  history of reforms at, 118–124, 139
  mission and vision statements of,
    110–112, 140, 151
  role of teachers at, 113–114, 123,
    132–133
  school climate at, 116–118
  social justice mission of, 114–115
  student outcomes at, 140–141
  student self-knowledge at, 116–118
  success and failure at, 134–140
  Summer Bridge program, 123–124
  technology use at, 182–183
social mobility, 99, 194
social reformers, 58
societal reform, 19
software, 32
Soviet Union, 85, 196, 212
Spaulding, Frank, 15–16, 28
Spengler, Matt, 149
sports, 67–71, 187
Sputnik, 20, 79, 196
standardization, 30
standardized testing, 4, 15, 24, 26, 78,
    90, 91, 194
Starr, Bart, 69–70
stock market, 63
student agency, 212
student-centered learning, 153
student outcomes, 3–5, 21, 22, 26, 31,
    76, 89, 90, 97, 140–141, 150–151
students
  differentiation of, 186, 191
  with disabilities, 76
  low-income, 82, 91, 100
  minority, 25–26, 74, 82, 91, 100
  poor, 26
  self-actualization by, 116–118,
    141–144
  teacher "adoption" of, 123
  as workers, 198
success
  conflicted, 189–190
  criteria for, 110, 137–138, 189
  definitions of, 185–187, 190–191,
    213, 214
  determining, 5–10
  differences in defining, 11–12, 22,
    136, 181
  expanding definition of, 110,
    181–182, 211–212
  individual, 77, 99, 181, 185–186,
    187, 208, 210–212
  judging overall, 136–140, 187–190
  measures of, 5, 83, 90, 138, 177,
    210–211

at MetWest High School, 174–181
money and, 41, 46
origins of views on, 41–60
at Social Justice Humanitas Academy, 134–140
Success Academies, 213
Success For All, 11, 12, 25
successful schools
  contemporary examples of, 109–184
  contemporary views of, 20–22
  criteria for judging, 81–108
  effectiveness and, 22–27
  judgments on, 76–77
  past views of, 12–20
  personalized learning and, 33–39
Summer Bridge program, 123–124
Super Bowl ads, 66
superintendents, 88
Super School Project, 204
Survivor, 67
Sylmar High School, 119–120, 121, 139

Taylor, Frederick Winslow, 27–28, 30, 32, 88
Taylorism, 30–31
teachers
  accountability of, 101, 106
  adaptability of, 93–94, 96, 97, 104–105
  "adoption" of students by, 123
  autonomy of, 95, 96, 97
  as coaches, 198
  demographics of, 3, 4
  effectiveness of, 31, 99–108
  evaluation of, 103–104, 106
  at MetWest High School, 145–147, 161
  pay schemes for, 100
  school reform and, 96–97, 206
  at Social Justice Humanitas Academy, 113–114, 123, 132–133
  standards for, 74
teachers' unions, 96–97, 140
teaching machines, 28–29, 31

Teach to One, 34–35, 201
technical rationality, 94–95, 96
technocrats, 21
technologies, 27–32, 182–183
television, 67
Teng, Lawrence, 161–165
test scores, 26, 27, 31, 34, 83, 84, 90, 91, 97, 101, 103–104, 106, 177
Thayer High School, 199
Thirteenth Amendment, 51
Thorndike, Edward, 18, 28, 33
Three-Fifths Compromise, 57, 58
time-and-motion studies, 15, 27–28
Title I funds, 91–92
Tomasky, Michael, 53
Torres, Monica, 41
Trump, Donald, 55–56
Tyack, David, 184, 193

United Teachers Los Angeles (UTLA), 121, 140
Urban Academy, 203
urban school districts, 148, 182, 213–214
Urban Teacher Corps, 2–5, 188–190
US Constitution, 56, 57
US Department of Education, 91

Vega, Robert, 115
Ventilla, Max, 209
Vietnam War, 20, 90
vocationalism, 79
Vonnegut, Kurt, 186
Voting Rights Act, 20
voucher programs, 84

wages, 52, 64–65
Waldorf schools, 214
War on Poverty, 91
Washburne, Carleton, 17
Watson, John, 33
Waukesha STEM Academy, 36–38
wealth, 52–53, 55–56, 58
Wealth of Nations (Smith), 53
Welsh, Patrick, 11
white teachers, 3, 4

whole child, 33–34, 38–39, 98, 123, 212
William and Flora Hewlett Foundation, 207
Winnetka Plan, 17, 195

working class, 65
workplace, 81
World War II, 19

XQ Institute, 204